APPEALING TO SCRIPTURE
IN MORAL DEBATE

Appealing to Scripture in Moral Debate

Five Hermeneutical Rules

CHARLES H. COSGROVE

WILLIAM B. EERDMANS PUBLISHING COMPANY
GRAND RAPIDS, MICHIGAN / CAMBRIDGE, U.K.

Wm. B. Eerdmans Publishing Co.
255 Jefferson Ave. S.E., Grand Rapids, Michigan 49503 /
P.O. Box 163, Cambridge CB3 9PU U.K.
www.eerdmans.com

Printed in the United States of America

07 06 05 04 03 02   7 6 5 4 3 2 1

Library of Congress Cataloging-in-Publication Data

Cosgrove, Charles H.
    Appealing to scripture in moral debate : five hermeneutical rules /
    Charles H. Cosgrove.
        p.   cm.
    Includes bibliographical references.
    ISBN 0-8028-4942-3 (alk. paper)
    1. Ethics in the Bible.   I. Title.

  BS680.E84 C67 2002
  241.5 — dc21

                                                    2002067925

Unless otherwise noted, the Scripture quotations in this publication are from the New
Revised Standard Version Bible, copyright © 1989 by the Division of Christian Education
of the National Council of Churches of Christ in the U.S.A., and used by permission.

For my parents,
Charles and Marjorie Cosgrove

Contents

PACNM

Acknowledgments

I wish to thank the following people, who read portions of this book and gave me valuable feedback and encouragement: my brother, Joseph Cosgrove; my former students Raymond and Lawrence Mattera; my colleague Douglas Sharp; and members of the Association of Chicago Theological Schools New Testament Group.

Introduction

Important studies of the use of the Bible in Christian ethics have appeared in the thirty some years since James Gustafson noted a lack of attention to this area.[1] Among these are particularly fine general studies by Thomas Ogletree, Bruce Birch and Larry Rasmussen, and J. I. H. McDonald,[2] to name a few. There have also been some notable studies of ethics in the Bible that have taken up hermeneutical questions, such as Walter Harrelson's superb examination of the Ten Commandments, and books on New Testament ethics by Allen Verhey and Richard Hays.[3]

1. James M. Gustafson, "The Place of Scripture in Christian Ethics: A Methodological Study," *Interpretation* 24 (October 1970): 430-55. Reprinted in James M. Gustafson, *Theology and Ethics* (Philadelphia: United Church Press, 1974), 121-45.

2. Thomas W. Ogletree, *The Use of the Bible in Christian Ethics: A Constructive Essay* (Philadelphia: Fortress Press, 1983); Bruce C. Birch and Larry L. Rasmussen, *Bible and Ethics in the Christian Life,* rev. and expanded ed. (Minneapolis: Augsburg Fortress, 1989); J. I. H. McDonald, *Biblical Interpretation and Christian Ethics* (Cambridge: Cambridge University Press, 1993).

3. Walter Harrelson, *The Ten Commandments and Human Rights* (Philadelphia: Fortress Press, 1980); Allen Verhey, *The Great Reversal: Ethics and the New Testament* (Grand Rapids: Eerdmans, 1984); Richard B. Hays, *The Moral Vision of the New Testament: Community, Cross, New Creation: A Contemporary Introduction to New Testament Ethics* (San Francisco: HarperSanFrancisco, 1996). I have distinguished between studies on the use of the Bible in Christian ethics (notes 1 and 2 above) and books on biblical ethics that take up hermeneutical questions (this note). The line between the two is somewhat fuzzy.

A number of scholars have compared how Christians appeal to scripture with their avowed theories (or doctrines) of the role of scripture in constructive theology and ethics. In a now classic study, David Kelsey compared what several modern theologians have said about the nature and proper use of scripture with how they actually interpreted and used scripture, suggesting that their theories (doctrines of scripture) were not fully compatible with their uses. Kelsey did not focus on the use of scripture in ethics, but his study has direct relevance for moral appeal to scripture. In a topical approach, Willard Swartley examined how Christians in the nineteenth and twentieth centuries developed arguments from scripture on different sides of debates over slavery, sabbath-keeping, war, and the status of women. Swartley used his analyses of argumentative practice to develop guidelines for the use of the Bible in Christian ethics. More recently, Jeffrey Siker has looked at eight twentieth-century theologians, comparing what they say about using the Bible in Christian ethics with how they actually appeal to it.[4]

It has long seemed to me that one could learn something important by supplementing examinations of particular theologians and ethicists (Kelsey's and Siker's approach) or particular topics (Swartley's approach) with identification and analysis of *common hermeneutical assumptions* in appeals to the Bible as scripture in moral debate. I am especially interested in the *tacit* hermeneutical assumptions at work in appeal to the Bible as scripture. This book exposes and examines some of these assumptions by formulating them as hermeneutical rules. I identify five such rules, setting forth their rationales, and subjecting each to a critique.

By "appeal to the Bible as scripture" I mean a use of the Bible that presupposes its authority for the church.[5] The hermeneutical rules which are the subject of this study do not require a particular definition or theory of biblical authority, but they do assume the bare minimum of the traditional conception of authority as "carrying weight." I will say more about this below.

---

4. David H. Kelsey, *The Uses of Scripture in Recent Theology* (Philadelphia: Fortress Press, 1975); Willard M. Swartley, *Slavery, Sabbath, War, and Women: Case Issues in Biblical Interpretation* (Scottdale, PA, and Waterloo, Ontario: Herald Press, 1983); Jeffrey S. Siker, *Scripture and Ethics: Twentieth-Century Portraits* (Oxford and New York: Oxford University Press, 1997).

5. As Kelsey observes, "authority" is analytic (definitional) to the concept of scripture (*The Uses of Scripture in Recent Theology*, 97).

By "hermeneutical assumptions" I mean shared but typically unexamined plausibility structures. A hermeneutical assumption gives force to an appeal to scripture. Appeals to scripture can be persuasive only if speaker and audience share the same hermeneutical assumptions. These shared assumptions have a particular shape and logic, which depend on other presuppositions. The term "plausibility structure" expresses this complexity by which a particular hermeneutical assumption makes a given appeal to scripture appear valid.

The five hermeneutical assumptions examined in this study are the following:

1. The Rule of Purpose. The purpose (or justification) behind a biblical moral rule carries greater weight than the rule itself.
2. The Rule of Analogy. Analogical reasoning is an appropriate and necessary method for applying scripture to contemporary moral issues.
3. The Rule of Countercultural Witness. There is a presumption in favor of according greater weight to countercultural tendencies in scripture that express the voice of the powerless and the marginalized than to those tendencies that echo the dominant culture of their time.
4. The Rule of the Nonscientific Scope of Scripture. Scientific (or "empirical") knowledge stands outside the scope of scripture.
5. The Rule of Moral-Theological Adjudication. Moral-theological considerations should guide hermeneutical choices between conflicting plausible interpretations.

These formulations are hermeneutical "rules" in the sense that they state certain norms for valid use of scripture in moral argument. They are not "my" rules of validity, except in the sense that they are my formulations (and perhaps sharpenings) of what I take to be common assumptions. Others may wish to put the basic ideas behind these rules in different language.

Some of the rules have opposite counterparts that could be formulated as rules that are also in use today. For example, the rule of purpose stands opposed to a "rule of the letter" that is assumed by many who invoke scripture. The rule of nonscientific scope stands opposed to the view that where scripture addresses (or makes assumptions about) empirical matters, such as cosmology, it carries greater authority than modern science or should be used as a guide to Christian discrimination between competing scientific theories. The rule of moral-theological adjudication stands opposed to the hermeneutical assumption of "one correct" (one historically demonstrable) meaning. These opposing rules naturally come in for at least some direct and indirect discussion in the course of the analysis of the five rules that are the focus of this study.

I have identified the five rules primarily by examining and analyzing how modern biblical scholars and ethicists use the Christian Bible in making moral arguments. But I have also been guided by my own experience of living debate in various Christian contexts, including churches and seminary classrooms. The rules are not the special property of professional interpreters but are common hermeneutical coin. My choice of these five particular rules is due to the fact that I find them especially interesting and am more inclined to affirm them than their opposites. My analysis will reveal where I have reservations about some of them. My aim is not so much to recommend the rules as to examine them.

One last comment about the choice of the five rules. When Augustine took up Tyconius' *Book of Rules,* he complained that the seven rules of Tyconius scarcely cover all the problems ("obscurities") that one encounters in scripture.[6] I hope I do not open myself up to the same criticism when I present only five rules. My selection is meant to be illustrative and not comprehensive. In an appendix, I suggest some "other rules."

The Use of the Bible in Christian Ethics

Some twenty years ago James Childress lamented that the function of the Bible in moral deliberation and justification had been neglected in favor of an overemphasis on "vision and perspectives, images and metaphors, stories, loyalties, and character" as features of the moral life that scripture shapes or influences.[7] The justificatory function of appeal to scripture is still often neglected and stands under something of a cloud in nonconservative circles.

Disinterest in or suspicion of the justificatory functions of appeal to

6. Augustine, *On Christian Doctrine* 3.92-97 (3.XXX.42-43). Augustine was probably not completely fair to Tyconius. See Pamela Bright, *The Book of Rules of Tyconius: Its Purpose and Logic* (Notre Dame, IN: University of Notre Dame Press, 1988), 119-57.

7. James F. Childress, "Scripture and Ethics: Some Reflections on the Role of Scripture in Moral Deliberation and Justification," *Interpretation* 34 (1980): 371.

scripture owes much, I think, to two developments in the field of Christian ethics. First is the consensus among Christian ethicists that the Bible ought not be used "prescriptively." This consensus was firmly in place at least by the 1980s.[8] It has to do primarily with appropriating scripture at the moral-rule level (i.e., treating scripture's moral rules as moral rules for us).[9] The consensus is that scripture speaks to the moral life at the level of basic values and principles, not at the level of moral rules. But even as this consensus was emerging, a disenchantment with deontological ethics was setting in, the effect of which was to cast doubt on not only the usefulness of rules but also the utility of principles. The newer narrative/virtue-oriented ethics is usually presented as an alternative to conventional deontological and consequentialist ethics to the extent that the latter involved reasoning from rules or principles to concrete cases. The association of arguments from scripture with appeals to rules or principles seems to have led some to reject or become largely disinterested in the justificatory function of scripture. This is unfortunate for several reasons. First, justificatory uses of the Bible abound in actual Christian practice. Second, as Childress observes, deliberation and justification are important constituents of moral responsibility. Third, the newer approaches should not be viewed as inherently incompatible with moral argument; they simply call for a different mode of argument, namely, inductive or case-based reasoning.

Argumentative Appeal

I have located the function of the rules in appeal to scripture in moral argument. This raises the question whether the rules have merely rhetorical value, as strategies of persuasion, or are also means of interpretive discovery and judgment.

We sometimes suspect that the arguments someone makes in favor of a particular view or course of action are different from one's own reasons

8. See William C. Spohn, S.J., *What Are They Saying About Scripture and Ethics?* (New York: Paulist Press, 1984). Spohn summarizes the results of his survey of Christian ethics as follows: "Most of the authors we investigated propose an illuminative rather than a prescriptive use of Scripture" (134).

9. The tendency to define "prescriptive use" as appeal to the moral-rule level no doubt owes to the typology presented in Gustafson's influential essay, "The Place of Scripture in Christian Ethics."

and motives for favoring that view or action. Do Christians typically make (or inherit) moral judgments that they subsequently seek to defend by scripture, so that the original reasons for their convictions are not the same as their arguments for those convictions? I think the answer to this question is a qualified "yes." This does not mean, however, that argument from scripture is simply a rhetorical game. In many fields of knowledge the logic or method of discovery differs at least somewhat from the logic of justification. We come to convictions by many routes. Sometimes we test an idea after we have at least tentatively embraced it. In many cases we come to convictions as heirs of a particular tradition or subculture. Testing our convictions often involves efforts to justify them to ourselves and others. If the justificatory arguments succeed, they shore up our confidence in our conviction. If these justificatory arguments fail, we may abandon our original judgment and seek to form a new one or we may seek out fresh justifications.

Arguing from scripture is one of the public ways in which Christians test their moral judgments. When we speak of scripture as authorizing a particular moral position, we do not (or should not) mean that the logic of this authorization fully or even partly expresses the logic by which we arrived at that moral position "in the first place." We mean (or should mean) that the logic of this authorization is part of the rationale by which we hold to that position as members of a community to which we are accountable.

For example, I may hold to a position against capital punishment and trace the origins of this conviction to what my family taught me when I was a child. As an adult Christian I may work out biblically informed warrants for this position. In defending my view "from scripture" to other Christians, I am not expressing the whole course of the personal journey that led me to hold and maintain a position against capital punishment. Rather, I am giving a defense of my position to other Christians in terms I think they will find persuasive. The biblical argument I mount against capital punishment is *now* part of my own rationale against this institution, but it is not the only part of that rationale; nor does it represent the whole story of how I arrived at my conviction. In this sense, the logic of my appeals to scripture is not identical with the logic by which I arrived at my position "in the first place" but part of the rationale by which I hold to that position and defend it to others.

To elaborate the preceding example, let us suppose that at some point I lose confidence in my conviction against capital punishment and subsequently restore my confidence through a profound reflection on the teaching of scripture. From that point on, my arguments from scripture against capital punishment may well be a kind of account of how scripture led me back to my original conviction. But even in this case, I will likely be adjusting my case from scripture through dialogue with others and shoring up my conviction from other sources as well. Hence, it is important to distinguish the biography of individual or group convictions from the rhetorical justification of those positions. The two may be related (especially when an argument is cast in a biographical form), but they are not identical.

By "rhetorical" justification I mean the arguments one makes to a public or community (actual or imagined). I include here *the arguments one makes to oneself* in maintaining a position. We are never alone with our arguments, even when we are making them silently to ourselves. We are always conditioned by the common plausibility structures we share with others, and often we test the justifications we hold for a particular position by considering whether others would find them persuasive. Admittedly, the public arguments that Christians make may not always reflect the strength or form of their own convictions. Sometimes Christians engage in cynical acts of rhetorical persuasion, trading on a status of scripture in their community that they do not personally endorse and arguing *ad hominem,* i.e., on the basis of hermeneutical assumptions that they do not hold but their audience does. Sometimes they proceed this way not cynically but as a matter of fidelity to the norms of a particular community's discourse, treating that community's rhetoric of justification as more important than their own (or, more accurately in social terms, as more important than the justificatory logic of other communities to which they have not committed themselves). These and related aspects of the "rhetoric" of appeal to scripture are worthy subjects of inquiry, but they are not my focus here. My interest is the justificatory logic of appeal to scripture in public moral argument. What are some of the hermeneutical "rules" of such appeal and can they stand up to critical scrutiny?

Rules

It is probably fair to say that, outside of games and sports, many people (especially Americans) don't like rules — or say they don't. This owes largely to the common experience that most people have with rules: we become aware of them usually when they pinch us. In the church, antipathy to rules is sometimes also due to their association with legalism.

The negative connotations attaching to "rules" may make the subject of this book off-putting to some. If so, I have no quarrel with anyone substituting "principles" or "guidelines" (as I myself will do from time to time) for the five "rules" under discussion here. Nevertheless, I choose to speak of rules for several important reasons.

First, I wish to place my study in the long Christian tradition of devising "rules of interpretation," a tradition that has parallels in other religions (notably Judaism and Islam) and also in law. The rabbis devised rules of interpretation, such as the seven rules of Hillel and the thirteen rules of Ishmael. On the Christian side notable examples are the Seven Rules of Tyconius, Augustine's revision and expansion of Tyconius' rules in *De Doctrina Christiana,* and the "rules of recognition" *(regulae cognoscendi)* and "directives for intelligent reading" *(præcepta de ratione legendi)* of Matthias Flaccius Illyricus.

Identifying hermeneutical rules is also an important part of the historical-reconstructive task for any era of Christian interpretation. Such rules are not always stated explicitly, reflected upon, or even "thought" by those who use them. For example, James Kugel has identified five widely-shared tacit rules of ancient Jewish and Christian interpretation of scripture.[10] I aim to do something similar for contemporary interpretation of scripture, without claiming that my account is in any way comprehensive.

A third reason is substantive. Hermeneutical rules are one way we promote consistency and fairness in the way we use scripture. Their most basic *raison d'être* is that fundamental moral principle of our existence which says, *Treat like things alike.* Formulating rules makes explicit the plausibility structures inherent in our discourse, so that those structures can be subjected to analysis and critique for coherence and consistency.

A fourth reason is practical. It is not feasible to rehearse in every situation (including hermeneutical ones) all the considerations that informed us the last time we encountered a similar question or set of circumstances. Hence one purpose of giving rules to ourselves is to allow past experience

---

10. James L. Kugel, *Traditions of the Bible: A Guide to the Bible as It Was at the Start of the Common Era* (Cambridge, MA: Harvard University Press, 1998), 14-19. See also John Barton, *Holy Writings, Sacred Text: The Canon in Early Christianity* (Louisville, KY: Westminster/John Knox Press, 1997), 134-45.

and reflection to guide future deliberations and decisions. The force of rules viewed under this fourth aspect of practicality is the confidence we place in our own wisdom. In ordinary conversation, such rules (or at least the implicit plausibility structures they represent) are important conditions of efficient communication. Shared interpretive rules are part of the *sensus communis* (common sense) that makes communication and persuasion possible at all. Behind this reason for rules, then, lies the value of the Christian community as a morally responsible corporate agent, a deliberative community.

It is unfortunate that the term "rule" — and hence the idea of hermeneutical rules — carries negative connotations for many in our day, smacking of formula without judgment, logic without creativity, perhaps of an effort to control or circumscribe language and subject matter whose very nature is boundary-breaking. As I have suggested and hope to show in the body of the study, hermeneutical rules are not formulas; they require judgment, even creativity. Moreover, one can fruitfully use the concept of hermeneutical rules without reducing the role of scripture in the church to its operation under such rules. Hermeneutics is about much more than "arguing from" scripture, and scripture also serves the moral life by revealing, motivating, challenging, and persuading quite apart from our "arguments from scripture." Hermeneutical rules have a place in the moral use of scripture; they are not applicable to all the powers of scripture.

Hermeneutical Rules and the "Rule" of Scripture

There are many kinds of rules of interpretation. I have in view hermeneutical rules that make moral arguments *from* scripture plausible, valid in the eyes of those who find the arguments persuasive. This species of rule assumes some kind of authority of scripture. David Kelsey speaks of the "rulish" function of the Bible in the church.[11] Using Frederick Schauer's analysis of rules, we can say that rule-quality is a reason to act (in conformity to the rule) that is independent of any other reasons to act, in-

---

11. "And the concept 'scripture' brings with it a concept of 'authority', for to call a set of writings 'scripture' is to say that they ought to be used in certain normative and rulish ways in the common life of the church" (Kelsey, *The Uses of Scripture in Recent Theology*, 164).

cluding those in and behind the *content* of the rule.[12] We can also describe this as "status" authority. When someone in authority over me commands me to do such and such, there may be various reasons, besides the fact of the command, for me to comply. *That* I am commanded by someone with status authority is itself an independent reason for compliance. Because it is one kind of reason among others, it may not be a compelling reason. The political doctrine of civil disobedience, for example, holds that under certain conditions conscience overrides status authority.

Status or rulish authority can be absolute, presumptive, or relative. An absolute authority admits no exceptions based on consideration of other authorities or reasons. A presumptive rule is one that we hold unless persuaded to abandon it in a particular case. Under the doctrine of civil disobedience, the rule of law is not absolute but presumptive. Presumptive authority can be near absolute, requiring especially powerful countervailing considerations under extraordinary circumstances, before we will make an exception. Or presumptive authority may be weak, enjoying the benefit of the doubt but easily overcome by other reasons. Between these two lies a continuum. Relative authority is one voice among others. Obviously, weak presumption shades into relative authority.

The five hermeneutical rules do not themselves entail positions on the kind of authority scripture has except to assume that scripture has some sort of status authority. Persons and communities that affirm the status authority of scripture, but differ in how they conceive that authority, nevertheless make arguments from scripture in some common ways. Identifying common hermeneutical rules reveals the family resemblances among these ways of arguing from (appealing to) scripture. It is for this reason — to get at the resemblances while accommodating differences — that I suggest "weight" as the basic meaning of status authority for purposes of this study. In the chapters to follow, "authority" refers to the practice of *giving weight to scripture simply because it is scripture*. This usage has the advantage of allowing me to show how the rules function for Christians who hold to a variety of views on the authority of scripture.

A final clarification of terms is in order. To say, with Kelsey, that scripture has authority of a rulish kind does not mean that scripture contains

---

12. See Frederick Schauer, *Playing by the Rules: A Philosophical Examination of Rule-Based Decision-Making in Law and in Life* (Oxford: Clarendon Press, 1991), 5-6. I give a further discussion of rule-quality in chapter one.

rules in a formal sense or that, if it does, scripture's authority operates in these rules. To describe scripture as a rule is a metaphor that does not override the many different *genres* of scripture (or forms of speech in scripture), most of which are not rulish. To avoid possible confusion, let me point out that this study uses the concept of the rule in three different subject areas: hermeneutical rules, scripture as "rule" (authority for faith and practice), and moral rules *in* scripture. My general focus is on hermeneutical rules. These rules assume that scripture is a "rule" for faith and practice. The first hermeneutical rule (treated in chapter one) happens to deal with appropriation of moral rules in scripture.

We ourselves are the authors of our shared hermeneutical rules. We are constantly, if usually indirectly, negotiating them. We don't all agree about all of them. Not everyone who invokes the rules tacitly in argument is able to articulate them clearly or at all. Sometimes we know the logic of our arguments without being able to express it. The purpose of this study is to put some of these rules on the table and subject them to critique, exposing their strengths and weaknesses. The identification and explication of these rules should, at the very least, reveal why arguments sometimes work and sometimes don't, showing those gaps in assumptions that make us sometimes talk past each other. The critique of these rules can also help us examine our assumptions for coherence and defensibility. Finally, paying attention to the rules we tacitly invoke can help us discover how consistent we are in how we appeal to scripture.

Each rule has virtues. Each also has its problems. Those who decide to stick by (or adopt) any one of these rules, after reading this study, will do so because they perceive that the alternative is even more troublesome. Those who decide to reject any one of these rules will, I hope, at least come away with a better understanding of the rule and some appreciation for why others embrace it.

ONE

The Rule of Purpose

The purpose (or justification) behind a biblical moral rule carries greater weight than the rule itself.

Christian moral debate often involves appeals to the moral prescriptions of the Bible. Sometimes these appeals are to the "letter," other times to the "spirit" of a biblical prescription. The language of "letter" and "spirit" can be put more precisely as *rule* and *rule purpose*. The purpose or aim of a rule is also the justification or rationale for the rule.[1] Hence, I use the terms "justification," "purpose" (or "aim") and "rationale" almost interchangeably. For example, a rule requiring traffic to stop at an intersection probably has as its purpose the safe and orderly flow of traffic. This purpose is the justification or rationale for the rule. That rationale could be worked out more fully as the logic or reasoning that supports having a rule to ensure safety and efficient order. The rationale in this case might include reasons why safety and order are valued in this context (over, say, freedom), what "safety" and "order" mean here, why a rule is needed to promote safety and order, and so forth. The justification or rationale for a

---

1. On rules and their justifications, see Frederick Schauer, *Playing by the Rules: A Philosophical Examination of Rule-Based Decision-Making in Law and in Life* (Oxford: Clarendon Press, 1991), 53-62.

rule always includes its purpose: it is the purpose of the rule and the reasons supporting that purpose.

There are basically three ways of conceiving the force of rules in relation to their justifications:

1. Rules carry greater force than their justifications.
2. Rules and their justifications cannot be ordered in a hierarchy; where they conflict in a particular decisional situation, one must weigh the claims of each for that situation.
3. Rule justifications carry greater force than rules.

The subject of this chapter is a rule about rules: a hermeneutical rule — the "rule of purpose" — about appeal to moral rules (prescriptions) in the Bible. The rule of purpose states the third position listed above as a normative principle of biblical hermeneutics: rule justifications (purposes) carry greater weight than the rules they support. The implication is that whatever force biblical moral prescriptions carry in Christian ethics resides at the level of rule justifications, not rules.[2]

In what follows I explore the meaning of the rule of purpose, set forth its warrants, and elaborate its implications by examining three biblical moral rules (the Old Testament law against lending at interest, the rule against homoerotic behavior assumed by Paul in Romans 1, and the Levitical purity rules). I will not take up the question of how the Bible itself, e.g., through the witness of the New Testament regarding the law, limits or nullifies the authority of moral rules found in either Testament. This is obviously a critical question, but it is not my purpose to discuss it here.

---

2. The rule of purpose fits to a certain extent with the view of many Christian ethicists (along with some of the biblical scholars who have treated the use of the Bible in Christian ethics) that it is a mistake to think of biblical authority as extending to the moral-rule level. This common view is summarized in Allen Verhey, "Scripture and Ethics: Practices, Performances, and Prescriptions," in *Christian Ethics: Problems and Prospects,* ed. Lisa Sowle Cahill and James F. Childress, 18-21 (Cleveland, Ohio: The Pilgrim Press, 1996). Nevertheless, as I will show, there is an important sense in which the rule of purpose also preserves the traditional view that biblical authority does extend as far as biblical moral rules.

The Bible and Moral Rules

As I noted in the Introduction, prescriptive rules (unlike, for example, the "laws of physics") are backed by authority. Hence, when a prescription is a rule, its rule-quality supplies a reason to act (or not to act) that is separate from substantive considerations (including the substantive justification for the rule).[3] Rule-quality does not confer the *only* reason to follow a prescription. Prudential consideration of the content of the prescription may also support following the rule. Moreover, rule-quality does not necessarily supply a *sufficient* reason to follow the rule. Countervailing reasons may exist that outweigh the authority of the rule. Sometimes these countervailing reasons are found in the *justification* (purpose) of the rule.

Before proceeding further with our examination of the relation between rules and their justifications, it may be helpful to introduce two additional terms — "fact pattern" and "case" — that can assist us in describing what prescriptive rules do. Rules govern "fact patterns." I borrow the term "fact pattern" from the field of law to denote specific human behavior within a specific set of circumstances (as in Person X doing action Y under conditions Z). A fact pattern is a set of relations between the elements making up an event, a way of construing a human event as an integrated whole.

For analytic purposes, we can use the term "fact pattern" to cover not only actual but also hypothetical and fictitious events. Prescriptive rules assume fact patterns; they command or prohibit particular behaviors under particular circumstances. An actual fact pattern to which we have applied or seek to apply a rule is a "case." Applying a rule requires judging whether the case before us falls under the fact pattern assumed by the rule.

Applying rules to cases involves judgments, which in turn rest on basic convictions about how rules ought to function in given domains. This brings us to the focal issue of this chapter. In a situation where a case falls under a given rule but the rationale for that rule argues against applying the rule in that particular case, we must ask whether the rationale for the rule carries greater weight than the rule itself. For example, suppose my physician imposes on me the rule "No eggs!" because eggs are bad for the cardiovascular system, but I later conclude from reading an article in the *New England Journal of Medicine* that the studies supporting the claim that

---

3. See Schauer, *Playing by the Rules,* 4-6, 51-52, 112-18, 128-34.

eggs are unhealthy may have been flawed and that perhaps better research supports modest consumption of eggs. If I accept the claims of this article, the justification for the rule "No eggs!" now argues against the rule. In this situation, which carries greater weight for me, the rule or its justification?

To take a biblical example, in the Sermon on the Mount Jesus says, "if anyone forces you to go one mile, go also the second mile" (Matt. 5:41). Let us assume the common view that Jesus has in mind a soldier's right to compel a person to carry his gear for a mile. I think almost everyone today who reads Jesus' words in Matt. 5:41 takes them not as a rule but as a pointer to a deeper principle, a principle to which the other verses in the immediate context also point. "Going the extra mile" has become proverbial for serving others beyond conventional expectations or requirements. Nevertheless, Matt. 5:41 is in the form of case law (a command given in a conditional construction: "if . . . then"). Those who reject the idea that the Sermon on the Mount is meant to function as case law (or a "code") view Jesus' commands as examples standing for principles.[4] We could term these commands "paradigm cases." Do the principles exemplified by these paradigm examples have greater weight than the specific prescriptions? We may conclude that they do for at least some of the commands, after considering situations in which performing those commands would violate their purposes. For instance, suppose at the conclusion of carrying a soldier's pack the first mile, the disciple learned that the soldier was on his way to rob and murder a widow in the next village. In that case, it would no longer serve the purpose of the rule (showing love to the soldier, doing justice, combating evil[5]) to carry the soldier's pack any further because doing so would aid him in an evil purpose.[6]

4. Hans Dieter Betz appropriately calls the commands in 5:39-42 "examples." See Hans Dieter Betz, *The Sermon on the Mount: A Commentary on the Sermon on the Mount, including the Sermon on the Plain (Matthew 5:3–7:27 and Luke 6:20-49)*, Hermeneia (Minneapolis: Augsburg Fortress, 1995), 289. It is an interesting and important question whether the Sermon on the Mount contains rules (in form-critical terms) and if so, whether these rules were originally intended to carry force *as* rules for the disciples (or for Matthew's community). If so, a second question is whether Matthew thought of rules as carrying their weight in their underlying principles. Unfortunately, space does not permit me to explore these interesting questions. See further n. 23 below.

5. These are some of the ways in which Betz characterizes the underlying principle or concern of Matt. 5:38-41 (*The Sermon on the Mount*, 277-89).

6. Another way to analyze this situation is to say that the value of the widow's life outweighs any obligation to assist the soldier. Obviously, both analyses are correct.

mandatory rule → no exception

Rules may be "mandatory" ("absolute," "final," "conclusory," "exceptionless") or "presumptive" ("prima facie," "revisable").[7] A mandatory rule is a prescription whose authority by definition outweighs any reasons for setting the rule aside in a particular case; it admits no exceptions (e.g., game rules, such as the rules of chess). A presumptive rule is a prescription whose authority is simply *one* reason (not an absolute reason) for heeding it. More precisely, presumptive force makes a rule controlling unless and until sufficiently countervailing reasons are adduced against its application in a particular instance. Moreover, the force of rules exists on a continuum from absolute to virtually exceptionless to robustly presumptive and so forth on down to the most weakly presumptive.

Most rules in law and morality are presumptive, owing to the nature of rules in these domains.[8] A rule is a generalization covering a class.[9] In a game (chess, Monopoly), it is possible to establish rules that cover in advance every conceivable situation. But life doesn't operate like a game. Rules covering life situations are often both *over-inclusive and under-inclusive* with respect to their purposes. That is, once formulated, such

---

7. The most common way of referring to this distinction is "absolute" vs. "prima facie." Schauer prefers the term "presumptive" to "prima facie" because the latter suggests that the force of the rule may evaporate once one has penetrated beneath its surface impression (*Playing by the Rules*, 5-6, 113-14). Some use the term "exceptionless" to describe absolute or mandatory rules. See Donald Evans, "Paul Ramsey on Exceptionless Moral Rules," in *Faith, Authenticity and Morality* (Toronto: University of Toronto Press, 1980), 160-96. A typology of five kinds of rules is offered by Abraham Edel, *Ethical Judgment: The Use of Science in Ethics* (Glencoe, IL: The Free Press, 1955), 42-49. Edel distinguishes "must rules," "always rules," "break-always-with-regret rules," "for-the-most-part rules," and "complex-singular-situation rules."

8. In a debate with Paul Ramsey (one of the most vigorous and formidable advocates for according a place for mandatory rules in Christian ethics), Donald Evans makes a strong case that we ought not to adopt any moral rules as exceptionless, but Evans grants that we should hold some rules as "virtually exceptionless." He gives the following examples: (1) "Never carry out a medical experiment on someone without his consent"; (2) "Never punish a man whom one knows to be innocent of a crime for which he would be punished"; (3) "Never rape (i.e., force sexual intercourse on someone who is unwilling)." With enough imagination, one can think of exception cases for all of these, but the exceptional situations appear to be so rare to Evans as to make the rules virtually exceptionless. See Evans, "Paul Ramsey on Exceptionless Moral Rules," 182-83. On the fact and force of what might be called robust presumptive moral rules, see also Alasdair MacIntyre, "Does Applied Ethics Rest on a Mistake?" *The Monist* 67 (1984): 508-09.

9. On rules as generalizations, see Schauer, *Playing by the Rules*, 17-37.

rules often turn out to include some things that their purposes do not warrant and to exclude other things that their purposes would otherwise support.[10] Moreover, even if we could know in advance every conceivable set of circumstances that might arise, taking all cases into account would deprive rules of their useful generality. We would have to formulate a rule for every situation or pile up exception clauses; in either case, our rules would lose their utility. The idea of a perfectly comprehensive set of rules is merely hypothetical in any event, impossible to achieve and always reaching a point of diminishing returns in systems that seek to approach it.

Should we accord biblical moral rules the status of rules for us (rules carrying at least presumptive force)? Christians have traditionally assumed that since the Bible carries authority for faith and practice, biblical moral prescriptions carry authority as rules at least for the peoples and times to which they are spoken. Many Christians have also judged that the moral law of the Old Testament and the moral teaching of the New Testament express moral rules for God's people in all times and places. Others, at least in modern times, have rejected the view that the Bible speaks authoritatively to the church at the moral-rule level. Some who hold this position argue that since the Bible is not a systematic code of ethics — indeed even the pentateuchal law is not a systematic code — it is therefore wrong to appropriate biblical morality at the moral-rule level. This conclusion (while it may be correct for other reasons) does not follow from its stated premise. One might as well argue that the command I give my nine-year-old daughter to "come straight home from school" carries no force *qua* command because I insert it in a note in her school lunch box containing mostly chit-chat, endearments, and a funny story. The fact that the Bible is not a code of ethics does not imply that it does not intend to bind at the moral-rule level *when it speaks at that level.* I take this to be Richard Hays' point when he insists that "New Testament texts must be granted authority (or not) in the mode in which they speak."[11] Hays apparently means that *if* we grant moral authority to New Testament texts, we must grant that authority in the mode in which they speak; otherwise, we violate the intentions of the text. Hence, as Hays sees it, we ought not to turn one mode of

10. On under- and over-inclusivity, see Schauer, 31-34.
11. Richard B. Hays, *The Moral Vision of the New Testament: Community, Cross, New Creation: A Contemporary Introduction to New Testament Ethics* (San Francisco: HarperSanFrancisco, 1996), 294.

17

textual discourse into another of its modes or use appeals to one mode to override other modes.

Hays identifies four modes of moral appeal to biblical texts and apparently regards these as modes in which the text itself also speaks: rules, principles, paradigms, and symbolic world.[12] Although Hays treats these as more or less distinct, they are in fact interrelated in ways that make it difficult or impossible to speak of one apart from another. For example, biblical "paradigms" may be construed in different ways: as precedents (rule-bearing normative cases), as narrative embodiments of values, or as clues to an informing symbolic world. To the extent that a paradigm is a normative instance or case, it implies a rule. Likewise, every rule assumes a paradigm case (or set of cases) that embodies it. Seeing the connection between rules and their paradigm cases requires grasping the principles behind the rule. These principles are in turn embedded in the larger (more general) symbolic world of the text.[13] These principles are also defined by the paradigm cases themselves (see chapter two).

If we affirm the rule of purpose, then biblical moral rules impinge on us not in their rulish formulations but in their justifications, which may be principles. In that case, we cannot accept Hays' claim that "New Testament texts must be granted authority (or not) in the mode in which they speak." If we take the justification for a biblical moral rule as weightier than the rule, the justification always trumps the rule, even though the rule remains the marker of the authority of rule justifications, the place where the authority of those justifications "appears" in the biblical text.

Rules and Their Justifications

The rule of purpose calls for giving greater weight to biblical rule justifications (their purposes) than to the rules themselves. The effect at the

---

12. Hays, *The Moral Vision of the New Testament*, 208-9; see also 293-98.

13. Symbolic worlds bear on ethical questions in two ways: they articulate (and shape) values, and they answer the foundational question, "Why be moral?" Thus, symbolic worlds can be said to speak at two levels: at what ethicist Henry David Aiken has termed the ethical level, where we inquire into the justifications for a particular course of conduct, and at what he calls the post-ethical level, where we explore the ultimate foundations of being moral. See Henry David Aiken, "Levels of Moral Discourse," in *Reason and Conduct: New Bearings in Moral Philosophy* (New York: Alfred A. Knopf, 1962), 65-87.

hermeneutical level is that biblical rules lose their force *qua* rules and serve instead as signs of their justifications. The warrant for treating the justification for a biblical rule as weightier (for us) than the rule itself is that transferring biblical rules from their ancient cultural contexts into modern contexts tends to disrupt the relation between the rules and their justifications so severely that confidence in the rules is undermined (or ought to be).

In some rule-governed domains (notably law and morality), the reasons for changing rules (including making exceptions, which in effect changes a rule) are also reasons for giving greater weight to the purpose of a rule than to the rule itself. Two types of reasons for rule changes are the following: (1) the appearance of fact patterns uncontemplated by the rule-makers calls for reformulating the rule to do better justice to its purpose or (2) the rise of new knowledge may call for rethinking not only the rule but its purpose as well. Let me illustrate these two types by taking them up in reverse order. As to the second type, new knowledge may be knowledge unavailable to the rule-makers (or uncontemplated by them), or it may be an alternative, competing knowledge. For example, if we follow Bernard Levinson,[14] we can view Deuteronomy's cultic innovations as an instance of a new knowledge (an alternative theology of centralization) leading to a change not only of the rules but of the rationales for the rules governing the cult. Deuteronomy forbids sacrifice at local altars in favor of Jerusalem as sole cultic center. This in turn makes other laws problematic. Centralization has changed the assumed facts upon which laws requiring judicial oaths were predicated. The legal requirements that litigants formally swear their innocence assumed the viability of the local sanctuary as the place for oath-taking "before Yahweh." This creates the sort of situation described by the first type of reason for rule changes. Now the rule about legal oaths must be modified in order to fulfill its purpose. Thus, the cultic legal innovations change the rules on the basis of new (or modified) purposes (type 2), while the changes in the laws governing oath-taking are efforts to fulfill original purposes under changed conditions (type 1).

Modifying a rule is noncontroversial where the rule-makers do the modifying. Rule modification becomes problematic only where both (a) there is a separation of powers between those who make rules and

---

14. Bernard M. Levinson, *Deuteronomy and the Hermeneutics of Legal Innovation* (Oxford and New York: Oxford University Press, 1997).

those who interpret and apply them and (b) the rule interpreters engage in rule modification. This is a much-discussed issue in law, and we can clarify our thinking about rules and their justifications by looking briefly at how rules function in different domains of law.

In Anglo-American[15] common law there is no separation of powers between rule-makers and rule-interpreters/appliers. In the common law, judges make and interpret the law. Nevertheless, they tend to adhere to the principle of *stare decisis*, i.e., they honor precedent until there are compelling reasons to change the received law. In the domain of enacted law, where a separation of powers exists between rule-makers (e.g., a legislature) and rule-interpreters/appliers (a judiciary), the traditional Anglo-American theory of law holds that duly constituted lawmakers enact law and judges only interpret and apply law. In fact, however, judges do make law through their interpretation and application of enacted law.

It is important to distinguish two ways in which appeals to the purpose of a law can bear on the application of the law. In most instances, the meaning of the law is in some dispute. In such instances, the purpose (or intent) of the rule-makers is often adduced to clarify the meaning of the law. In some cases, however, the meaning and applicability of the law to the case at hand are clear, but applying the law would produce a harsh or absurd result. In such cases, judges may refuse to apply the plain sense of the rule, justifying their decision by appealing to the purpose of the rule. That is, perceiving that the law is over-inclusive with respect to its purpose, justices give greater weight to that purpose than to the plain sense of the law.

A famous instance of a court using the purpose of a law as a reason not to apply the plain legal rule in a particular case is *Riggs v. Palmer*,[16] a civil suit involving a nephew who murdered his uncle and stood to inherit from his uncle. The legal question was whether the law of wills required that the donee of a will who murdered the donor be granted his share of the inheritance. The court concluded that under the plain sense of the applicable statute the murdering donee should receive his share, but it decided not to apply the statute, relying in part on the judgment that the legislature that enacted the statute could not have intended this immoral

---

15. I choose Anglo-American law for purposes of illustration because it is more or less familiar to English-speaking readers, not because other traditions of law might not be equally illuminating.

16. *Riggs v. Palmer*, 115 N.Y. 506, 22 N.E. 188 (1889).

result. Hence, the court gave greater weight to the purpose of the rule than to the rule itself.[17]

Cases like *Riggs* are not typical. Courts are generally reluctant to use their own judgments about the purpose of a law as a reason for not applying a law in a particular case. When they consider the purpose or justification for a law, it is usually to clarify the meaning of an ambiguous law, not to avoid the letter of the law (although the difference between these two uses of rule justifications is not always clear). Courts tend to be deferential to the rights of lawmakers to establish the law; judges, at least in theory, exercise a lawmaking function only "in the gaps"[18] (where there is no applicable law) and through interpretation.[19]

There are parallels between how judges make law and how at least some Christians use scripture to construct ethical positions. They look to the Bible as an authority in matters of the moral life. Where the Bible does not speak to a particular moral question, they legislate (for themselves) "in the gaps." They often do so by considering general biblical principles. Where the Bible speaks to a particular moral question, they engage in interpretation as a way of developing their moral positions. Interpretation in such cases entails judgments about whether certain biblical texts really do treat the issue at hand and, if so, what those texts mean (for example, whether the Bible addresses the question of abortion and if so what it says).

Then there are cases where the Bible speaks at the moral-rule level but its plain-sense application to our own situation seems harsh or problematic in a way that leads us to ask whether the rule ought to be applied (e.g., the

17. The majority interpretation may have been wrong in its construal of the purpose of the law of wills. The dissenting opinion argued that a fundamental principle of inheritance law is that donors have a right to devolve their property on whomever they wish, including morally unworthy recipients. The dissent probably took the view (it's not clear from the opinion) that the legislature, in enacting the statute of wills, intended to incorporate this basic common law theory of wills. Thus, the dissent found no disjunction between the purpose of the rule of wills and the application of the rule to the fact pattern in *Riggs*.

18. For the classic statement of this view, see Benjamin N. Cardozo, *The Nature of the Judicial Process* (New Haven and London: Yale University Press, 1921), 113-14.

19. I dissent from the extreme "legal realist" view which holds that what judges do simply *is* the law, as if the separation of powers between legislative and judicial functions is a complete fiction. I think the realist position gives an especially flawed account of statutory law. It is closer to the mark in constitutional law; it does apply to the common law, where there is no separation of powers.

rules on divorce in the Gospels). Much debate about the teaching of the Bible on specific moral questions focuses on cases of this type, where an application of the letter of scripture to us in our situation strikes some as harsh or even absurd. It is typically here that we find appeals behind the letter to the justification or purpose of a biblical moral rule. One can call this "interpretation," but only if one distinguishes it from the kind of interpretation that seeks to clarify the meaning of the rule as a prescription. That is, there is a difference between establishing what conduct a rule commands, permits, or proscribes and judging how far it succeeds in embodying its justification. For example, there is a difference between the question, "What behavior is meant by the term 'kill' in the sixth commandment?" (whether the term means simply "kill" or carries the narrower meaning of "murder") and the question, "What is the rationale for this rule?" These two types of inquiry may be related. Often an inquiry into rule purpose helps one clarify rule meaning. But the two sorts of questions are not identical. Otherwise, rules and their justifications would never be at odds.

The rule of purpose, therefore, is not simply a way of describing the need to interpret a rule before applying it. The rule of purpose speaks to the situation where a moral prescription has been interpreted, its rationale has been identified, and a discrepancy between the prescription and its rationale appears when one contemplates applying the prescription to a particular case. For example, it has been argued that in ancient Israel wives were regarded as, in some sense, the property of their husbands and that the purpose of the commandment against adultery was to protect this property right. Identifying this purpose helps to define the seventh commandment as prohibiting sexual relations between a man and the wife (or betrothed) of another man and between a married woman and any other man.[20] This clarifying appeal[21] to an unstated aspect of the purpose of the

20. See J. J. Stamm and M. E. Andrew, *The Ten Commandments in Recent Research* (London: SCM Press, 1967), 100. Walter Harrelson registers some cautions about the assumption that it is primarily a property right concern that motivates the prohibition against adultery. See Walter Harrelson, *The Ten Commandments and Human Rights* (Philadelphia: Fortress Press, 1980), 124-25. Anthony Phillips argues that the purpose of the rule is to protect not property but the continuance of the husband's "name" through his offspring. See Anthony Phillips, *Ancient Israel's Criminal Law: A New Approach to the Decalogue* (Oxford: Basil Blackwell, 1970), 117.

21. Notice that the purpose of the rule helps one to define the concept of adultery used in the rule. This raises the question whether, when concepts employed in rules change, the

law of adultery differs, however, from using the law's purpose as an argument *against* following the law. For instance, the property-right purpose of the commandment against adultery might justify a husband giving permission to another man to have sexual relations with the husband's wife, something that the law against adultery would prohibit.[22] Thus, where a particular case reveals a tension between a rule and its justification, one has to decide whether the justification should be accorded greater weight than the rule. The rule of purpose decides this question in advance by specifying that the justifications for biblical moral rules always carry greater weight than the rules *qua* rules.[23]

---

rules change their meaning. In law, Ronald Dworkin has proposed that by distinguishing between a concept and its conception (conceptions evolve as changing understandings of concepts), we can understand how law changes through interpretation. See Ronald Dworkin, *Law's Empire* (Cambridge, MA: Harvard University Press, 1986), 70-72. In Christian ethics, a similar idea is built into Paul Ramsey's understanding of mandatory rules. Evolving and deepening interpretations of the concepts employed in such rules allow for adaptation of the rule to unanticipated cases. Donald Evans argues, rightly, I think, that such an approach smuggles room for unspecified and unspecifiable exceptions into supposedly exceptionless rules. See Evans, "Paul Ramsey on Exceptionless Moral Rules," 169-74.

22. I suggest this merely as a hypothetical. Examination of biblical cases where this rule is violated suggests that the biblical writers did not reflect on the purpose of the rule. For instance, in the story of Abraham offering Sarah as his sister to Pharaoh in Gen. 12, Abraham's action could be justified on the basis of the rule's purpose. In the text, however, Abraham stands condemned not because he violated the purpose of the law but because he transgressed the rule itself. It may be, however, that we are to understand the husband's right over the wife as a quasi-property right, that is, a very limited kind of property right with special moral restrictions, including protection of the sexual bond between husband and wife. In that case, the purpose of the rule would not justify Abraham's action. It may also be a mistake to think that the husband's property rights in his wife must entail rights of transferability, etc. In modern law, for example, some kinds of property are thought to be inalienable (non-transferable). See Susan Rose-Ackerman, "Inalienability and the Theory of Property Rights," *Columbia Law Review* 85 (1985): 931-69. Perhaps some similar, morally restricted notion of a husband's property rights in his wife informed ancient Israelites in their conceptions of adultery. Gerda Lerner has argued that under the history of patriarchy women were never regarded as things; it was their sexuality and reproductive capacity that was reified and commodified. See Gerda Lerner, *The Creation of Patriarchy* (New York and Oxford: Oxford University Press, 1986), 213-14. It is not clear what implications Lerner's interpretation might have for the rights of a husband over his wife's sexuality in Israelite culture.

23. One important question, which I leave aside here as a subject in its own right, is whether (and if so to what extent) ancient Israelite interpreters of the law accorded greater weight to the purposes of legal rules than to the rules themselves. Our sources may not permit an answer to this question. As far as I can tell, Michael Fishbane's study of inner-biblical in-

As the property-right interpretation of the commandment against adultery shows, rule justifications may not always strike us as morally "better" than the rules themselves. Sometimes the justifications for biblical moral rules (at least as scholarship is able to reconstruct those rationales) contain assumptions that we find morally problematic and that conflict with moral principles found elsewhere in the Bible.

The Warrant for the Rule of Purpose

Thus far I have been describing the meaning of the rule of purpose. As I have noted, its practical effect is to undermine all biblical moral rules at the rule-level, since assigning greater weight to rule justifications than to the rules themselves means that the justifications always trump the rules. I have also given some indications of the warrant for the rule of purpose. It is now time to look more closely at this warrant.

It may be that most people who operate by the rule of purpose do so on the assumption that if a particular application of a rule does not fulfill its purpose, even contradicts it, one ought to follow the spirit and not the letter of the rule. This makes sense where the rule-appliers are also the rule-makers (as, for example, when I make exceptions in applying rules that I have imposed on myself). As I noted, however, where there is a separation of powers between rule-making and rule-application, it does not necessarily follow that the rule-appliers should always follow the purpose of the rules where doing so would mean going against the rule. The domain of enacted law is one sphere where the rule is at least presumptively superior to its purpose or justification when it comes to application.

Similarly, Christians have understood themselves as standing under scripture as a norm to which they are accountable. According to the traditional conception of the relation of the church to the norm of scripture, Christians today (and Christians for most of the church's history) stand under scripture as a rule that others made or that God made through human instruments, not a rule that Christians today have authority to make

terpretation in the Hebrew Bible does not include examples of this sort of interpretation (Michael Fishbane, *Biblical Interpretation in Ancient Israel*, paperback ed. with new material [Oxford: Clarendon Press, 1988]). More information is available on how later Hellenistic Jewish interpreters treated the questions of meaning and purpose in law. See, for example, the highly illuminating discussion of the *lex talionis* by Betz, *The Sermon on the Mount*, 274-93.

or unmake. The church is the interpreter and applier of scripture, not the maker or reviser of scripture. Assuming this traditional view, one might conclude that a separation of powers exists between those with the authority to make the rule of scripture (ancient servants of God guided by divine providence) and those with the authority to interpret and apply the rule of scripture. Operating on this assumption, one might further hold that this separation of powers extends to the level of moral rules in scripture. In that case, the rule of purpose, which accords greater weight to rule justifications than to the rules themselves, violates the proper relation of the church to scripture.

It might be instructive to show, in greater detail than I have already done, that by analogy with separation-of-powers doctrines in law the rule of purpose can have a limited place in Christian hermeneutics even on the assumptions laid out in the preceding paragraph. But it is more important at this stage to see that the traditional assumption of scriptural authority is in fact presupposed by the rule of purpose. The idea that rule justifications trump rules depends on the presupposition that biblical rules implement an authority, specifically, the authority of scripture. For if biblical moral rules do not implement an authority, then one cannot argue that their justifications carry greater authority. The justifications exist for us only as justifications of the rules. Hence, the rule of purpose is meaningful only for those who grant authority to the Bible *in some sense* at the moral-rule level. Or to put it differently, to appeal to the justification of a biblical moral rule in a constructive moral argument is necessarily to presuppose that the scope of biblical authority includes the moral-rule level.

This brings us to the crucial question of warrants for the rule of purpose. If biblical moral rules enjoy authority, on what grounds can Christians accord greater authority to the justifications of the rules than to the rules themselves?

En route to answering this question, it is helpful to consider the alternatives. One could hold that Christians ought never to use the justification for a rule to trump the rule in a particular case. This position can take one of two forms. First, one could regard biblical moral rules as conclusory, meaning that insofar as one is able to determine their domain and scope, they ought to be followed without question. Of course, judging the domain and scope of rules is an interpretive act that allows for differences of opinion (and invites imaginative ways of finding wiggle room for avoiding rule applications one doesn't like), but it does not permit one to decide not to follow a rule because other considerations are more important. Second, one could hold that (perhaps with a few exceptions, such as the very general commands to honor God and to love one's neighbor as oneself), biblical moral rules are presumptive, not mandatory. In that case, one would be obliged to follow biblical moral rules except in atypical cases where other compelling reasons called for setting aside the rule. We can all think of hypotheticals (or actual examples) in which Christians who otherwise accept biblical morality for themselves would be prepared to make exceptions to specific biblical moral rules in order to honor some other more compelling set of considerations. An example made famous by Joseph Fletcher is whether a female prisoner of war (with a husband and children waiting for her return) should seek to become pregnant by one of her guards if the choice presented to her is a medical release and return home if she becomes pregnant but likely death if she remains a prisoner of war.[24]

Treating biblical moral rules as presumptive is a workable approach so long as the cases that seem to require exceptions are infrequent. But once the apparently exceptional cases begin to pile up, it is difficult to maintain the presumptive force of the rules. Under such conditions, one is likely to fall into the bad form of casuistry, where only lip service is paid to the rules and making exceptions is what actually governs everyday behavior. It is under conditions of this sort that recourse to the justification for rules looks appealing as a way to honor the rule by honoring the authority behind the rule, when literal adherence to the rule no longer seems right to us.

There are two ways in which we justify our decisions to follow the justification of a moral rule against its prescriptive intent. First, we may argue that we live in circumstances that are so different from those of the original rule-makers that the gap between the rules and their purposes in our situation is too wide for us to place even presumptive confidence in the rules *qua* rules. For example, at the moral-rule level, the witness of the Bible is against lending at interest, but the vast differences between ancient agrarian economies and modern postindustrial economies are grounds for

24. Fletcher's example is reported by him as the actual experience of a Mrs. Bergmeier. During WW II, Mrs. Bergmeier was a German prisoner of war in the Ukraine. Learning that the Russians released prisoners (and returned them to Germany) if they were pregnant and wishing to be reunited with their husband and children, Mrs. Bergmeier asked a sympathetic guard to impregnate her. See Joseph Fletcher, *Situation Ethics: The New Morality* (Philadelphia: Westminster, 1966), 164-65.

not accepting the biblical law against interest as a rule for modern economies. Recognizing the tremendous socioeconomic gap between then and
now shakes (or ought to shake) any presumptive confidence we might have
that the rule against lending at interest could routinely fulfill its purpose if
taken over as a rule for people living under modern economic conditions.

As I have said, treating rules as presumptive makes sense if we have
confidence that the purpose of the rule is routinely fulfilled by applying
the rule. That is, one has a presumptive confidence that the rule is not too
over-inclusive with respect to its purpose. But the perception of a significant sociocultural gap between the original contexts of biblical moral rules
and a new cultural context tends to erode this confidence, causing us to ask
how best to fulfill the purpose of the rules (whether by formulating new
rules or by simply letting the justifications for the rules serve as guiding
principles and values). This perception of sociocultural discontinuity between the ancient context(s) in which the rules were given and our own
context may be general, leading us to adopt the rule of purpose for all biblical moral rules. Or it may be selective. For example, one could hold that
while economic conditions have dramatically changed since ancient times,
sexuality has not. Nevertheless, the perception that the world has radically
changed in one domain tends to put question marks over our acceptance
of biblical morality in other domains, especially if we think that the various domains of social, cultural, and economic life are not easily separated
and even more so if we view all aspects of human existence as in some
sense "socially constructed."

A second way in which we justify treating the purposes of biblical
moral rules as weightier than the rules themselves is by considering how
new knowledge changes our perception of a rule. For example, another
way to look at the question of lending at interest is to consider that perhaps the ancient advocates of this rule did not have an adequate economic
theory. Thus, Richard Posner remarks of the early medieval theologians
who embraced this rule that "[i]f economics had been a well-developed
science at the time, an economist could have explained to the theologians
in a few minutes why interest was compensation rather than theft. . . ."[25]
Perhaps one could interpret the biblical prohibitions against lending at interest as likewise motivated by the theory that interest is inherently theft.

25. Richard A. Posner, *Overcoming Law* (Cambridge, MA: Harvard University Press,
1995), 523.

Modern economic theory of interest refutes this assumption, thus under-mining the rule but not its purpose to prohibit economic exploitation of the poor (see below).

The preceding example shows that in moving to the justificatory level, we sometimes also make judgments about whether all of a rule's premises are correct. Posner thinks the rule against lending at interest is wrong-headed because it depends on false economic assumptions. But his analysis does not imply that the purpose of the rule — to protect the poor against exploitation — is wrongheaded. If we accept (for the sake of illustration) Posner's analysis of the ancient rule against lending at interest and map the logic of the rule's justificatory basis, we discover that its economic theory resides in the backing for its minor premise, its concern for protection of the poor in its major premise:

Major premise: Do not exploit the poor.
Minor premise: Lending at interest exploits the poor.
Backing: Lending at interest is theft; therefore lending at interest to the poor exploits (robs) the poor.
Conclusion (the rule): Do not lend at interest.

If the minor premise collapses, the rule no longer follows, but the major premise still stands. These observations bring us to another aspect of rules, namely, levels of generality in the justifications for rules.

Before turning to the subject of levels of generality in rule justifica-tion, one more brief comparison of legal and theological hermeneutics may shed some light on our subject. This will also help prepare for some analogies I will draw in the discussion to follow. In Anglo-American com-mon law, judges are rule-makers and rule-interpreters. This means that they can adapt the law to changing sociocultural circumstances. In the case of statutory law, the role of the judiciary is to interpret and apply law, not to make it. As I have said, judges do have a kind of law-making function in statutory interpretation (and negatively in judicial review), but it is cir-cumscribed by enacted law. The check in the domain of enacted law against law becoming alienated from sociocultural conditions, with the consequence that rule purpose and rule justification slip further and fur-ther apart, is that the legislature is always on hand to change the law. In the American legal system, the United States Constitution presents a different form of the problem of law's place in the stream of historical change. The

Constitution is very difficult to amend. In view of this, the United States Supreme Court has generally not treated the Constitution like a statute. The history of the Court's interpretations of the Constitution shows that in most periods (and especially in the twentieth century), the Court has elaborated constitutional law in a way that goes far beyond anything courts regularly do with statutes. The dramatic change in American society from preindustrial to industrial and postindustrial conditions is one of the main reasons for this.[26] On the other hand, the Court cannot treat the Constitution on the model of common law, since the Constitution is enacted law. Hence, the Court again and again finds itself confronted with how to reinterpret the Constitution in the light of changed socioeconomic conditions, exercising far greater freedom than is customary in statutory interpretation without treating constitutional law as a kind of common law. It would be illuminating, I think, to consider the "rule of scripture" in the church by comparing it to the history and doctrines of constitutional interpretation. Both the similarities and differences would be enlightening. One point of analogy worth pondering is that the Bible, like the Constitution, is not (or is no longer) tradition that can be revised over time but is an ever more ancient text that must be interpreted again and again to fit changed circumstances. To speak metaphorically, the Bible as canon is neither "statute" nor "common law" but "constitution" for the church.[27] The question is what modes of interpretation are appropriate for such a "constitutional" document, and how do they differ from modes of interpretation that are appropriate to other rulish texts.

26. For a readable and engaging introduction to the history of the Supreme Court's interpretation of the Constitution, see Archibald Cox, *The Court and the Constitution* (Boston: Houghton Mifflin, 1987). For a briefer but very cogent analysis of constitutional interpretation, see Robert C. Post, "Theories of Constitutional Interpretation," in *Constitutional Domains: Democracy, Community, Management* (Cambridge, MA: Harvard University Press, 1995).

27. To call the Bible a kind of constitution is best taken not as a literal statement but as a metaphor. The metaphor of the Bible as "constitution" has been suggested by a number of people. See, for example, Robin Scroggs, "The Bible as Foundational Document," *Interpretation* 49 (1995): 17-30; Francis Schüssler Fiorenza, "The Crisis of Scriptural Authority: Interpretation and Reception," *Interpretation* 44 (1990): 363.

Levels of Generality in Rule Justifications

Frederick Schauer notes how the justifications for rules tend to be lay-ered.[28] For example, the rule, "No dogs allowed in the restaurant," has, per-haps, as its most proximate justification the aim of excluding noisy and an-noying agents. This justification has its own rationale, say, increasing or preserving the enjoyment of the restaurant by its customers, which is justi-fied in turn by an anterior purpose, such as increasing the restaurant's profitability, which also depends on some more general justification, and so on.[29]

An interesting example of how levels of justification come into play in appeals to authoritative texts is the lively debate in American constitu-tional law about what *level of generality* of the framers' intentions should govern interpretation of the Constitution. Some "originalists" distinguish between the specific and general intentions of the founders, maintaining that the framers' general political theory (not their specific ideas about the practical implications of that theory) is most fundamental to the Consti-tution.[30] Other interpreters (non-originalists) see the Constitution as in many ways free from even the general political theories of the framers. Thus, Justice William Brennan speaks of the "majestic generality" of the Constitution and argues that the "genius of the Constitution rests . . . in the adaptability of its great principles to cope with current problems and current needs."[31] There is a certain parallelism between these views of the

28. See Schauer, *Playing by the Rules,* 73-76.

29. Schauer, *Playing by the Rules,* 73.

30. On the distinction between specific and general intentions in the context of debates about originalism, see Bruce Ledewitz, "Judicial Conscience and Natural Rights: A Reply to Professor Jaffa," in Harry V. Jaffa et al., *Original Intent and the Framers of the Constitution: A Disputed Question* (Washington, D.C.: Regnery, 1994), 109-13; Scott Gerber, *To Secure These Rights: The Declaration of Independence and Constitutional Interpretation* (New York: New York University Press, 1995), 12-15. While I think the distinction between general and specific intent is generally valid, I dissent from the overall originalist approaches (of Jaffa, Gerber, and others) in which this distinction figures. See my article, "The Declaration of In-dependence in Constitutional Interpretation: A Selective History and Analysis," *University of Richmond Law Review* 32 (1998): 107-64.

31. William J. Brennan, Jr., "The Constitution of the United States: Contemporary Rati-fication," in *Interpreting the Constitution: The Debate over Original Intent,* ed. Jack N. Rakove, 27 (Boston: Northeastern University Press, 1990). Brennan borrows the phrase "majestic gen-eralities" from Justice Robert Jackson.

level at which the Constitution speaks authoritatively and different models of the use of the Bible in Christian ethics. Many conservatives advocate (at least in theory) a strict originalism in scripture interpretation that is akin to the strict originalism (of specific intent) advocated by Edwin Meese and Robert Bork for constitutional law.[32] Others, both liberal and conservative interpreters, stress the priority of the general principles of the scripture text over the biblical writers' specific applications of those principles. Still others treat the Bible more the way Brennan treats the Constitution. An example is Reinhold Niebuhr, whom Richard Hays aptly characterizes as attentive to "big theological ideas and themes" rather than to the results of "close exposition of biblical texts."[33] Of course, this schematization is an oversimplification, but it points to a significant interpretive issue and illustrates a rough range of options.

These observations about levels of justification raise a very important question about appeals to scripture in Christian ethics. If the justifications for biblical moral rules carry more weight for us than the rules themselves *qua* rules, at what level(s) of justification does this greater force reside? The most proximate or the most general? Or should we rather think of a continuum of diminishing force, whether in the direction from the most general justification toward the most proximate or from the most proximate toward the most general? Schauer points out that often a given level of justification may contain an implicit rule. For example, the rule against dogs in the restaurant may be justified by the aim of maximizing patron enjoyment, an aim that lends itself to formulation as the rule, "Conduct the business in ways that best maximize patron enjoyment." But this rule likely has its own justification, for example, profitability, a value that can also be stated as a rule. Under the rule of purpose, these observations require the following conclusion about weighing levels of justification. Where any justification admits formulation as a rule, it carries less weight than the next more general justification.

---

32. An interesting study (by an anthropologist) of similarities between Fundamentalist interpretation of scripture and legal jurisprudence in America is Vincent Crapanzano, *Serving the Word: Literalism in America from the Pulpit to the Bench* (New York: The New Press, 2000). The book is an illuminating survey, although it probably exaggerates the prevalence of literalism in law and religion in America and is not sufficiently nuanced in its analyses of religious and legal hermeneutics. For a review, see Edmund S. Morgan, "Back to Basics," *New York Review of Books* 47:12 (July 20, 2000): 47-49.

33. Hays, *The Moral Vision of the New Testament*, 220.

Ultimately, moral-rule justifications must contain at least one implicit rule as part of their major premises, since one cannot derive a moral rule from premises that themselves do not contain at least one rule or normative principle at the major-premise level.[34] An implication of this is that formalization of the justifications for moral rules will produce a hierarchy of syllogisms, each of which contains at least one major premise normative. One keeps moving back until one arrives at ultimate norms for which no further arguments can be given. This is not to imply that those who formulated biblical moral law went through a formal syllogistic process! It is simply to say that justifications for moral rules can be analyzed logically if we are able to reconstruct their assumptions.

A qualification on the preceding is that the movement from a higher level of generality to a lower level involves judgment, not analytic deduc-

---

34. R. M. Hare argued against reigning views in analytic philosophy that there is such a thing as deductive moral logic by making a similar point about imperatives. For an imperative to be a valid inference, Hare argued, at least one of the premises on which it is based must be an imperative. See R. M. Hare, *The Language of Morals* (Oxford: Clarendon Press, 1952), 17-55. D. S. Clarke has criticized this argument and has cast doubt on Hare's equation of imperatives with normatives. See D. S. Clarke, Jr., *Practical Inferences* (London: Routledge & Kegan Paul, 1985), 87-108. Without getting into a lengthy discussion of Clarke's critique, it is helpful to note his own proposal for how to map a moral argument syllogistically:

> If 'B' stands for a general type of action (e.g., telling a lie), 'A' for a more specific action of this type (telling a lie to Jones on a specific date), and if $C_1, C_2, C_3 \ldots C_n$ stand for exempting circumstances, then the negative and positive inferences used are typically of the form,
>
> (1) No one ought to do B unless $C_1, C_2, C_3 \ldots, C_n$
>   For X to do A is for X to do B
> $C_1, C_2, C_3 \ldots, C_n$ do not obtain
>   _____
>   X ought not to do A
>
> and
>
> (2) Everyone ought to do B unless $C_1, C_2, C_3 \ldots, C_n$
>   For X to do A is for X to do B
> $C_1, C_2, C_3 \ldots, C_n$ do not obtain
>   _____
>   X ought to do A
>
> Clarke, *Practical Inferences*, 142.

Since $C_1, C_2, C_3 \ldots, C_n$ may be undefined or indefinable, the inferences are not strict logical entailments but judgments.

tion.[35] Ethical judgments typically require some degree of insight or perception that cannot be fully conceptualized and assimilated to logical analysis. I will say more about this in the next chapter. Here it is necessary only to point out that the most general level of justification for a biblical moral rule is not by itself sufficient to represent the biblical witness, as if the chain of lower-level conclusions were simply logically entailed by the most general premise (for a given set of factual minor premises). For example, to say that a general social justice value stands as the higher-level warrant behind the biblical concern for the poor does not mean that we can grasp the biblical concern for social justice without attending to its "lower level" examples in such things as the law against lending at interest, the provisions for the sabbatical year and Jubilee, or Jesus' ministry of exorcisms and healings in the Gospels. The lower levels tell us something about the higher levels. Moreover, the question of weighting comes into play not as a general argument for taking scripture only at the highest levels of generality but rather in those instances where a given level of generality calls for something different from the level(s) below it in view of changed circumstances.

In what follows, I examine the levels of generality in the justifications

35. The movement from premises to conclusions is typically not a matter of strict logic but of probabilistic and interpretive judgments (see the preceding note). Noting the role of judgment (interpreting and weighing) in practical reasoning, Stephen Toulmin has proposed to characterize practical reasoning as *informal*, in distinction from formal logic. See Stephen Edelston Toulmin, *The Uses of Argument* (Cambridge: Cambridge University Press, 1964). Toulmin proposes a way to map informal arguments by laying out in a spatial scheme the place of data, warrants, backing for warrants, rebuttals, and conclusions and by marking probabilistic or interpretive judgments with qualifiers (*The Uses of Argument*, 94-145). Warrants, however, are major premises, which in turn function as minor premises in relation to their backings, etc. Hence, informal arguments can also be laid out in syllogistic form, so long as one does not treat the inferential relationships as analytic. Hence, in what follows, I will use the more familiar language of the syllogism, although each of the examples to follow could just as easily be described using Toulmin's categories. Vernon Robbins has begun mapping the argumentative logic of ancient Jewish and Christian discourse using the categories of Rule — Case — Result developed for informal logic by Richard Lanigan. See Vernon K. Robbins, "From Enthymeme to Theology in Luke 11:1-13," in *Literary Studies in Luke-Acts: A Collection of Essays in Honor of Joseph B. Tyson*, ed. R. P. Thompson and T. E. Philips (Macon, GA: Mercer University Press, 1998), 191-214; Richard L. Lanigan, "From Enthymeme to Abduction: The Classical Law of Logic and the Postmodern Rule of Rhetoric," in *Recovering Pragmatism's Voice: The Classical Tradition, Rorty, and the Philosophy of Communication,* ed. Lenore Langsdorf and Andrew R. Smith (Albany, NY: SUNY Press, 1995), 49-70.

behind three examples of biblical rules: the variations of the Old Testament law against lending at interest, the rule against homoerotic behavior assumed by Paul in Romans 1, and the Levitical purity rules. The examples are diverse, displaying the variety of hermeneutical issues that arise when we grant greater weight to biblical rule justifications than to biblical rules themselves.

The Biblical Rule against Lending at Interest

We have already looked briefly at the question of lending at interest in the Bible. A closer examination shows how consideration of levels of generality figures in appeals to the justificatory basis for a moral rule. In Ezek. 18:5-18, the prophet gives a description, twice repeated, of what it means to live justly. Among other characterizations, he describes the just person as one who "does not take advance or accrued interest" (18:8; cf. 18:13, 17; 22:12). Here Ezekiel echoes and intensifies an older rule against lending money or goods at interest (see Ex. 22:25 and Deut. 23:19-20).[36]

From the time of the church fathers and well into the Middle Ages, Christian moralists viewed lending at interest in virtually every form as sinful.[37] Deut. 23:19-20 figured importantly in the establishment of this opinion. It reads as follows:

> You shall not charge interest on loans to another Israelite, interest on money, interest on provisions, interest on anything that is lent. On loans to a foreigner you may charge interest, but on loans to another Israelite you may not charge interest, so that the LORD your God may bless you in all your undertakings in the land that you are about to enter and possess.

Patristic moralists reasoned that under the era of Christ, the distinction between Israelite and stranger was no longer valid; since all human beings were now brothers and sisters, lending at interest was absolutely forbidden. Psalm 15:5 supplied another argument from scripture by pronouncing a

---

36. On Ezekiel's use of earlier legal traditions, see Michael Fishbane, *Biblical Interpretation in Ancient Israel*, 293-94. On the other pentateuchal laws governing loans, see Fishbane, 174-77.

37. See Albert R. Jonsen and Stephen Toulmin, *The Abuse of Casuistry: A History of Moral Reasoning* (Berkeley and Los Angeles: University of California Press, 1988), 181-94.

blessing on those "who do not lend money at interest and do not take a bribe against the innocent" (see also Prov. 28:8[38]). Moreover, Ezekiel assumes a universal form of the rule, one that does not distinguish between loans to Israelites and loans to non-Israelites (Ezek. 18:8, 13, 17; 22:12).

At least part of the rationale for rejecting lending at interest was that charging interest was a means by which the wealthy exploited the poor. Albert Jonsen and Stephen Toulmin propose the following plausible reconstruction of the moral basis for the prohibition:

> In the subsistence economies that existed from the time of the writing of Deuteronomy up through the early Middle Ages, the failure of a crop or the loss of a flock could threaten the life of a poor man and his family; and the loan of seed, of an ewe for breeding, or of food might be lifesaving. In such circumstances, to demand "more than was given" would clearly be exploitation of one's "brother" or neighbor. While loans were certainly given in other circumstances, the paradigm for the moral analysis of usury appears to have been aid in time of distress.[39]

The parallel texts to the rule in Deuteronomy focus on loans to the poor (Ex. 22:25 and Lev. 25:36-37), making no specific provisions for other kinds of loans (e.g., commercial loans). Thus, within the canonical form of the law, the provision in Deuteronomy stands as the more general rule, comprehending in scope the prohibitions in Exodus and Leviticus. The promulgators of the Deuteronomic form of the law probably also had the vulnerability of the poor in view, since the poor were typically the recipients of loans.[40] Moreover, construing these laws from the perspective of the

38. The NRSV translates the formula *neshekh w^e-tarbît* in Prov. 28:8 as "exorbitant interest," but it more probably means "advance and accrued interest" (as the NRSV has it for Ezek. 18:8). Or *neshekh* and *tarbît* may simply be synonyms for interest. See Daniel I. Block, *The Book of Ezekiel, Chapters 1–24*, The New International Commentary on the Old Testament (Grand Rapids: Eerdmans, 1997), 573. For a general discussion of the Old Testament texts dealing with interest, see Walter C. Kaiser, Jr., *Toward Old Testament Ethics* (Grand Rapids: Zondervan, 1983), 212-17.

39. Jonsen and Toulmin, *The Abuse of Casuistry*, 183. See also Jeffrey H. Tigay, *Deuteronomy*, The JPS Torah Commentary (Philadelphia and Jerusalem: The Jewish Publication Society, 1996), 217.

40. One might construe the references to the poor in Ex. 22:25 and Lev. 25:35-37 as suggesting that originally loans were prohibited only to the poor and that Deuteronomy was the first to bar interest lending to all Israelites (as part of the reform under Josiah). But as Tigay observes, "nonlegal passages consistently regard the taking of interest from one's

New Testament (notably Paul's emphasis on the end of the Jew/gentile distinction) provides grounds for taking the rule beyond its restriction to Israelite dealings with other Israelites. In fact, we see a universalizing of the rule already in Ps. 15:5, Prov. 28:8, and Ezekiel. Hence, the patristic conclusion that under the era of Christ the various scriptural teachings on lending warrant a universal rule against loans at interest seems a reasonable inference, one already supported in Israelite legal tradition before the rise of Christianity. Similar universalizing tendencies are also evident in subsequent Jewish law. Although in Talmudic law, the permissibility of lending at interest to foreigners was extended to include resident aliens, there were also voices discouraging lending at interest to Jew *or non-Jew*.[41] In the post-Talmudic period, interest lending to non-Jews was judged to be permissible only because political conditions in Europe severely restricted the trades and professions open to Jews. Under eased political circumstances, it was held, lending at interest to non-Jews would also be prohibited.[42]

The medieval casuists worked out a theory of interest lending that permitted various exceptions thought to be prudent in the light of prevailing economic conditions. We now recognize that these conditions differed markedly from earlier agrarian economies. With the shift from a European economy based largely on subsistence farming toward a mercantile and commercial economy, the Catholic moral theologians recast the earlier doctrine from an absolute prohibition of loans at interest to a prohibition only against "gratuitous distress loans."[43] The modern Western church is heir to this changed perception of lending at interest. Hence, when we examine the biblical prohibitions against interest loans, we are inclined to argue that those proscriptions were aimed at the "paradigm case" of exploitative loans to the poor.[44] In so doing we reject the rule against lending at

countryman as wrong, without differentiating between solvent and poor borrowers. . . . Most likely Exodus and Leviticus specify the poor simply because it was they who normally borrowed" (Tigay, *Deuteronomy*, 217).

41. H. H. Cohen, "Usury," *Encyclopaedia Judaica*, vol. 16 (New York: Macmillan, 1971), 31.

42. Cohen, "Usury," 32.

43. Jonsen and Toulmin, *The Abuse of Casuistry*, 192.

44. I have been treating the purpose of the rule as protection of the poor. As I noted in an earlier discussion, one can construe the rationale for the rule as the idea that lending at interest is a kind of theft. If this idea lies behind the rule, the primary concern was no doubt that the poor person (but perhaps on occasion the wealthy person caught in an economic predicament) was especially vulnerable to exploitation through this kind of theft.

interest, but treat its purpose or justification as carrying abiding moral force.[45]

Closer inspection shows that this purpose or justification is layered. The most immediate purpose is to prevent economic exploitation of the poor in lending practices. Behind this purpose is a more general biblical concern for protection of the poor and powerless. That concern is in turn grounded in a distinctive conception of God as defender of the powerless (more precisely, defender of the less powerful against exploitation by the more powerful). Behind this stands the theological assumption that our relation to God entails moral obligations that are to take their cues from God's own character, for example, from the character of God as "defender of widows and orphans." This entire justificatory scheme warrants the position that lending at interest can be morally permissible and, as an instrument of economic utility, is morally desirable insofar as it ameliorates rather than exploits poverty.

The Rule of Romans 1 on Homoerotic Behavior

The preceding analysis of the biblical rules against lending at interest offers a relatively straightforward example of identifying the justification for a biblical rule and according it greater weight than the rule itself. A more difficult example is the Pauline rule against homoerotic behavior in Rom. 1:26-27. Some might claim that there is no rule against homoerotic activity in Romans 1, pointing out that Paul does not formulate any such rule and that his purpose is not to make a pronouncement about homosexuality per se but to illustrate the nexus of sin and judgment in which human beings are caught by their own rebellion against God. This is, of course, correct. Nevertheless, it does not touch the question of whether Paul operates in this text with a moral rule against homoerotic behavior. It is more accurate to say that Paul's argument, while it does not lay down moral rules, necessarily assumes a rule against homosexual relations (in 1:26-27). Likewise, the wider context, Rom. 1:18-32, assumes other moral rules: e.g., a prohibition of idolatry, a command to live in truth, a command to practice righteousness, etc. What is notable about Romans 1:18-32 is the way in which it conceives the divine sanctions for violating such rules. Paul's ex-

45. This is the approach of Kaiser, *Toward Old Testament Ethics*, 212-17.

amples suggest that our infidelity to God entails its own intrinsic price or punishment. God does not impose extrinsic penalties but exercises judgment by giving us up to our infidelity and its natural consequences. In that divine abandonment is the human predicament to which the gospel speaks.

Paul probably regards the prohibition of homoerotic behavior as an absolute rule. Under the rule of purpose, however, we are to treat the justification for this rule as weightier (for us) than the rule itself. Since Paul was a Hellenistic Jew, a first step toward identifying the justification behind the rule is to consider the reasons why Hellenistic Jews condemned homoerotic practice:[46] (1) because it was linked with idolatry; (2) because they thought of it as an expression of unbridled passion (passion uncontrolled by reason); (3) because they regarded it as unnatural, i.e., against the divinely-created order. The second and third of these are related, since Hellenistic Jews understood reason as a power by which human beings are to order their passions, bringing them in line with the divine order. Moreover, one way in which people of Paul's time conceived homoerotic behavior as unnatural was in its confusion, to their minds, of the proper male and female roles. We can fill out the logic of this scheme as follows. Sexual passion inclines toward sexual fulfillment and is inherently indiscriminate. Those who have taken rational control of their passions direct their erotic desire toward those of the opposite sex. This is "natural" in the sense that it accords with the rational order of nature (God's designs in and for creation); the sexual act between a man and a women puts the male in his properly dominant role over the female, who is and also symbolizes the irrational, passion-driven dynamic of human existence that needs the rational, ordering control of the male for its proper expression.

46. The following discussion of Paul's view of homosexuality is indebted to Robin Scroggs, *The New Testament and Homosexuality* (Philadelphia: Fortress Press, 1983); Bernadette J. Brooten, "Paul's Views on the Nature of Women and Female Eroticism," in *Immaculate Conception: The Female in Sacred Image and Social Reality,* ed. Clarissa W. Atkinson et al., Harvard Women's Studies in Religion (Boston: Beacon, 1985), 61-87; idem, *Love Between Women: Early Christian Responses to Female Homoeroticism* (Chicago: University of Chicago Press, 1996); Victor Paul Furnish, *The Moral Teaching of Paul: Selected Issues,* 2d ed. (Nashville: Abingdon, 1985), 52-82; idem, "The Bible and Homosexuality: Reading the Texts in Context," in *Homosexuality in the Church: Both Sides of the Debate,* ed. Jeffrey S. Siker (Louisville, KY: Westminster John Knox, 1994), 18-38; Dale B. Martin, "Heterosexism and the Interpretation of Romans 1:18-32," *Biblical Interpretation: A Journal of Contemporary Approaches* 3 (1995): 332-55.

We should not suppose that all of the views just sketched are assumed by Paul just because he is a Hellenistic Jew. Instead we should look for language in Rom. 1:18-32 that suggests one or more of these views as informing the references to homoeroticism in his argument. Romans 1:18-32 is clearly indebted to the view that homoeroticism is passion that has moved into unnatural forms because it is unchecked by reason. Paul thinks of the reasoning faculty as having become "darkened" through its turning away from the light of God. It is also evident that Paul links homoerotic behavior with idolatry, although it is not clear that he is thinking exclusively of sexual relations with cult prostitutes. He may have in mind that the turn to idolatry plunges the mind into darkness, thus opening the way for the passions to issue in unnatural acts. This is the more probable interpretation, since homosexuality was not linked exclusively with cultic practices in Paul's social world.

If we accept the preceding, for the purpose of illustration, we can analyze the justificatory basis for the assumed rule against homoerotic behavior in Romans 1. First, the view that homoerotic behavior is a consequence of idolatry depends on the view that idolatry lies at the root of that deformation of God-honoring reason that leads to a passional usurpation of the mind's proper control of the passions. Second, homoerotic activity is passion in disorder, an unnatural expression of erotic desire. Third, the underlying justification becomes intelligible only if there is a reason why homoerotic behavior is unnatural, for only that reason explains why Paul regards it as an expression of unbridled passion freed from the grip of a divinely illumined mind. That underlying reason is no doubt the assumption that the scriptures (notably Gen. 2:18-25, Lev. 18:22, and Lev. 20:13) and creation itself[47] establish heterosexual union as the divine norm of creation. It may also be that Paul shared the pervasive view that the female represents the irrational and passional, the male the rational which is to order eros for both the male and the female.[48] However, nowhere in Romans 1 does Paul hint

---

47. Paul asserts that knowledge of God is available to humanity through the created order (1:18-21). At the end of his description of how human beings have rejected that knowledge and given themselves up to their passions, Paul presents a vice list and declares that humanity knows "God's decree" about such things (1:32). This suggests that he operates with some kind of natural law theory (see also Rom. 2:14-16). God has decreed in a way that can be known by human beings through the created order. God's decree is, of course, also in scripture.

48. For a detailed elaboration and defense of this interpretation, see Brooten, *Love Between Women*, 215-66.

that the problem with homoeroticism is that it puts males in improper passive roles and females in improper dominant roles.[49]

Some who argue that Romans 1 and other biblical texts do not touch the question of homosexuality in its modern forms do so by claiming that what the biblical writers understood by homoerotic behavior is something altogether different from the modern conception of homosexual "orientation."[50] Some who make this point also go on to stress that the ancient polemic against homosexual behavior had in view nothing like modern homosexual adults uniting in committed monogamous relationships. Consider, for example, these remarks by William Placher: "If two men in the contemporary United States . . . come to love each other, move in with each other and share their lives while having regular sexual intercourse, they are almost certainly doing something unlike anything *anybody* in ancient Israel did."[51] This observation is correct, but it does not remove the

---

49. The inclusion of *malakoi* ("weak, soft" persons) in the vice list of 1 Cor. 6:9-10 may suggest that Paul shared the widespread view that males ought not to assume passive sexual roles. However, Paul may have used the term *malakos* simply to denote those who engage in homoeroticism. Moreover, Dale Martin has cogently argued that the word is probably best translated effeminate and does not denote specifically homoerotic qualities. See Dale B. Martin, "*Arsenokoitês* and *Malakos*: Meanings and Consequences," in *Biblical Ethics and Homosexuality: Listening to Scripture*, ed. Robert L. Brawley (Louisville, KY: Westminster/John Knox Press, 1996), 124-28. Hence, one should be cautious about attributing to Paul a full-blown theory of sexuality based on his use of a single word, open to more than one interpretation, especially since other texts in Paul show that at the very least he had come to question gender hierarchy or at least to revise traditional conceptions of it. Texts that suggest this rethinking are (1) Gal. 3:28; (2) those passages in which Paul acknowledges female authority, as in the cases of Phoebe, a minister of the church at Cenchreae and a patron of Paul's mission (Rom. 16:1-2), and Junia, an apostle (Rom. 16:7); (3) his recognition of female exercise of prophetic gifts in 1 Cor. 11:2-16. Since 1 Cor. 11:2-16 also contains hierarchical language, the picture of Paul's attitude toward women and authority is mixed. He may well hold competing "theories" of male and female roles in tension. 1 Cor. 11:2ff. itself suggests some sort of compromise between competing conceptions of male and female. See Wayne A. Meeks, "The Image of the Androgyne: Some Uses of a Symbol in Earliest Christianity," *History of Religions* 13 (1974): 165-208.

50. See Furnish, "The Bible and Homosexuality," 18-19, and Scroggs, *The New Testament and Homosexuality*; Furnish and Scroggs stress that the primary (or perhaps even exclusive) form of homoerotic behavior known to Paul was pederasty.

51. William C. Placher, "Is the Bible True?" a paper of the Center of Theological Inquiry, Princeton, N.J., as quoted by Thomas G. Long, "Living with the Bible," in *Homosexuality and Christian Community*, ed. Choon-Leong Seow (Louisville, KY: Westminster/John Knox Press, 1996), 69.

modern form of homosexuality that Placher describes from the scope of the moral *rule* in Romans 1.

As to the rule, Paul speaks only of homoerotic activity, not of any particular social form of homosexuality. The rule implied by Paul's language includes by its sheer generality all forms of homoerotic behavior. (Similarly, a statute that prohibited "vehicles from entering the park" would include fire engines and ambulances, even if the city council did not mean to include emergency vehicles but simply forgot to consider them.) Such a rule, depending on its purpose, could be over-inclusive (as a city ordinance prohibiting all vehicles in the park would no doubt be over-inclusive). This would be the case, for example, if the justification for the rule were the association of homoerotic behavior with cultic prostitution, or if its aim were simply to prohibit uncontrolled passion on the assumption that homoerotic behavior is always eros run wild, or if Paul's concern were with pederasty as an exploitative and dehumanizing form of sexuality. On any one or any combination of these justifications, the *rule* would still cover forms of homosexuality that were not idolatrous, were not driven by unfettered passion, and were not exploitative of boys. Failure to distinguish the implicit rule in Romans 1 from its justification accounts for much of the disagreement over whether this text warrants a blanket prohibition of all homoerotic behavior. The *rule* does, even if its justification may not.

One important consideration stands against what I have just argued. If homosexual practice is "socially constructed," so that the ostensibly identical homoerotic act is in fact not the same from culture to culture, then Paul's blanket rule may have to be taken as culturally specific. Here we confront the problem of what to do when we judge that a biblical writer means to speak universally but we perceive that there is relevant factual information unavailable to that biblical writer which might be grounds for limiting the applicability of what the biblical writer says. I will not linger over this question here because it really belongs to the discussion of two other hermeneutical rules: the rule of analogy and the rule of scope.

As to the justification for the rule, a close examination of the underlying logic of Romans 1 shows that the rule is probably not over-inclusive with respect to its underlying rationale. Transforming the earlier analysis into deductive logic, we can describe Paul's view as follows.

First Major Premise: Heterosexual union is the creational norm; homosexual behavior is against the creational norm.

Second Major Premise: Idolatry is the root of all disorder, the initial cause of all departures from the creational norms for human life.

Conclusion: Therefore, homoerotic behavior is an expression of disordered passion signifying a mind given over to idolatry.

If this analysis captures the implicit logic of Paul's argument, then the assumed rule against all forms of homoerotic behavior is apparently not over-inclusive since the justification for this rule is that such behavior is inherently unnatural. Moreover, if we ask what further levels of justification inform Paul's rationale, we discover that we have probably reached a limit since it seems almost impossible to determine how Paul construed the reasons (if he even thought about them) for the norm of heterosexuality. It may be that a Hellenistic-Jewish theory of gender roles informs Paul's reading of Genesis (even though Romans 1 gives no hint of this). He may think that the creation of woman "out of" man in Gen. 2:21-22 signifies *some* order of male over female that in turn is to be honored in sexuality. I think we should be very cautious here since the only other text in Paul that provides a clue to his reading of Gen. 2:21-22 is 1 Cor. 11:2-16, a passage that seems to cut both ways. Moreover, it may be that Paul simply took the rule against homosexual behavior from scripture, connecting Lev. 18:22 and 20:13 with the creation story, and did not reflect or even think it important to reflect on *why* scripture has such a rule. In that case — which seems the most likely possibility — Romans 1:26-27 assumes this creation rule without any further rationale.

In saying that Romans 1:26-27 may assume a creation rule against homoerotic behavior without any further justification for this rule than that it is in Paul's Bible (as Paul reads it), I do not preclude that our reading of Romans as part of our Bible may lead us back to Genesis and Leviticus and to an inquiry about human sexuality that Paul does not undertake. In that case, Romans 1 may also stand for the necessity of developing a biblical conception of sexuality as a framework in which to judge the significance and weight of Paul's statements about homoerotic practice in Romans 1.

To summarize, assuming the analysis above, Romans 1 presupposes a blanket *rule* against homoerotic behavior. But if we grant that the purpose (or justification) behind a biblical moral rule carries greater weight than the rule itself, then this rule, like all biblical moral rules, no longer carries force *as a rule*. Its force lies in its purpose or justification. However, in this case, it happens that the justification itself (a creation norm) warrants a blanket form of the rule. The justification is therefore a reason (insofar as we grant authority to the Bible at the level of its rule justifications) in favor of our adopting a moral rule against homosexuality.

I say "a" reason because other considerations have to be taken into account as well. For example, we may modify our assessment of the weight of Romans 1 if we hold to the hermeneutical principle that a presumption exists in favor of according greater weight to countercultural voices in scripture than to those that merely echo the dominant culture of their time.[52] Whatever Paul's exact understanding of the created "order" of sexuality, his view seems clearly indebted to a dominant antipathy in his culture against homosexuality. By contrast the baptismal formula he quotes in Gal. 3:28 challenges dominant notions of sexual identity. Some have found in Gal. 3:28 a countercultural vision calling for a radical rethinking of traditional understandings of human sexuality. Likewise, those who hold to the hermeneutical principle that empirical knowledge (scientific knowledge) stands outside the scope of scripture[53] may conclude that the conceptions of "nature" and of the social phenomenon of homosexual behavior in Paul's day are open to correction by various branches of modern science. By themselves, modern scientific disciplines cannot settle the moral question; but they can provide knowledge that recasts certain factual premises of the question. Of course, not everyone accepts the two hermeneutical principles I have just mentioned (to be discussed in subsequent chapters). Moreover, some who do accept them are not led by these principles to the conclusion that homoerotic behavior can be a morally appropriate form of sexual expression. My point here is simply that the rule of purpose, as a hermeneutical principle for appropriating biblical moral prescriptions, does not stand alone but is properly used in consort with other principles.

Some may conclude that my reconstruction of Paul's implicit logic, rooting the moral rule against homosexual behavior in a creation norm, is faulty or at least is not the only plausible way to construe the text. They may reconstruct the ultimate rationale differently and in a way that shows the moral rule against homoerotic behavior to be over-inclusive with respect to that ultimate rationale. Or they may argue that the creation norm is present but that behind the creation norm is a rationale with respect to

---

52. On this hermeneutical principle, see chapter three.
53. On this hermeneutical principle, see chapter four.

which the rule against homoerotic behavior is over-inclusive. I have suggested a few of these rationales for the creation rule above. This kind of approach has an ally in the argument (noted briefly above) that homoerotic activity cannot be defined apart from its social meaning and therefore differs from culture to culture to such an extent that Paul's rule, however universally understood by Paul himself, should be treated as having in view only the forms of homosexuality known to Paul. Another response might be to recognize that the rationales for the implicit rule against homosexual activity are so difficult to reconstruct — there being multiple possibilities — that one should not use Romans 1 as a guide in developing a Christian position on contemporary homosexuality(ies).

The Purity Rules

In his *Theology of the Old Testament,* Walter Brueggemann comments on the significance of the Levitical law for contemporary theology and ethics.[54] His discussion offers a particularly illuminating example of attending to different justificatory levels of biblical commands. The predominant teaching of the New Testament argues against the purity rules as rules for the church. Nevertheless, cautions Brueggemann, this does not necessarily make the purity laws irrelevant. To put Brueggemann's argument in the terms of our present discussion, we can hold that the Levitical rules are not *rules* for us, but that conclusion does not foreclose the question whether they carry weight, for the church's life and witness, at some level of their *purpose.*

Brueggemann notes that there is a tension between the justice and purity traditions in the Bible, and he holds that if compelled to choose between them he affirms justice over purity, as Jesus did. Nevertheless, Brueggemann offers three considerations against dismissing altogether the "holiness" concern embodied in the purity laws of the Torah. First, the imagery of the holiness witness provides Christians with categories for understanding the atonement in Christ (an interpretive move already evident in Hebrews and Paul). Second, the commands of justice may need the special religious orientation of the holiness traditions to keep them from be-

54. See Walter Brueggemann, *Theology of the Old Testament: Testimony, Dispute, Advocacy* (Minneapolis: Fortress Press, 1997), 193-96.

ing reduced to a purely political program. Thus, the Old Testament purity regulations stand for an orientation of ethics *in holiness* that is necessary to keep our fidelity to the justice traditions of the Bible from collapsing into a "self-propelled human crusade."[55] Third, the Israelite concern for purity reflects our human need for a kind of reconciliation and restoration to God that cannot be satisfied by moral action alone. "[W]hat the 'sacrificial system' seeks to do is not outgrown through enlightenment and sophistication. After human efforts at righting wrongs and making reparations have been done as fully as possible, an unsettled 'residue of ache' remains that requires another kind of action, action in a priestly domain."[56] Or, as Paul Ricoeur observes, even though we no longer operate with the conceptual frameworks that made ancient notions of pollution intelligible, we still experience moral culpability as a "stain," which makes the symbolism of ancient understandings of moral pollution relevant to us and recoupable through hermeneutics.[57]

Taking our cues from Brueggemann and Ricoeur, we can distinguish three different kinds of justification for the biblical purity regulations. One is the particular ancient Israelite conception of human existence in right relation to divine holiness. A second is a biblical-theological conception that Christians construct by attending to the way in which the atonement in Christ is articulated in the language of the Israelite purity tradition and by considering how holiness and justice are related to each other in the Bible. In this perspective the original plain sense of the holiness traditions is reinterpreted in the light of the biblical witness to Christ as the agent of our atonement and the one who subordinates purity to justice without renouncing the motive for purity. A third justification of the purity rules is the philosophical or phenomenology-of-religion level where purity is justified through a more general philosophical anthropology. This perspective can also be cast in theological terms through a correlation of the Christian symbols in the biblical witness with certain features of the human experience of guilt and shame.

If we use the second and third justifications for the purity rules as a way of appropriating them for our own time and culture, they will not

55. Brueggemann, *Theology of the Old Testament*, 194.

56. Brueggemann, *Theology of the Old Testament*, 195.

57. Paul Ricoeur, *The Symbolism of Evil*, trans. Emerson Buchanan (Boston: Beacon Press, 1967).

function as rules for us but rather as symbols informing our life and thought. Understood in this way, the purity rules symbolize a special religious witness against letting justice commitments turn into a purely political program, and they disclose that dimension of our ethical life that cannot be dealt with in purely ethical terms. They also speak at what Henry David Aiken has called the post-ethical level,[58] answering the question "Why be moral?" in a specifically religious or theological way: the call to be holy because God is holy.

Concluding Summary and Assessment

The idea that the purpose (reason or justification) for a moral rule is weightier than the rule itself is a widely held assumption. It belongs to a shared set of plausibility structures that cause us to find some kinds of arguments from scripture more persuasive than others. Making these implicit plausibility structures explicit as hermeneutical rules helps us to understand the nature of moral argument from the Bible, to examine its bases, and to test for consistency in our tacit hermeneutical theories and argumentative practice.

I have pointed out that prescriptive rules may be mandatory or presumptive. Mandatory rule-quality excludes any other reasons for not following a prescriptive rule. Presumptive rule-quality signifies that the rule *qua* rule is a reason for following it but does not exclude departure from the rule on the basis of other considerations. The rule of purpose undermines the rule quality of both mandatory and presumptive rules by according greater weight to rule justifications. To treat a rule as presumptive leaves room for considering its justification but only in atypical situations. The presumptive force of a rule may weaken over time to the point where it no longer carries any practical weight in decision-making. When that happens to a biblical moral rule, those who affirm the rule of purpose may treat the rule as a marker of its justification, the justification thus becoming the bearer of the rule's authority.

The warrant for treating the justification for a biblical rule as weightier than the rule itself is that transferring biblical rules from their ancient cultural contexts into modern contexts tends to disrupt the relation be-

---

58. Aiken, "Levels of Moral Discourse," 83-87.

tween the rules and their justifications so severely that confidence in the rules is undermined (or ought to be). This warrant for the rule of purpose is insufficient without a second necessary assumption, namely, that *in some sense* the scope of scriptural authority reaches to the moral-rule level. In depending on this presupposition, however, the rule of purpose also modifies it by relocating, for all practical purposes, the authority of the rule to its justification. That is, if the justification is weightier than the rule, it always trumps the rule, even though the rule remains the marker of the authority of rule justifications, the place where the authority of those justifications "appears" in the biblical text.

Rule justifications are layered, proceeding from more specific proximate reasons to more general ones. In explicating the levels of justification behind biblical moral rules, we typically discover a movement from the more culturally-specific to the less so, which argues for giving greater weight to more general justifications. Moreover, insofar as any justifications contain implicit rules, *their* justifications carry greater weight, but not in such a way that lower justificatory levels become irrelevant. The question of weighting comes into play not as a general argument for taking scripture only at its highest levels of generality, but rather in those cases where a given level of generality calls for something different from the level(s) below it in view of changed circumstances in our time and place.

Identifying a hierarchy of justifications behind a biblical prescription is itself a methodologically complex matter. It can be very difficult to make probability judgments about what conceptual frameworks existed in the minds of those who originally shaped and read the biblical texts.

This brings up a further question that we have not yet considered. Is it legitimate to objectify rationales that the original writers and readers probably did not think through, rationales that we discover as part of the implicit, even non-conscious, logic of an ancient perspective? This seems fair where we are making explicit what is implicit, giving the most coherently logical reading in terms indigenous to the ancient setting of the text. But sometimes our objectifications involve modern concepts foreign to the thinking of the ancient writers and hearers. Our modern interpretations of why ancient peoples developed rules of purity are an example of this. From the standpoint of the ancient Israelites themselves, the purity rules are to be obeyed because God commands them, but we are able to discover other plausible reasons why the Israelites developed a purity system. It is doubtful that our ways of describing the Israelite concern with cosmic order represents how the Israelites themselves thought about purity. Most sociological and cultural interpretations of biblical texts are not merely descriptive of ancient perspectives but entail analysis that depends on modern categories unavailable to ancient people. This is probably unavoidable if we are to let the ancient texts speak to us, but it is important to be aware of how far we are using our categories and not ancient ones. Only with that awareness can we make a fair judgment about whether we are doing justice to the text.

This brings us to a further issue. Are the justifications for biblical moral rules only those rationales that can be probabilistically reconstructed behind the rules in their original historical settings? And if not, what are the implications for the rule of purpose? We find examples within the biblical tradition itself of the giving of new rationales for old rules. Moreover, it has long been common for Christians to provide new rationales for ancient scriptural moral rules. A particularly sophisticated contemporary example is the post–Vatican II *Catechism of the Catholic Church* in its teaching on human sexuality.[59] The catechism defends what it construes as universal biblical rules governing the sexual life by adducing social and personalistic rationales growing out of the history of Catholic moral reflection. Hermeneutical approaches of this type appropriate biblical moral commandments as rules, but by adducing extra-biblical rationales for the rules, the *Catechism* also signals the importance of rationales for rules. This raises the question whether the more modern rationales of the *Catechism* are *guides* to moral decision-making, which may at times be more important than the rules, or are only interpretive arguments intended to back up the rules.

When it comes to biblical moral rules, Christians tend to divide hermeneutically over the function of identifying the purpose behind a moral prescription. Some see that function as limited to aiding in the interpretation of the prescription and making it more attractive by revealing its good sense and place in God's moral economy. For others, the function of identifying the purpose of a biblical command is also to discover the only thing about the command that should properly guide us in seeking to fit our practice into God's moral economy. For those who affirm the hermeneutical rule of purpose, the question is how to relate reconstruc-

---

59. *Catechism of the Catholic Church,* English translation (Washington, D.C.: United States Catholic Conference, 1994), 560-76.

tions (which are sometimes rather speculative) of ancient purposes behind biblical prescriptions to other traditional and contemporary ways in which the church has come to understand those prescriptions. For example, it is not immediately evident how to relate conceptions of human sexuality based on ancient notions of cosmic order (involving judgments about clean and unclean things) to the later (and arguably quite modern in some respects) view given by the Roman Catholic *Catechism* that sexuality "especially concerns affectivity, the capacity to love and to procreate, and in a more general way the aptitude for forming bonds of communion with others."[60] Moreover, we are likely to have more difficulty grasping the significance, for us, of the ancient cosmic approach to sexuality than in making sense of the *Catechism's* way of defining sexuality. The traditions to which we belong, including emerging modern or postmodern traditions of Christian moral self-understanding, always mediate how we "take" the meaning (for us) of ancient conceptions. Hence, there is an important constructive dimension to any use of biblical moral commands according to the hermeneutical rule of purpose. This will become even more evident in the next chapter when we consider the necessary place of constructive analogizing in the use of the Bible in Christian ethics.

A related question is whether it is legitimate to identify the rationale behind a biblical prescription by recourse to the Bible as a whole. An example is the argument that behind the prohibition of lending at interest lies an understanding of God as defender of the poor and oppressed. Without being able to show that this understanding of God in fact informed those who promulgated the law against interest lending, is it nonetheless appropriate to argue that the Bible as a whole invites us to adduce this theology as the best way of understanding that law, where "best" is a value judgment? Does the Bible as a scripture "whole" (an "integrity" as Kelsey terms it) create its own symbolic world and thus "refigure" the texts and traditions that it comprises? In searching for the justifications behind biblical morality, the church confronts the question whether the meaning of discrete biblical texts changes or deepens through their incorporation into the scriptural canon.

A further issue has to do with the scope of the rule of purpose. If we treat some biblical prescriptions according to the rule of purpose, is it consistent to treat others as retaining their rule-force? For example, if we treat

---

60. *Catechism of the Catholic Church*, 560.

the prohibitions of lending at interest according to the rule of purpose, can we nevertheless treat the Ten Commandments as carrying rule-force? Do the moral rules of the Ten Commandments belong to a special class of rules? Treating some biblical moral prescriptions as retaining their rule-force *qua* rules and treating others according to the rule of purpose requires some set of differentiating criteria. Short of such criteria, one who accepted the applicability of the rule of purpose to all biblical moral prescriptions might nevertheless use the Bible as a whole, together with any other sources he or she admitted as appropriate to the construction of Christian ethics, to arrive at an ethical conclusion in rule form. For example, he or she might conclude that the commandments "Thou shalt not steal" and "Thou shalt not commit adultery" should be embraced as moral rules but not because they appear in scripture in rule form. Hence, those who do not conceive the authority of scripture as conferring rule-quality on biblical moral prescriptions could nonetheless accord a place for moral rules in their own moral vision, including some rules that the Bible also affirms. Or, to put it differently, the affirmance of the rule of purpose does not entail the view that there is no place for moral rules *qua* rules in Christian ethics; it speaks only to the question whether what we take from biblical moral prescriptions is their rule content or, alternatively, their rationales.

Finally, the use of the rule of purpose is not sufficient by itself as an approach to the use of biblical moral prescriptions in Christian ethics. There are cases where our best construction of the rationale for a rule uncovers a set of cultural assumptions that we cannot accept and may reject for other biblical-theological reasons. For example, the ancient justification for the prohibition of adultery in the seventh commandment may include an assumption that husbands enjoy property rights in their wives, an assumption that we reject on broader biblical-theological grounds. Rejecting that assumption is compatible with the rule of purpose. The rule does not mean that any or all of the assumptions contained in rule justifications must be *accepted*; it means only that the justifications are weightier than the rule *qua* rule.

TWO

The Rule of Analogy

Analogical reasoning is an appropriate and necessary method for applying scripture to contemporary moral issues.

The use of analogical reasoning is common in Christian ethics, yet its logic has rarely been analyzed and its importance has not always been fully recognized. One of the few discussions is the brief treatment in James M. Gustafson's influential article, "The Place of Scripture in Christian Ethics."[1] Gustafson defines a form of argument from the Bible that runs as follows: "Those actions of persons and groups are to be judged morally wrong which are similar to actions that are judged to be wrong or against God's will under similar circumstances in scripture, or are discordant with actions judged to be right or in accord with God's will in scripture."[2] Although Gustafson does not label this approach, it is a form of case-based reasoning, an "action" (or set of actions) being a fact pattern making up a "case."

Case-based reasoning uses an analogical method, a showing of similarity between two fact patterns to argue that one, which we may term the

---

1. James M. Gustafson, "The Place of Scripture in Christian Ethics: A Methodological Study," in *Theology and Ethics* (Philadelphia: United Church Press, 1974), 121-45. Originally published in *Interpretation* 24 (October 1970): 430-55.

2. Gustafson, "The Place of Scripture," 133.

paradigm case, should govern the other, which we may call the problem case. Biblical paradigm cases can be analogized to any number of problem cases, often quite diverse ones. Examples are analogizing from the exodus story (as paradigm case) to the problem cases of slavery in antebellum America, the plight of the poor in Latin America,[3] or the bombing of Cambodia during the Viet Nam War;[4] analogizing from New Testament debates over gentile inclusion (as paradigm cases) to the problem cases of racism[5] and the question of homosexuality;[6] and analogical use of the paradigms of the Good Samaritan and the New Testament's special concern for the poor in making judgments about how the church should respond to abortion.[7]

According to Gustafson, two problems beset analogical reasoning from scripture. One is demonstrating sufficient similarity across the epochal gaps between biblical times and our own. A second is that of control: on what basis do we select some biblical stories and not others? If *present events* (and our prior moral judgments about them) determine the selection of those stories in scripture that will serve as paradigms, then the selection tends to be self-serving. If we seek to let the *Bible itself* be controlling, that still requires some normative judgments by us about which stories from the Bible are most truly expressive of the Bible's witness as a whole.

In discussing "control" as primarily a problem of *selection*, Gustafson seems to assume that the problem of control arises only after one has solved the first difficulty he mentions: demonstrating sufficient similarity between ancient biblical stories and our contemporary problem case. This

3. I discuss these two examples below.
4. Gustafson presents this example ("The Place of Scripture in Christian Ethics," 123-29, 133-34).
5. I have treated this question in *Elusive Israel: The Puzzle of Election in Romans* (Louisville, KY: Westminster/John Knox Press, 1997), 65-90.
6. Jeffrey S. Siker, "Homosexual Christians, the Bible, and Gentile Inclusion," in Siker, ed., *Homosexuality in the Church: Both Sides of the Debate* (Louisville, KY: Westminster/John Knox Press, 1994), 178-94; see also Luke Timothy Johnson, "Debate and Discernment, Scripture and the Spirit," *Commonweal* (January 1994): 11-13 (reprinted in *Virtues and Practices in the Christian Tradition: Christian Ethics after MacIntyre*, ed. Nancey Murphy, Brad J. Kallenberg, and Mark Thiessen Nation [Harrisburg, PA: Trinity Press International, 1997], 215-20).
7. Richard B. Hays, *The Moral Vision of the New Testament: Community, Cross, New Creation: A Contemporary Introduction to New Testament Ethics* (San Francisco: HarperSanFrancisco, 1997), 451-52.

problem of selection does not really touch the *logic* of analogical reasoning, which is my main focus in this chapter. Moreover, selection is not a special problem of appeal by analogy. We always have the problem of selection and weighing no matter what kinds of appeals to scripture we make. Moreover, the implication that we can (and perhaps should) avoid analogical reasoning in favor of some other method or approach assumes that non-analogical uses of scripture are available to us. I will show that analogical reasoning is entailed in every kind of moral appeal to scripture where there is a gap between biblical culture and the culture of those making the appeal. We must analogize not only when we appeal to biblical stories but also when we appeal to biblical laws, wisdom sayings, prophetic judgments, and so forth.

The problem of demonstrating sufficient similarity, across the cultural gap, between a biblical paradigm case and a contemporary case is one form of an even more fundamental problem with analogizing. Even within a single cultural framework, it is possible to analogize in artificial or irrelevant ways. Hence, even deeper than the question of the cross-cultural gap is the problem of how to determine whether a perceived similarity or set of similarities warrants treating two cases alike. It is this problem — the *logic* of analogizing — that has not been sufficiently clarified for the use of the Bible in Christian ethics.

I phrase the rule of analogy as follows: Analogical reasoning is an appropriate and necessary method for applying scripture to contemporary moral issues. The term "appropriate" speaks to debates about whether analogizing is a valid form of reasoning; the term "necessary" addresses (and rejects) the assumption that one can reason from identity in applying scripture to contemporary problems. We reason from like to like, not from identical to identical.

The Nature of Analogical Reasoning

In moral thinking, analogical reasoning[8] has a long history in the use of the case method, one form of which is traditional casuistry. Casuistry ac-

8. There is little acute scholarly analysis available, as far as I can tell, on the logic of analogizing in moral reasoning. A brief discussion of the logic of analogical reasoning as a process of predicting likely outcomes based on past experience can be found in Stephen F. Barker, *The Elements of Logic,* 2d ed. (New York: McGraw-Hill, 1974), 233-36. A philosophi-

quired a bad reputation in the early modern period when it was subjected to merciless critique by Pascal and others. Today it is associated with overly complex rule-making that loses sight of principles. Case comparison, however, is a mainstay of close moral analysis. Recently, Albert Jonsen and Stephen Toulmin have extolled the virtues of case-based moral reasoning as a form of practical reasoning especially well-suited to our current pluralistic environment.[9] They argue that the case method facilitates dialogue that leads to shared moral insights among those who otherwise hold to very different philosophical or religious views. One begins with a case about which all participants agree. This provides a departure point for analogizing to cases about which there is disagreement. The process leads to shared moral insight about particular cases.[10]

The analogical method, which is widely used in law, has also recently been described and assessed by Cass Sunstein. Sunstein sets forth the logic of analogical reasoning as follows:

(1) Some fact pattern A has a certain characteristic X, or characteristics X, Y, and Z; (2) Fact pattern B differs from A in some respects but shares

cal treatise on analogy is J. F. Ross, *Portraying Analogy* (Cambridge: Cambridge University Press, 1981). Ross does not treat moral analogizing, but he does discuss the role of analogy in law (*Portraying Analogy*, 202-11). His discussion of law does not, however, lay out the logic of analogizing; it only demonstrates its pervasiveness in law in order to show the extent to which legal reasoning does not proceed deductively according to rules of language and conceptual logic (legal formalism). A classic treatment of legal analogizing is Edward H. Levi, *An Introduction to Legal Reasoning* (Chicago: University of Chicago Press, 1949). See also Cass Sunstein, "On Analogical Reasoning," *Harvard Law Review* 106 (1993): 741-91; and Richard A. Posner, *The Problems of Jurisprudence* (Cambridge, MA and London: Harvard University Press, 1990), 86-100; idem, *Overcoming Law* (Cambridge, MA and London: Harvard University Press, 1995), 174-77 and 518-23. I discuss Sunstein and Posner below.

In the field of ethics, the Aristotelian tradition of practical reason exemplifies the analogical mode. Modern advocates of this approach include Stephen Toulmin, Martha Nussbaum, and Alasdair MacIntyre (all of whom are referred to below). Although none of these philosophers has discussed the logic of analogizing as such, their analyses of the nature of practical reasoning are very illuminating for any examination of the role of analogical reasoning in the moral domain.

9. Albert R. Jonsen and Stephen Toulmin, *The Abuse of Casuistry: A History of Moral Reasoning* (Berkeley: University of California Press, 1988). For Toulmin's understanding of the nature of moral reasoning as practical reasoning set forth through informal argument, see Stephen Toulmin, Richard Rieke, and Allan Janik, *An Introduction to Reasoning*, 2d ed. (New York: Macmillan, 1984; London: Collier Macmillan), 393-421.

10. Jonsen and Toulmin, *The Abuse of Casuistry*, 1-20.

characteristic X, or characteristics X, Y, and Z; (3) The law treats A in a certain way; (4) Because B shares certain characteristics with A, the law should treat B the same way.[11]

Determining which characteristics are relevant for comparison requires grasping the principles exemplified by the analogue. But this does not mean that the principles stand independent of the case or that they derive from a general moral theory. Analogical reasoning works inductively to discover "low-level" principles that may or may not be easily related to some larger moral theory. This perception leads Sunstein to characterize analogizing as involving the following four features: (1) principled consistency (the discovery of a principle that governs all the cases said to be relevantly alike), (2) reasoning from particulars (deriving principles inductively from concrete facts), (3) incompletely theorized judgments (judgments not deriving from or leading clearly to a more general moral theory), and (4) principles operating at a low or indeterminate level of abstraction (i.e., without any general principles of the right and the good).[12]

Analogical, case-based reasoning is ubiquitous in law and unlikely to be replaced by any other method. Nevertheless, case-based reasoning has its detractors. Jurist Richard Posner characterizes analogical reasoning as a form of induction masquerading as deductive logic and bedeviled by the uncertainties of conflicting interpretive intuitions.[13] Hence, he advocates a quantitative economic approach to legal decision-making as more scientific and objective.[14]

If economic efficiency is suitable to law (I think it is inadequate by itself), it is no answer to the problems of moral reasoning. Nevertheless, Posner is right that argument from analogy is not valid unless it moves to the level of principles, where we ask whether the reasons that apply to the

11. Sunstein, "On Analogical Reasoning," 745.

12. Sunstein, "On Analogical Reasoning," 746-47. As Sunstein summarizes the legal use of analogical reasoning, "Without relying on general theories, and without achieving reflective equilibrium, lawyers develop low-level principles to account for particular judgments, and apply those low-level principles to new cases in which there is as yet no judgment at all" (758).

13. Posner, *The Problems of Jurisprudence*, 87-98.

14. Richard Posner is a leading theorist of the economic approach to law. For an example of how he treats legal problems from an economic point of view, see his examination of the law and homosexuality in *Overcoming Law*, 552-78.

analogue also apply to the case at hand.[15] In conducting valid fact comparisons, we search for principial relevance by considering the significance of the facts, facts always being subject to interpretation.

We may conceive analogizing as a form of "bottom-up" reasoning that helps one discover low-level principles to deal with concrete cases that share a family resemblance. Let me give a pedestrian example. Mrs. Burns has three children: seven-year-old Tom, five-year-old Julie, and four-year-old John. Mrs. Burns is in the habit of baking a cake every Friday afternoon after Julie returns from kindergarten. On these occasions, Julie and John take turns, week by week, eating whatever remains in the mixing bowl used for the cake topping (a treat called "licking the bowl"). Older sibling Tom is in school during these cake-making sessions. But on the first Friday after the end of the school year, Tom is home all day, and when the cake making is underway and the topping has been put on and the bowl ready to be "licked," Tom asks for the bowl. Julie balks since it is "her turn." She says that Tom should wait his turn, that is, be sequenced into the rotation in third position. Tom claims that since he missed all the other cake-making sessions, he should get to lick the bowl all summer. Mom rules that Tom should have the bowl this time and then take his place in the rotation.

On the last Friday in June, Julie brings her friend Libby to the cake-making event. Julie and Libby have become inseparable friends and it seems likely that Libby will be around for many of the cake-making sessions. On the Friday in question, Julie asks whether Libby can have the bowl. When John protests because it is "his turn," Julie says, "But Tom got the bowl when it wasn't his turn." Does the precedent established with John apply to the case of Libby? Mom says that Libby gets the bowl because she is the guest. But John protests, "What if she comes next week, will she get the bowl next week, too?" Here is what mom decides. Libby gets to lick

---

15. As Posner sees it, the process of analogizing itself gets us only to the threshold of reasoning, the place where we can inquire into principles that might supply the premises for drawing a conclusion about the case at hand (*Overcoming Law,* 521-22). Hence, according to Posner, analogical discernment or imagination is not, strictly speaking, a form of reasoning; it is a heuristic tool that supplies useful material for reasoning. "One can call this reasoning by analogy . . . but what is really involved is querying or quarrying the earlier case for policies that may be applicable to the later one and deciding the later one by reference to these policies" (*Overcoming Law,* 518). Others, such as Sunstein, however, include consideration of principles or "policy" as part of the method and stress the usefulness of the approach for discovering and clarifying legal principles and extending them to novel cases.

the bowl this week because she is the guest. If she is around on any other Fridays, then it will be her turn only if John, Julie, and Tom have each had at least one turn since Libby last had a turn. This satisfies Julie, but John blurts out to his mother that he doesn't think Libby should be allowed into the sequence of turns because "she's not a member of the family."

The fundamental justification for analogizing is a rule of fairness that says, treat like cases alike. Are the cases of Tom and Libby sufficiently alike to justify treating them the same way? The preceding shows that comparisons of fact similarities and dissimilarities do not go very far without consideration of governing principles. There are several principles implicitly or explicitly at work in the cases of Tom and Libby. A first principle is Tom's implicit claim that each of the children should have an equal share. Mom rejects the absolute application of this norm. She formulates a more local rule: All those who are around for the cake making should have an equal share. When confronted with Julie's appeal to the case of Tom as a reason for giving Libby the bowl, mom ignores this precedent and introduces a different principle: the guest gets the bowl. This decision, however, has implications for the future. Does the guest always get the bowl, even if she is present every time? Mom decides that this would be unfair to the other children, so she proposes a solution that more closely resembles the result in Tom's case. Libby, after being treated as a guest this one time, will be put into the rotation. This means that Libby will be treated more like a family member than a guest. Should nonfamily members be treated like family? Mom does not decide this question at a general level; she decides only for the case at hand. In a situation like this one, she judges, the friend of one of the children should be treated more like a family member than like a guest.

Let us look at this last question more closely. Suppose that on Saturday mornings, mom doles out the children's allowances. One Saturday morning, Libby is present for this event, and Julie asks whether Libby can have an allowance, too. Mom explains that receiving an allowance is different from getting to "lick the bowl." But wherein lies the difference? My guess is that most parents would find it easy to make an immediate judgment in this case but might find it difficult to articulate the exact reasons for it, without time to reflect. That is, having intuited that the two cases call for a distinction, we may need time to think through how the two cases are different in ways that call for a different result. Or perhaps we have a set of rules or social conventions for such cases. Rules or social conventions help us make all sorts of immediate decisions. But behind conventions stand basic convictions about the moral life. Sometimes we may need help identifying these convictions and seeing how they fit together.

Some of our basic moral convictions may be in tension. For example, most societies hold that a person owes a different allegiance to his or her family than to nonfamily persons and groups (neighbors, strangers, the state, etc.). In some cases, this difference of allegiance means that the obligation to one's family is superior, in other cases that it is inferior. In still other cases, it may be unclear which claim is superior. Or, even if the order of claims is clear according to conventional norms, an individual or group may challenge those norms on the basis of the fundamental shared convictions of the community or by advocating some new principle.

For example, suppose that Julie later asks her mother why she did not give Libby an allowance when "Jesus teaches us to love everyone." Mom begins her response by asking whether Libby already receives an allowance from her parents. It turns out that Libby does not receive an allowance. Julie thinks this is a reason for her parents to give Libby an allowance, but mom explains that loving one's neighbor includes respecting parents' rights to make such decisions for their children. Julie responds by saying that Libby's family is very poor and her parents can't afford to give their children allowances. Mom still insists that it is "not our place" to act like parents to Libby by giving her an allowance. Nevertheless, she suggests, perhaps including Libby in family events would be a way to share things with her that she might not otherwise have. Julie offers, "Libby says her family is too poor for her to go to college. When I go to college, can we give Libby's family money secretly, without them knowing it's from us, so she can go to college, too?" Although Mom is not prepared to do any such thing, she finds it tough to answer this question, which focuses the conflict between allegiance to one's own family and the universality of Jesus' love commandment. That tension is present in all the cases dealing with Libby: licking the bowl, getting the allowance, being helped with college expenses. Moreover, behind the question of how the Burns family ought to treat Libby is the larger issue of distributive justice at the societal level, given the structures of power that affect the economic fortunes of the Burns family and Libby's family.

None of the decisions in these cases can be justified simply by comparing similarities and differences between them. Justification requires identification of the principles governing the cases. Moreover, as Sunstein observes, it requires identification of not only broad principles but also low-level ones, the kinds of special considerations that come to light through case comparison. For example, in the case of licking the bowl, mom works out the principle that a guest who is around all the time should be treated more like a family member. In declining to give Libby an allowance, however, she modifies this rule with another low-level principle: equal treatment for a child who is a regular guest so long as that treatment does not usurp the rights and privileges of the child's parents.

The preceding discussion reveals two important features of the moral life. First, one can learn to make good analogical judgments without being able to articulate fully the logical rationale for those judgments. There is a difference, then, between the ability to make good judgments (prudence) and the methods by which judgments can be rationally defended (justification). Prudence is the virtue that enables one to discern what is right. Justification is the method by which we test our prudential decisions for consistency and fairness; it is also the way we gain wider community support for a practice or course of action. This testing — to ourselves and to our community — in turn reshapes our prudential sensitivity. Although it is possible to work up a justification merely in order to amass reasons in favor of a conviction that we already hold (and have no intention of abandoning), justification through genuine dialogue with ourselves and others can alter our understanding and lead us to a revised moral understanding.

Second, general moral principles are inadequate in the abstract. They provide guidance only when grasped, even if tacitly, in relation to concrete examples.[16] There is a reciprocal relation between principles and cases. Judgments about cases are not properly moral if they are not principled. By the same token, we form and revise our principles by considering and comparing cases. For example, human beings do not grasp what is immoral about "cruelty" simply by having a theory about it. Moral intuition based in experience is to some extent logically prior to any principled definition of cruelty. At the same time, the moral conception of cruelty depends on the formation of a principled account of it. Nevertheless, any analysis of the principles that ground a particular judgment about what is

16. This point is made effectively by Jonsen and Toulmin (*The Abuse of Casuistry,* 5-11). Jonsen and Toulmin also make a strong argument that even purportedly general theories (such as John Rawls' theory of justice) make sense only in relation to particular kinds of problem cases and that their claim to generality is to that degree limited (*The Abuse of Casuistry,* 279-303).

cruel ultimately reaches a bedrock where we can no longer argue from principles but can only point to what we know to be indisputable examples of cruelty.

In making this argument I do not mean to espouse a kind of naive moral intuitionism disembodied from the social construction of reality. The definition of cruelty differs from culture to culture.[17] Our moral knowledge is always shaped and reshaped in a social context in which a moral tradition is already present and at work in our intuitive judgments and the evolution of our moral concepts. Nevertheless, in any given cultural context, the justification of any moral principle will always depend in part on judgments that are at least in some sense prior to principles, judgments about concrete cases that function more or less as paradigms. This does not mean that the paradigms are unassailable. Paradigm cases are themselves open to reinterpretation. The point is that we cannot grasp the meaning of principles in the abstract apart from cases. Hence, the application of a principle is never a matter of simple "deduction"; it is always, at least implicitly, a way of seeing principial relations between cases.

Alasdair MacIntyre makes this same point with respect to rules.[18] A rule is always a prescription about some fact pattern or set of fact patterns. When we adapt a rule (revise it) to cover an unanticipated fact pattern, we are expanding the set of applications that constitute the meaning of the rule. At the same time we are discovering or revising our perception of the purpose of the rule. In moral reasoning, as in other forms of practical reasoning, "we move to and fro from the rule to some range of examples of its application and from these particular applications back to the rule."[19] Hence, grasping a rule's purpose is not independent of applications any more than the rule itself is. In this sense, "applied ethics rests on a mistake."[20]

MacIntyre focuses on moral rules, but his arguments cover principles as well. Principles are explicit or implicit rules. A principle in the form of a

17. Thus the scope of the protection in the U.S. Constitution against "cruel and unusual punishments" (Eighth Amendment) is different and larger today than it was in the eighteenth century because our national sense of "cruelty" has changed.

18. Alasdair MacIntyre, "Does Applied Ethics Rest on a Mistake?" *The Monist* 67 (1984): 498-513.

19. MacIntyre, "Does Applied Ethics Rest on a Mistake?" 503.

20. "Applied ethics is not only based on a mistake, but upon one that has proved to be harmfully influential" (MacIntyre, "Does Applied Ethics Rest on a Mistake?" 512).

concept, X, is the implicit rule, "Act in accord with normative concept X." The meaning of even the most general principle, such as "love" or "utility," depends on a sense of what love or utility requires concretely in some situations. These examples, carried in the fund of our experiential knowledge, serve as paradigms of the meaning of the principle. Moreover, this fund of examples, when drawn upon and explicated, always turns out to include low-level principles that constitute our specific sense of how a general principle applies in specific cases. It is the anchoring of the principle in examples, not the mere abstract formulation of the principle, that completes our grasp of the principle. Hence, principles are not "applied" — if that means moving from their abstract formulation to a concrete fact pattern; the principles come usefully into play only when exemplified to our minds in concrete cases. Hence, analogizing is the natural reflex of any use of principles to decide a specific moral question.

We may hold a principle as a presumptive rule, for example, by including the proviso, "unless principle X conflicts with principle(s) A, (B, C, etc.), in which case principle A takes precedence or the two principles must be balanced, etc." Holding principles presumptively because we know that they often conflict depends on a prior knowledge of situations in which principles do conflict. For example, we know the meaning of justice only in relation to mercy or promise-keeping in relation to truth-telling because we have experience with cases in which these pairs of principles compete.

We sometimes use the term "exemplification" to denote the identification of paradigm cases that inform our sense of a principle. I know of no word for the opposite form of reflection, from the case to its principles.[21] For convenience, I propose the term "principiation" for the act of discerning the principles of a paradigm case. We may call the relationship itself the "principiate." The principiate is a case grasped as an exemplification of a principle. Principiation is the exercise of practical wisdom (Aristotle's con-

---

21. Aristotle's use of the term ἐπαγωγή (typically translated "induction") comes close (see note 22 below). Some may suggest Pierce's term "abduction" (which is more or less the logic of discovery), but I am hesitant to bring this term into the framework of moral analysis given the word's scientific associations in Pierce's work. Those who wish to pursue the question of "abduction" in moral reasoning can begin with Richard L. Lanigan, "From Enthymeme to Abduction: The Classical Law of Logic and Postmodern Rule of Rhetoric," in *Recovering Pragmatism's Voice: The Classical Tradition, Rorty, and the Philosophy of Communication,* ed. Lenore Langsdorf and Andrew Smith (Albany, NY: SUNY Press, 1995), 49-70.

ception of *phronēsis*) through induction (in Aristotle's sense of ἐπαγωγή[22]). A principiate is what one knows concretely but in a tacit way about a particular kind of moral problem. While it is possible to state a principle and to describe a case, a principiate lies beyond formulation. It is our intuitive grasp of the *relationship* of a principle to a case, that is, of what the principle means concretely and of how a paradigm case is principled. If I try to put my moral knowledge into an exact and comprehensive formula, I am on the road to casuistry and its endless rule revisions, none of which can ever fully state *the knowledge that enables me to recognize the necessity of an exception.* If I imagine that I can contain my moral knowledge solely within principles, I forget that principles are *empty without examples.*

When, in our story of taking turns with the mixing bowl, John blurts out to his mother that he doesn't think Libby should be allowed into the sequence of turns because "she's not a member of the family," John shows that he has principiated the practice of taking turns. He has intuited its principle. His sister Julie has done the same thing, attributing a different principle to the taking of turns (something like "having missed out on previous rotations qualifies one for an immediate turn"). All the participants, including the mother, who has to adjudicate the conflicts, rely on an intuitive sense of the fairness of the original rotation. When a novel situation presents itself, each participant is challenged to articulate the fairness of that paradigm case, to identify its principle(s). They agree that the original rotation was fair and to that extent already operate with a principle of fairness exemplified by the rotation. But in seeking to articulate the fairness of the case more precisely, they begin discovering additional, more specific principles. This is principiation.

Principiation and exemplification are ways of attending to what is always a unity. The practical difference between the two lies in two different aspects of the method of analogizing: the art of discovery and the art of judgment. Principiation and exemplification describe pathways of thinking that correspond, respectively, to discovering an analogue and judging the fit of an analogue. To show what this means, I will first divide analogies drawn from scripture into two rough types: ostensible and oblique.

22. For Aristotle, ἐπαγωγή is induction not in the sense of generalizing to an abstract principle from the particulars but as grasping the form, principle, or essence as exemplified in the concrete individual. I wish to thank my brother Joseph Cosgrove for referring me to this concept in Aristotle.

Ostensible analogues are identified by "same subject," that is, by a kind of concordance method based in part on translation conventions. Many would see this as simply matching up identities, but our consideration of the cultural gap and the nature of case-based reasoning has shown that we are always dealing with analogies at best. For instance, if we wish to bring the question of divorce under the rule laid down in Matt. 19:3-9, we discover that the rule is really a paradigm case in which "divorce" has a specific sociocultural meaning. The term "to divorce" *(apolysai)* refers to an established cultural practice that is both similar to and different from "divorce" in, say, twenty-first-century America.[23] The English translation term "divorce" masks these differences and may encourage us to imagine that an appeal to Matt. 19 in a contemporary debate about divorce is an appeal from identity, not analogy. A closer look would reveal to us that Matt. 19 is about what English-speaking people today know as "divorce" only analogically, since ancient Mediterranean "divorce" (and "marriage" and all the other practices and institutions that together define ancient divorce) is not the same as divorce in contemporary English-speaking societies. Traditional interpretation and conventional English translation terms make it "obvious" that Matt. 19 and other biblical texts that speak of "divorce" are applicable to Christian debates about divorce in English-speaking settings. We should instead describe these passages as *ostensible* (not obvious) and treat them as offering ostensible *analogies* to divorce in an English-speaking setting.

By contrast, *oblique* analogies do not depend on translation terms. We discover them through moral-theological categories that help us find connections that are not immediately (linguistically) evident. These categories are often abstract subjects, providing a kind of theological concordance — a concordance not of biblical words/subject terms but of concepts attached in our minds and discourse to various biblical stories, themes, etc. A notable example is the category of "the marginalized" in contemporary theology. One will not find the term "marginalized" in a Bible concordance, but many biblical stories attach to this concept in circles where it is used as a

23. For a discussion that brings out some of the issues of sociocultural similarities and (especially) differences between ancient and modern "divorce," with attention to the question whether "divorce" is an adequate translation term in biblical passages traditionally identified as "divorce" texts, see Gerald L. Borchert, "1 Corinthians 7:15 and the Church's Historic Misunderstanding of Divorce and Remarriage," *Review and Expositor* 96 (1999): 125-29.

hermeneutical key. Moreover, the concept of marginalization carries moral-theological freight. For example, the notion of "stories of Jesus' practice toward the marginalized" is a particular way of principiating a cluster of Gospel stories. The category of the marginalized, with its paradigm Gospel stories, facilitates the discovery of oblique analogies to contemporary ethical concerns. For instance, the concept of marginalization has sparked discernment of a parallel between victims of AIDS and the lepers of the Gospel stories.

It should be evident from the preceding that once an oblique analogy has become established, it is no longer oblique but obvious, just like ostensible analogies based on translation terms. Obvious and oblique are relative terms, describing a relation to the tradition of interpretation. Analogizing to the obvious is a repetition of the tradition with perhaps minor variations. Oblique analogizing is the discovery of novel associations based on traditional or emerging theological categories. Thus, identifying victims of AIDS with lepers in the Gospel stories is an oblique analogy that has now become so established in some circles that it looks obvious.

The modern concept of "culture" has opened up fresh possibilities for oblique analogizing. In contemporary cultural anthropology, a culture is an integrated system, which means that one cannot "remove" something from one cultural system and "transfer" it to another cultural system without changing it in some way. Even the basic act of linguistic translation is analogical where the receiver language is situated in another culture. This means that sometimes things that appear to be the same — or very similar — are really very different because they function[24] so differently in their respective cultural systems. By the same token, things that appear to be different may share profound functional similarities.[25]

---

24. I use the term "function" in a nontechnical sense to denote how a part of a culture has its meaning in relation to other parts. I do not use the term "function" to refer to "functionalism" as a particular school in cultural anthropology.

25. An interesting and important question, but one that cannot be pursued here, is whether contemporary critical analogical reasoning has any affinities with the kinds of analogical reasoning characteristic of premodern interpretation. The chief difference between modern and premodern analogizing is that the former looks to function within a system while the latter looks to surface resemblance on the theory that each thing is a sign of many other things. The two kinds of analogizing — I am speaking very broadly — have in common the search for similarities not only between things that are close (or obviously related) but also between things that are otherwise distant from one another, but they define "simi-

We can state the possibilities of functional similarity and difference as follows with reference to ostensible and oblique analogies:

Ostensible analogizing:
   A in culture X analogizes to A′ in culture Y.
   (It turns out, on closer inspection, that A in culture X does not analogize to A′ in culture Y.)
   A in culture X does not analogize to B, C, D, . . . in culture Y.
Oblique analogizing:
   A in culture X is functionally analogical to B in culture Y.
   (It turns out, on closer inspection, that A in culture X is not functionally analogical to B in culture Y.)

We are now in a position to consider exemplification and principiation as pathways of thinking in the art of analogizing. We principiate when the paradigm case and problem case have already been given to us — by the tradition, by someone proposing their association, or by our own prior association of them. Under these conditions, we look for the principles exemplified by the cases to judge whether the analogy holds. By contrast, when we have a problem case and are in search of a biblical paradigm case, we typically use moral-theological categories or principles as guides to exemplification. Hence, we use exemplification as our primary pathway of thinking in discovering oblique analogies. We use principiation as the primary pathway in judging ostensible and oblique analogies.

On the basis of the preceding, I offer the following generic (and simplified) description of the analogical method. First, we identify, from the tradition or through exemplification, a potential biblical paradigm case to govern our problem case. Second, we explicate the principles of the paradigm case.[26]

---

larity" very differently. On premodern analogizing, see Umberto Eco, *Interpretation and Overinterpretation*, with Richard Rorty, Jonathan Culler, and Christine Brooke-Rose, ed. Stefan Collini (Cambridge: Cambridge University Press, 1992).

26. One must be extremely cautious when principiating biblical stories. Many biblical stories do not express moral judgments; others express moral judgments in at most very subtle ways. Moreover, the status of a moral judgment in scripture must be evaluated by considering who makes the judgment, e.g., whether the judgment comes from a character in the story, from the author, from an implied author (narrator), etc. These are matters for sensitive exegesis. These questions also involve theological judgments about whose voices in scripture carry weight.

Third, we determine to what extent these principles apply to the problem case. Fourth, we make a judgment about the problem case, based on our comparison of the two cases. The comparison entailed in the third step involves *assimilating* (likening) and *distinguishing* the two cases. We may conclude that the two cases are sufficiently similar to justify the same outcome, that they are so different that the paradigm case sheds no light on the problem case, or that they are alike in certain illuminating respects that provide limited guidance. The term "analogizing" refers to showing a type and degree of *likeness* that warrants letting the paradigm case govern the problem case. The term "distinguishing" refers to showing a type and degree of *unlikeness* that puts the problem case outside the scope of the paradigm case.

Distinguishing means demonstrating that what looks similar (or what is claimed to be similar) is really not so. Paradigm cases govern problem cases only insofar as their rationales bind the problem case; hence, to distinguish the case underlying an authoritative rule is to show that the rule does not apply to the problem case or that the rationale for the rule applies differently. Showing that it applies but does so differently means discovering a higher level of generality at which some principle governs both cases but leads to different outcomes. Assimilation may mean that two ostensibly similar fact patterns really are so. But it can also mean showing that the principles governing some settled case apply to a case that treats a different subject matter (oblique analogizing).[27]

Analogizing to the Bible

The preceding analysis has far-reaching implications for the use of the Bible in Christian ethics. First, it shows that to argue that the Bible should be ap-

---

27. A striking example from the field of law is the argument by Akhil Amar and Daniel Widawsky that the Thirteenth Amendment's prohibition of slavery logically includes a prohibition against child abuse. As they define it, child abuse is a relation of dominance that involves degradation and physical abuse. Reasoning by analogy, they propose that since slavery is a relation of dominance that entails degradation and physical abuse, child abuse is a form of slavery and is therefore prohibited under the Thirteenth Amendment (to show that child abuse is a violation of a *constitutional* provision is the aim of their essay). See Akhil Reed Amar and Daniel Widawsky, "Child Abuse as Slavery: A Thirteenth Amendment Response to *DeShaney*," *Harvard Law Review* 105 (1992): 1359-85. For a critique, see Posner, *Overcoming Law*, 211-12. Judge Posner wrote the court opinion in *DeShaney* that Amar and Widawsky criticize.

propriated not at the level of its moral rules but rather at the level of its broad principles entails a logical mistake. Biblical principles are not disembodied concepts to be applied from above; they are explicit or implicit rules (however general) that assume some set of their applications. That is, the idea of "applied biblical ethics" rests on a mistake if it means that there are biblical principles and normative concepts that exist apart from applications. Applications are already resident in the principles themselves. The extension of biblical moral principles to problem cases in our own situation is possible only so far as we grasp principles in relation to paradigm cases.

Second, the preceding discussion casts in a positive light what might otherwise appear as a deficiency of the Bible as a source of moral guidance, namely, the seemingly ad hoc and unsystematic nature of its moral teaching. Speaking of the "moral programme" of the Old Testament, Barton comments that it

> is seldom expressed through the kinds of generalizations or statements of principle that we look for in Western moral philosophy. . . . Old Testament writers are maddeningly unsystematic. Asked for a general statement of moral principle, they reply with a little rule about local legal procedures, a story about obscure people of dubious moral character, or a hymn extolling some virtue in God with which human beings are supposed somehow to conform. Knowledge of the good for humankind lies through the observation of particulars, if Old Testament writers are to be believed.[28]

Likewise, the New Testament is ad hoc and largely occasional, rather than systematic, in its ethical teaching. If moral reasoning involves principiation, grasping moral norms through concrete examples, then the Bible's characteristic way of working from the particular to the general (and often concentrating on the particular without moving very far toward the general) is a virtue and not a liability.[29] Scripture itself encourages us to un-

28. John Barton, *Ethics and the Old Testament* (Harrisburg, PA: Trinity Press International, 1998), 14-15.

29. This is one of Barton's chief points, which he makes by reference to Martha Nussbaum's call for a return to an Aristotelian approach to ethics, where moral knowledge is knowledge of the particular. See Barton, *Ethics and the Old Testament,* 17-18; Martha C. Nussbaum, *Love's Knowledge: Essays on Philosophy and Literature* (Oxford: Oxford University Press, 1990).

derstand moral reasoning not as deducing practical inferences from abstract moral axioms but as discovering moral truth in the concrete and particular.[30]

Third, it is usually very difficult (sometimes impossible) to identify the cases assumed by biblical rules and principles with the degree of detail and precision that makes case-based analogical reasoning feasible. This poses a serious question. If all moral appeal to scripture must be analogical and case-based, how far can legitimate appeal to scripture be made where sufficient fact-sensitive detail is lacking? We will examine this problem more closely at a later point.

The preceding observations may seem to focus too much on problems associated with appropriating the Bible at the level of rules and principles. It could be argued that attending to the narrative cast of the biblical moral vision provides a more fruitful approach. However, what we have seen of the relation of rules and principles to cases shows that at whatever level of generality we are working, narrative or story is an essential element. Cases are stories. Whether we start with story or start with rules and principles, principiation always entails the back and forth movement between the two: generalizing from the story, discovering the paradigm stories that give meaning to the rule.

We can spell out this last point more explicitly by considering some of the different ways in which the Bible speaks its moral voice. The moral teaching of scripture is expressed in rules (general and specific prescriptive generalizations, including maxims), principles (normative concepts that are also more general rules), and narratives. Biblical rules and principles assume some set of their applications. Biblical narratives, insofar as they speak morally, can be understood as cases. Moreover, the moral teaching

---

30. Pauline scholars such as Leander Keck and J. Christiaan Beker have made similar points about the apostle Paul. Keck puts it this way: "If the interpreter first finds the particularity of the original occasions [of the Pauline letter] to be an obstacle to appropriating Paul, it is probably because one expects the letters to be articulate timeless truths and principles to be applied, rather than timely words to concrete situations which are prototypes for our own. In other words, in the long run it is precisely the particularity of the occasions that makes Paul's letters perennially significant." Leander E. Keck, *Paul and His Letters*, Proclamation Commentaries (Philadelphia: Fortress Press, 1979), 17; J. Christiaan Beker, *Paul the Apostle: The Triumph of God in Life and Thought* (Philadelphia: Fortress Press, 1980), 35 (quoting Keck's words with approval). Although neither Keck nor Beker sets forth a theory of the nature of moral reasoning, the approach I have been describing is an argument in favor of their claims.

of the Bible is also expressed in character (the character of God, Jesus, other exemplary figures). Biblical moral teaching through character is also case-based: the exemplary character acts in an exemplary way and is thus paradigmatic (of good, bad, or morally mixed behavior). A paradigm is an analogue, that is, a case whose application to other cases depends on our grasping it as a principiate. The moral teaching of the Bible is also framed by the symbolic world of the Bible as a whole (to the extent that a global biblical world can be constructed for scripture as a whole) and by the local symbolic worlds of the particular witness in which some moral teaching (rule, principle, paradigm, etc.) appears. A symbolic world contains rules, principles, and paradigms, along with various assumptions about the nature of reality — assumptions that shape conceptions of what is possible, supply motives for ethical action, and establish the meaning of the facts that make up biblical cases. A symbolic world is thus the context in which any given biblical case makes sense in its scriptural context. Or, to put it a bit differently, a case is a story (contained in a narrative or implicit in a prescriptive utterance) situated in a symbolic world made up of all the elements just enumerated, including other stories.

It should be clear, then, that case-based reasoning does justice to the predominantly narrative texture of the scriptural witness. Narrative carries prescriptive moral content[31] only to the extent that it can be taken as offering a paradigm case. One must show from the narrative that a particular action is approved by the text, that is, held out as exemplary.

---

31. Biblical narratives are also morally relevant beyond any moral prescription they may contain, or when moral prescription is not their main aim, and even when they do not purport to be (or do not lend themselves to being taken as) morally prescriptive. John Barton observes that one way in which biblical narrative is morally relevant is that it displays human characters in moral situations in ways that mirror analogically back to us the nature of the moral quest, with its struggles in the midst of a nexus of circumstances that can issue in chains of tragic or redemptive events. We learn not so much rules or principles or duties from such narratives as something about ourselves that can change our moral vision and shape our character and decision-making. "General moral principles are bound to operate in such stories, and they can be extracted and discussed. But the ethical interest of the stories does not lie there. It lies in the interplay of such principles with the flawed characters of the protagonists in the stories, producing complex actions in which we can recognize our own moral dilemmas and obligations" (Barton, *Ethics and the Old Testament*, 36). I agree with this, especially with Barton's comment about the "interplay" of the principles with the characters in the stories. Abstracting the principles is what I call principiation; the logic of that "interplay" is what I call the principiate.

We can now return to an observation made earlier about the detail available to us in principiating biblical moral teachings through the lens of cases. I have argued that every type of the biblical moral witness is explicitly or implicitly an expression of a case judgment. But the value of case judgments as *analogues* moves along a continuum where usefulness increases as the paradigm case approaches in *level of detail* that of the problem case. This can be illustrated by reviewing the nature and use of rules, principles, and examples.

Let us imagine that I am someone who takes a moral-rule approach to ethics and treats (almost) all moral rules as presumptive. Now a presumptive rule is a rule that holds for all known cases.[32] When I meet a novel case, I have no way of understanding whether the rule applies unless I have grasped the principiate of the rule. Grasping the principiate means seeing how the principle of the rule (its rationale) governs the cases I know. I then make a comparison with the novel case. In order to decide whether to assimilate or distinguish the novel case, the novel case and the cases to which I compare it must exhibit a sufficient level of detail to make the comparison possible.

Consider, for example, a presumptive rule against divorce except in cases of spousal violence. Let us say that I am an inexperienced pastor who holds this rule but have not given it a great deal of thought. I hold it as a presumptive rule in the sense that I do not rule out the possibility of other compelling grounds for divorce (although I do not specify what these might be) and I do not assume that in all cases where there is spousal violence, divorce is warranted. My seminary training has simply made me generally sympathetic to the view that spousal violence is often a compelling ground for divorce, and I see it as my duty to provide support to an abused wife to take this fateful step of separation for the sake of her own safety. In my first year of ministry, a parishioner, Alice Jones, comes to me for counsel and tells me that her husband beats her and she is considering divorcing him. In providing pastoral guidance and support to Alice, I must (among other things) make at least some tentative moral judgment about

---

32. As soon as we encounter a novel case that we conclude ought not to be governed by the rule, we modify the rule accordingly. We may do so formally or we may simply hold the novel case in our store of practical knowledge as an exception. The effect is the same. The rule, formally or implicitly modified, remains a presumptive rule, since we do not know what other novel cases we may encounter in the future. Hence, a presumptive rule is a rule that we take as true for all the cases we know.

what levels and kinds of spousal violence warrant divorcing a violent spouse. (I must do so even if I do not see it as part of my pastoral role to encourage her toward any particular decision, since guarding against insinuating my own judgments requires knowing what my judgments are.) I can analogize from my presumptive rule against divorce only if I can establish for myself the kinds of cases of spousal violence under which the rule against divorce ought to be observed. Listening to Alice's story will lead me to think of examples, at least hypothetical ones, to frame my judgment about her situation. Moreover, her story will probably include its own range of examples, a continuum of escalating abuse that at some point reaches what to her mind is a threshold point. Further, a host of other considerations will come into play — considerations about the children of the marriage, if there are any, the possibilities for a change in the spouse's behavior, and so forth. My presumptive rule against divorce is of little value unless I can concretize the meaning of my rule with some set of cases that contain relevant features of detail. If these cases are mostly hypothetical in my first real-life encounter with the question of divorce, future pastoral experience will provide a larger fund of more textured real-life examples. That is, I will develop practical wisdom in the form of a fund of principiates that inform my rule (or a revised rule) about divorce.

The highly contextual and fact-specific nature of so many moral questions leads many Christian ethicists to argue against using the Bible at the moral-rule level. Some who take this view advocate appropriation of scripture at the level of principles. But as we have seen, principles are equally useless unless they are anchored in a knowledge of concrete cases. For example, the principle of love sheds little light on the case of Alice unless it can be defined more concretely. Defining love in terms of other principles may move me in a particular direction, but it will not get me far enough unless those principles, too, are known through the principiates of practical (case-based) knowledge. For example, if I define love in utilitarian terms (the greatest happiness for the greatest number), I will seek in any moral situation to calculate the aggregate maximal utility of all concerned. But who are "all concerned"? The immediate family? Society as a whole? Or I may define love, at least in part, in terms of a rights-based ethic. But this requires defining rights (whether rights of marriage, rights of self-actualization, the right of security in one's person, etc.), recognizing in whom certain relevant rights lie (of spouses, children, and others, including perhaps some larger social entity — the church or society), and balancing rights where they conflict. It is for these reasons that many devoted to principles (as opposed to rules) argue for situation ethics. But situation ethics is a mere abstraction unless it operates by presumptive rules or principles anchored in practical experience with cases (one's own experience-based wisdom and that of others). The case is where principles and context intersect in principiation, which when funded by sufficient cases constitutes that practical wisdom to judge what is principially right in a given situation.

In what follows I examine some particular examples of analogizing to and from the Bible in order to delineate more precisely the nature of analogical reasoning as a hermeneutical method. The first example, analogizing to the exodus, describes a process of "augmentation" by which we give a biblical paradigm case a level of detail sufficient for a viable comparison to a contemporary problem case.

Analogizing to the Exodus

The exodus is preeminent among biblical stories of emancipation and has figured significantly throughout the history of reformist American Christian social and political discourse. In the history of race relations in America, the exodus has stood as a witness against literal chattel slavery and, by analogical extension, against the socioeconomic slavery of blacks under Jim Crow and like forms of racial oppression.[33] In more recent years both Latin American and black liberation theology have accorded a constitutive place to the exodus theme. Moreover, the theme of liberation is also pervasive and defining in theologies that do not go by the name "liberationist." "Liberation" has become so dominant in modern Christian theology, particularly in America, that it constitutes the distinguishing mark of the theological era in which we live.[34]

---

33. On the similarities and differences between chattel slavery and the economic condition of former slave populations, see the editor's introduction to *From Chattel Slaves to Wage Slaves: The Dynamics of Labor Bargaining in the Americas*, ed. Mary Turner (London: James Currey, 1995).

34. See also Ronald Goetz, "Confessions of an Academic Liberationist: Riding the Tiger of Liberation," in *Standing with the Poor: Theological Reflections on Economic Reality*, ed. Paul Plenge Parker (Cleveland: The Pilgrim Press, 1992), 61 (". . . the dominant characteristic of American philosophical, theological, and ideological discourse in this century has been in

A first consideration regarding the moral significance of the exodus is whether it stands as a witness against slavery. The moral content of the exodus story is found chiefly in two dimensions of the narrative: the action of God, who is the moral character par excellence in the story, and the responsibilities that attach to the people in the light of their liberation. As to the divine character, God acts to liberate the Israelites because (a) they are his people and (b) they are oppressed (Ex. 1:11-12; 3:7-9; 6:2-9). If the second motive is not an independent reason but depends on the first, then the moral significance of the story is limited to the relationship between God and Israel. Jon Levenson has argued that it is the election of Israel, not the moral repugnance of slavery, that supplies the basis for God's action. In Levenson's words, "The point is not that it is Israel's *suffering* that brings about the exodus, but that it is *Israel* that suffers."[35] Against this interpretation, John Collins quotes Ex. 3:7-8 as proof that the liberation theologians are right in construing the exodus as "first of all liberation from slavery and oppression."[36] The passage, however, is more ambiguous than the liberationist interpretation allows:

> Then the LORD said, "I have observed the misery of my people who are in Egypt; I have heard their cry on account of their taskmasters. Indeed I know their sufferings, and I have come down to deliver them from the Egyptians, and to bring them up out of that land to a good and broad land, a land flowing with milk and honey. . . ."

The use of the expression "my people" casts the exodus as the sort of act one does for one's own. There is no hint that God is committed in a like way to the deliverance of any other people who may suffer under slavery. On the other hand, the slavery of the Israelites is treated as a negative not simply because it separates Israel from its special destiny but also because the slavery itself is regarded as oppression (Ex. 1:11-12; 3:9; 6:5, 9). Thus, God acts because the Egyptians are *mistreating* Israel. Does this imply that slavery in any form is viewed as inhumane or only the kind of slavery prac-

---

one sense or another liberationist, i.e., an attempt to set individuals, classes, races, or genders free from bondage").

35. Jon D. Levenson, *The Hebrew Bible: The Old Testament and Historical Criticism* (Louisville, KY: Westminster/John Knox Press, 1994), 152.

36. John J. Collins, "The Exodus and Biblical Theology," *Biblical Theology Bulletin* 25 (1995): 154.

ticed by the Egyptians? The pentateuchal laws regarding slavery and manumission throw some light on this question (Ex. 21:1-6, 7-11; Lev. 25:39-55; Deut. 15:12-18). The laws apply a double standard to Israelites and non-Israelites, providing greater protections against slavery for Hebrews than for non-Hebrews. These privileges for Hebrews speak eloquently about the law's attitude toward slavery, indicating that slavery was seen as an undesirable and unworthy state for members of God's covenant community (including the poor).[37] Slavery is taken for granted as a social institution, the burden of which must fall chiefly on foreigners.

In tension with the double standard in the slave laws of Exodus and Deuteronomy are indications elsewhere in the Hebrew Bible that God's relationship to Israel is paradigmatic of God's relationship to other peoples (Amos 9:7; Isa. 19:18-25). Amos 9:7 is particularly pertinent to the exodus story:

> Are you not like the Ethiopians to me,
> O people of Israel? says the LORD.
> Did I not bring Israel up from the land of Egypt,
> and the Philistines from Caphtor and the Arameans from Kir?

This oracle is a word of judgment against Israel. It qualifies the idea of an exclusive election of Israel by suggesting that divine election is God's way

---

37. Both Ex. 21:1-6 and Deut. 15:12-18 make provision for the slave who desires to remain with the master at the time of release. The formulation in Exodus runs as follows: "But if the slave declares, 'I love my master, my wife, and my children; I will not go out a free person,' then his master shall bring him before God . . . and he shall serve as a slave for life" (vv. 5-6). This provision assumes that the slave came in single and received his wife from his master (v. 4). In such a set of circumstances, the slave who desires to remain and accept lifelong slavery can scarcely be regarded as preferring slavery to freedom; he desires to remain with his family. By contrast, Deut. 15:12-18 makes no reference to the marital status of the slave. It is at once ostensibly more liberal in not stipulating that family acquired after entrance into service remains with the master; at the same time it is likely to strike our ears as illiberal in its assumption that a slave might freely choose to stay and become a slave for life out of love for his master and satisfaction with his condition. Nevertheless, the two statutes may not be as far apart as my characterization suggests. Exodus 21 also mentions love for the master as a possible motivation of a slave to remain, and Deuteronomy 15 may assume the law that differentiates, at the time of manumission, according to the slave's marital status upon entrance into servitude. Lev. 25 abolishes Israelite enslavement of other Israelites altogether and provides for manumission (by redemption or in the jubilee year) in cases where an Israelite sells himself or herself to a resident alien.

with other peoples, including Israel's enemies. Moreover, the New Testament's use of the universalistic side of the Abraham tradition invites a universalizing of Israel's election, not necessarily in such a way that the election of Israel is simply relativized but at least in the sense that God's actions for the sake of Israel can be seen as disclosive of who God seeks to be toward all peoples.[38] This wider canonical perspective recasts the story of the exodus, making it exemplary of God's commitment to the liberation of all enslaved peoples. Thus, within the Bible as a whole the exodus story presents itself as a paradigm of God's opposition to slavery and thus as a warrant for human opposition to slavery.[39]

For purposes here, we will assume the preceding interpretation of the exodus as an anti-slavery symbol and focus on what constitutes *analogizing* to the exodus paradigm. We should note first of all that applying the exodus "case" to other situations of slavery, for example, cases of slavery in the Americas, is already an analogical extension. The term "slavery" designates a very wide and variegated semantic domain, since the institution has varied widely over time and place. Hence, any application of the exodus story to a modern question of chattel slavery must involve analogical reasoning. Slavery in ancient Egypt was not in all respects the same, for example, as slavery in antebellum America.

Analogizing requires principiation, that is, establishing the reasons for a judgment about a particular fact pattern. What is it about Egyptian slavery that God finds repugnant? The witness against slavery in the exodus story provides almost no moral analysis, except to characterize the situation of the Israelites as oppression and to attribute a motive of genocide to the Egyptian overlords. Since genocide can take many forms and is not itself a defining characteristic of ancient slavery, we must seek the meaning of slavery in the concept of oppression, which the biblical narrative describes as harsh forced labor. The texts assume that we can grasp what is immoral about this kind of oppression, but they do not tell us whether the defining term is the harshness of the labor or the fact that it is forced. The exodus story thus leaves it to us as readers to complete the meaning of the

38. For a detailed argument of this point, see Cosgrove, *Elusive Israel*, 65-90.

39. There are other ways to make the same point about the exodus as paradigm. For example, Gustavo Gutiérrez argues that the exodus is cast in the Bible in relation to creation in such a way as to exemplify the activity of the Creator. See Gustavo Gutiérrez, *A Theology of Liberation: History, Politics and Salvation*, trans. and ed. Sister Caridad Inda and John Eagleson (Maryknoll, NY: Orbis, 1973), 157-60, 294-95.

text by discovering, within the framework of clues given by the account, what makes harsh forced labor oppressive.

Modern readers, just like the ancient audience of this story, complete this meaning intuitively based on some prior understanding of slavery. Testing and sharpening these intuitive understandings require a social description of slavery and a moral interpretation of the judgment that slavery is oppressive. We begin by reconstructing the social structure of ancient slavery, as known to the community from which the exodus story comes. Here the data are scant, even nonexistent when it comes to reconstructing the slave's perspective and experience;[40] hence, social description must rely on models of slavery informed by knowledge of more recent slave societies, for which we have more information. Social description of ancient slavery can be fruitfully enriched by examination of slavery in other times and places, so long as we are careful to attend to the different ways in which slavery has been socially constructed. Thus, the interpretive process as a whole entails two basic features: (1) augmentation of our knowledge of the paradigm case through the disciplines of modern knowledge (e.g., historical sociology, historical cultural anthropology, etc.) and (2) principiation based on that expanded understanding.

Augmentation deals with the problem of "level of detail" mentioned above. Augmentation helps us fill out the exodus story so that it is sufficiently textured to serve as an analogue to contemporary cases. As we will see, augmentation is both reconstructive and constructive. It is reconstructive insofar as we are seeking to fill in the details of ancient slavery and attitudes toward it. It is constructive in that the biblical text is open to more than one plausible interpretation based on even our best historical knowledge.[41]

Augmentation depends on other examples from more accessible times

---

40. In appropriating scripture for contemporary guidance in Christian social ethics, it is always important to recognize and be honest about the limitations of our knowledge of ancient societies. As the great historian of Western antiquity M. I. Finley remarks, "the *severe limits* of what we can know about the ancient world can be pushed out a bit, even substantially, but they can never be broken" (emphasis added). See M. I. Finley, *Ancient History: Evidence and Models* (New York: Viking Penguin, 1986), 107. In his book, *Ancient Slavery and Modern Ideology* (New York: Viking Penguin, 1980), Finley notes the dearth of first-hand reports by slaves or former slaves of the experience of slavery (117).

41. Chapter five treats more fully the problem of appeal to scripture where we confront multiple plausible (reasonable) interpretations.

and places because the modern disciplines by which we understand ancient cases depend heavily on contemporary phenomena (and some well-documented past examples). This is manifestly true of *historical* applications of sociological, anthropological, psychological and other models. We are usually fitting relatively sparse ancient data into models based on richer contemporary data.

In the American context, the first thoroughgoing moral analysis of slavery was made by abolitionists, some of whom were ex-slaves and others of whom examined the conditions of American slavery first-hand. The abolitionists combined current American theories of justice with traditional Christian moral teaching as a framework for criticizing the institution. They argued for the "equality of man" as a basis for applying the Enlightenment doctrine of "the rights of man" to the situation of enslaved African Americans. They interpreted slavery as a state of domination enforced by violence in which the enslaved human being has the status of a thing, an instrument of production or service (like a beast of burden). These early-nineteenth-century social critics observed that slavery deprives slaves of basic rights of freedom: that it denies slaves the right to earn their own living and enjoy that independence through property so highly prized by early Americans; that it prevents slaves from marrying and disrupts common-law slave families; that it provides a protected context for rape (the unconsented use of slave women by white masters); that it degrades slaves by inculcating vices in the slave population (of lying, stealing, servility, sloth); that it provides a protected context for cruel physical abuse by masters; that it bars the way for slaves to receive education and develop their natural abilities; and that it generally imposes a humiliating stigma of inferiority under which any human being would chafe.[42]

Reviewing these antislavery arguments, we can identify the most basic problem with slavery as its treatment of the slave as an instrument, a piece

42. The preceding is a summary of recurrent themes in abolitionist writing. I have relied especially on the writings of black abolitionists, notably, the following: *The Black Abolitionist Papers,* ed. C. Peter Ripley, 5 vols. (Chapel Hill, N.C.: University of North Carolina Press, 1985-92); *The Life and Writings of Frederick Douglass,* ed. Philip S. Foner, 5 vols. (New York: International Publishers, 1950-75); *A Documentary History of the Negro People in the United States,* vol. 1: *From Colonial Times through the Civil War,* ed. Herbert Aptheker (New York: Carol Publishing Group, 1990). For a history of antislavery argument, focusing on arguments for equality, see Celeste Michel Condit and John Louis Lucaites, *Crafting Equality: America's Anglo-African Word* (Chicago: University of Chicago Press, 1993), 19-68.

of property, a thing. Specific social arrangements, labor practices, and forms of discipline — which vary from one institution of slavery to another — all follow from this basic *Verdinglichung* ("thingification"), this radical dehumanization of the slave. In the potent phrase of Orlando Patterson, the slave is treated as "socially dead."[43]

Patterson's work also suggests that the value of freedom is born out of slave societies. The free define themselves and treasure their freedom by reference to slavery.[44] In revolutionary America one sees this dramatically in the rhetoric of slavery applied by the colonists to themselves. To be denied what they regarded as the basic rights of Englishmen, the colonists argued, was tantamount to being made slaves.[45] Presupposed in this argument is the conviction that the colonists are the *equals* of Englishmen across the Atlantic and are therefore entitled to the same rights as Englishmen. The defense of the right of freedom rests on a claim to equality. Moreover, the argument against slavery as such, that is, against the enslavement of any people, depends on some notion of universal equality.

The biblical story of the exodus does not speak of thingification as a problem with slavery or of human equality as a reason to oppose slavery. We can argue that ancient slaves experienced what we call thingification, that they longed for freedom, and that the Israelite story-tellers who shaped the exodus account believed in some notion of human equality. Making this argument helps us to augment the exodus story so that we can analogize to it. But even if our augmentation is reasonable, based on available historical evidence and a judicious use of historical sociology, it is not the only plausible way to interpret the exodus story. In fact, it may be that the ancient Israelite authors and hearers of the story we meet in Exodus had somewhat different understandings of what it meant. The spare version we receive from the tradition leaves room for a range of original understandings. It seems likely that the story was already partly "indeterminate" (or "underdetermined") in its original setting, that is, open to more than one reasonable interpretation by original hearers.[46] In that case, our

---

43. Orlando Patterson, *Slavery and Social Death: A Comparative Study* (Cambridge, MA: Harvard University Press, 1982).

44. Orlando Patterson, *Freedom*, vol. 1, *Freedom in the Making of Western Culture* (n. p.: HarperCollins, 1991), xiii.

45. Examples can be found in Barbara W. Tuchman, *The March of Folly: From Troy to Viet Nam* (New York: Alfred A. Knopf, 1984), 154, 163, 179, 191.

46. I use "underdetermined" as a synonym in the sense that the original rhetorical set-

analogizing to the story entails an augmentation that is justified in part by a semantic openness that original hearers also confronted in the story.

The Exodus and Liberation Theology

Black, Latin-American, and Feminist liberation theologians have extended the exodus analogue to racial, economic, and gender oppression,[47] maintaining that the exodus provides a powerful biblical warrant for social revolution. In a sympathetic review of this appeal to the exodus story, Alfredo Fierro observes that for the liberationists, "the Exodus is a symbol of throwing off the yoke, breaking away from established institutions, and evincing the ability of a people to fashion or refashion a life for themselves."[48] He argues that although the biblical writers themselves did not give a political interpretation to the exodus, the event itself was political and can be analyzed as such by modern interpreters.[49] This is in effect to say that we are in a position to interpret the exodus story in ways that were not possible for the biblical writers. Our interpretation may take the biblical story as its basis or may look to a reconstructed history of Israel "behind" the story (or it may combine these two approaches). I will continue to focus here on the analogical use of the biblical narrative. In the biblical framing of the exodus, God is the primary actor. If the exodus, with its movement toward law and promise, is revolutionary, God is the revolutionary. The warrant for political revolution is therefore based in the character of God. Under modern conditions, the possibilities for political imi-

---

ting of the story did not provide shared assumptions (among original hearers) sufficient to support only one reasonable interpretation. One might also speak of "overdetermination," if one means that the assumptions the original hearers brought to the story were so varied as to allow for multiple reasonable interpretations of the story. Nevertheless, the term "overdetermination" has usually been applied to cause and effect relations where a single effect has multiple sufficient causes. For a discussion of indeterminacy and hermeneutical ethics, see chapter five. See further, Cosgrove, ed., *The Meanings We Choose: Hermeneutical Ethics and the Conflict of Interpretations* (forthcoming, Sheffield Academic Press).

47. See, for example, *Exodus: A Lasting Paradigm,* Concilium 189, ed. Bas van Iersel and Anton Weiler (Edinburgh: T. & T. Clark, 1987).

48. Alfredo Fierro, "Exodus Event and Interpretation in Political Theologies," in *The Bible and Liberation: Political and Social Hermeneutics,* rev. ed., ed. Norman K. Gottwald (Maryknoll, NY: Orbis Books, 1983), 476.

49. Fierro, "Exodus Event and Interpretation in Political Theologies," 478.

tation of the divine moral character appear much different than they did in the ancient world.

The application of the exodus story to the situation of the poor in Latin America involves extending the concept of chattel slavery to economic relations. This extension is plausible for several reasons. First, chattel slavery is itself an economic relation. Second, our constructive modern interpretation of what is wrong with chattel slavery provides a more elaborate framework for analogical extension. Where workers have no control of the means and conditions of production, they often find themselves in a situation like that of the chattel slave. If they organize to gain some bargaining power, they are typically threatened with violence. The physical well-being of the slave is protected insofar as it serves the economic advantages of those who control production and capital. This means that where economic considerations justify harm to workers — through dangerous or overly taxing labor or casting off workers who are no longer economically useful — the worker is unprotected. Moreover, workers kept at a subsistence level have no options for improving their lot. Their educational possibilities are restricted by the interests of those with economic power. Poor workers enjoy almost no leisure, and their freedom for cultural expression and creative cultural development is correspondingly restricted. Finally, to be poor is generally to suffer under a stigma of inferiority. To the extent that these conditions exist, the worker is treated as a thing and, through the mechanism of socioeconomic control, is a kind of slave.[50]

I take the preceding to be a fair summary of the general tenor of Latin American liberation theology's moral analysis of the situation of the poor in the light of the exodus. But a critical question remains. Does the exodus warrant a right to a certain kind of equal economic condition, as in the Marxist vision, or a right to equal freedom, as in the Kantian view? The former measures oppression against the ideal of a social arrangement in which the maxim, "from each according to their ability, to each according to their needs," obtains. The latter defines oppression in terms of equal freedom to obtain a fair share in the goods of society (distributive justice) and to keep one's share (corrective justice). There are, of course, mediating positions. The point here is to see that the exodus story cannot settle debates of this sort. Once we have interpreted the exodus as a symbol of God's opposition to slavery and have interpreted slavery through the

50. See *From Chattel Slaves to Wage Slaves.*

lenses of freedom and equality, we are still left with the debate about how to define freedom and equality. Terms such as "freedom," "equality," and "human dignity," as used today in the moral analysis of slavery, are not biblical concepts. At most, they have analogues in antiquity, making it possible to forge analogical links between certain biblical conceptions and contemporary conceptual frameworks.

My aim here is not to argue that the best approach to the story of the exodus is to work out biblical analogues to modern concepts of freedom and equality. The point is that, whatever our approach, it will require some moral framework that, if it is "biblical" at all, is biblical *in an analogical way* and relies on *augmentation* of the exodus story.

Analogizing to Scripture in the Work of Thomas Ogletree

The preceding discussion of the analogical method has focused on analogizing from a modern moral issue to a discrete biblical case. But analogizing is also involved in other uses of the Bible. In working out an ethical understanding of a particular issue or in constructing a more general Christian ethic, we often work with scripture at a broader level. For example, we develop biblical-theological constructions built on scriptural themes (e.g., covenant), major strands of tradition (e.g., the Priestly tradition), or large literary (or canonical) units (Mark, the synoptics), and so forth. In this way we seek to let the Bible as a *whole* inform ethical reflection. Whatever our broader approach, the movement that joins the scriptural witness to our modern world is analogical.

Thomas Ogletree's study, *The Use of the Bible in Christian Ethics*,[51] illustrates the broad approach and also exemplifies the analogical movement from the Bible to our current situation in a way that allows scripture to pose ethical questions to us rather than serve only as a source of relevant materials for the questions we are already asking. Ogletree seeks to interpret classic biblical themes as they relate to moral understanding. This aim requires framing the interpretation of the biblical materials in a way that shows their import for our moral understanding. The assumption of this task is that "there is a structure to moral understanding which is derived

---

51. Thomas W. Ogletree, *The Use of the Bible in Christian Ethics: A Constructive Essay* (Philadelphia: Fortress Press, 1983).

from constitutive features of the human way of being in the world" and that "that structure always appears concretely in forms and modes which are relative to a given history with its unique experiences and its distinctive cultural legacy."[52] To mediate the differences between the biblical moral world(s) and our own, Ogletree sets forth certain preunderstandings of the moral life and then uses them as a framework for analyzing classic themes in various blocks of canonical material — covenant and commandment in the law and the prophets, eschatological existence in the synoptic Gospels, and Christian freedom in Paul. The framework provides general categories for moral analysis: goal-oriented actions (the intentionalist structure of action and consequentialism), human interactions (intersubjectivity and deontology), the formation of the self (the implication of the self in action and perfectionist ethical theory), and the temporal horizon of experience (the historicity of moral understanding and the question of the meaning of being).[53]

The use of general preunderstandings of the moral life facilitates an interpretation of the biblical themes that makes them at least potentially intelligible to moral reflection in our modern situation. Ogletree uses these preunderstandings to establish types of moral discourse in the Bible. For example, in describing eschatological existence in the New Testament, Ogletree observes a dominant perfectionist motif to which deontological language is often assimilated. "Thus, laws and commandments function not simply as statements about what we are to do, but predominantly as specifications of who we are to become."[54]

Showing the presence of deontological and perfectionist language in the New Testament and describing their relation establishes, at a very general level, a basis for dialogue between ourselves and the Bible. Nevertheless, the eschatological framework that conditions the ethical language of the New Testament poses a significant hermeneutical challenge. Ogletree asks whether "contemporary interpreters of Christian faith [can] find common ground with eschatologically determined ethical perspectives."[55] His answer is that two central features of New Testament eschatological understanding do indeed speak relevantly to our own situation: "some de-

52. Ogletree, *Use of the Bible,* 36.
53. Ogletree, *Use of the Bible,* 15-45.
54. Ogletree, *Use of the Bible,* 90.
55. Ogletree, *Use of the Bible,* 182.

gree of alienation from the institutional arrangements of the larger society" characterizes the eschatologies of all the New Testament writers, and the counterpart to this alienation is "deep involvement with a community which is engaged in developing qualitatively distinct alternatives to those arrangements."[56] Ogletree further observes that neither social alienation nor the vision of alternative community has figured prominently in Christian ethics in America.[57] The eschatological structure of New Testament ethics, once it has been hermeneutically mediated into categories that are intelligible in a modern context, speaks a prophetic word to the modern church in America (and to its dominant patterns of social ethics).

Ogletree's approach depends on analogical thinking in that he reconstructs biblical ethics at levels that admit a likening of our situation to that of the biblical perspective. To take the example of eschatological thinking, the question of how the earliest church is related to and should relate to the institutions of its social world is like the question of how the modern church is related to and should relate to the institutions of its social world. This likeness must be shown through a use of categories that permit the abstraction of principles that can govern both the situation of the ancient church and that of the modern church. The categories Ogletree proposes are social alienation from the dominant society and alternative community within that society. The governing principle he derives from the New Testament, through the use of these categories, is that the church is an alien body in the world and ought to be an alternative community that stands as a witness against the institutions of its world. This principle of ecclesial alterity presents the modern American church with a fresh way of seeing itself. It can help the church discover neglected or suppressed areas of its experience (i.e., its own unexamined experience of alienation), and it can push the church toward a more critical witness within dominant culture.[58]

Ogletree's principiation of the biblical analogue operates at a very general level. He does not press the lower-level contents of New Testament eschatological existence: expectation of a (relatively) near apocalyptic end of the world, particular moral teachings (and moral assumptions) about what is wrong with the institutions of the world and how the community

56. Ogletree, *Use of the Bible,* 182.
57. Ogletree, *Use of the Bible,* 182.
58. Ogletree, *Use of the Bible,* 184.

ought to live. There are two reasons for this. One has to do with the nature of analogical reasoning itself. To the extent that the fact pattern of the problem case differs significantly from that of the analogue, the principles governing the analogue will appear irrelevant to the problem case or will lead to a different outcome for the problem case. In differentiation, we show that the principles governing the analogue do not apply *or apply differently* to the problem case. Showing that they apply but do so differently means grasping a higher (more general) order of principle that comprehends both analogue and problem case yet leads to a different judgment for each. Hence, the fact that the early church did not engage in efforts to reform the social structures of its time and place is not in itself an argument against a social gospel for the modern church because the political situations of the ancient and modern churches are so different. For example, the ancient church lacked the resources and social location to alter larger institutional patterns.[59] The eschatological critique of ancient societal institutions calls for a similar type of critique in our time, and the eschatological ethic of fidelity to God's justice calls for a different (and more activist) approach to social structures in our context.[60]

The second reason why Ogletree's analogizing operates at a general level is not a function of factual differences between the political situations of the ancient and the modern church. It owes rather to a perceived incompatibility between the modern Christian assumptions of Ogletree, within his Christian tradition, and certain assumptions in the ancient eschatological perspective. For example, the early church saw the present world as already in the process of passing away. We can analogize, as many millenarian movements have done throughout Christian history, and take a very similar view of the world in our day (with some adjustment of biblical timetables!), but the analogy should be rejected because we have better reasons to regard history as continuing indefinitely. Moving to a conceptual level where we construe alienation not in a narrowly "apocalyptic" sense but more broadly removes the impediment.

It is important to keep these two kinds of reasons separate. The first is a judgment belonging to analogical reasoning proper and follows from the logic of principiation. The second is a material judgment that has nothing

59. Ogletree, *Use of the Bible,* 117.

60. Ogletree, *Use of the Bible,* 177-92 (cf. also 116-34, where Ogletree treats social ethics and the synoptic Gospels).

to do with the possibilities or limits of analogical reasoning but follows rather from a critique of certain biblical assumptions based on modern knowledge and experience (perhaps also on more fundamental biblical-theological considerations).[61]

Conclusion and Assessment

I have described analogizing to scripture as follows. First, we identify, from the tradition or through our own imaginative discovery, a potential biblical paradigm case to govern our problem case. Second, we explicate the principles behind the judgment in the paradigm case. Third, we determine to what extent these principles apply to the problem case. Fourth, we make a judgment about the problem case, based on our comparison of the two cases. The comparison entailed in the third step involves assimilating (likening) and distinguishing the two cases. We may conclude that the two cases are sufficiently similar to justify the same outcome, that they are so different that the paradigm case sheds no light on the problem case, or that they are alike in certain illuminating respects that provide limited guidance. Doing justice to the case-based nature of analogical reasoning often has a limiting effect: the discovery of unforeseen differences that distance the paradigm case from the problem case.

Since analogical reasoning is not deductive, the completion of analogical meaning often involves judgments that can reasonably go in more than one way. This applies not only when we analogize to biblical stories, but also when we appeal to biblical moral rules, since the appropriation of a rule from one cultural context for application in another cultural context can only proceed analogically. Appeal to any mode in which the Bible speaks morally properly involves case-based analogical reasoning.

Two basic arguments against analogizing to scripture are (1) that ana-

---

61. It can be argued that at a deeper level, biblical theology itself calls for a rejection of any predictive eschatology except that which trusts God in radical openness to whatever future God may bring, "predicting" only that God lies always faithfully in our future just as God is with us in the temptations and sufferings of the present. This is Rudolf Bultmann's view. See Walter Schmithals, *An Introduction to the Theology of Rudolf Bultmann,* trans. John Bowden (Minneapolis: Augsburg Publishing House, 1968), 318-24; cf. also Walther Zimmerli, "Promise and Fulfillment," in *Essays on Old Testament Hermeneutics,* ed. Claus Westermann and trans. James Luther Mays (Richmond, VA: John Knox Press, 1963), 89-122.

logical reasoning is inferior to deductive forms and (2) that the gap between biblical times and our own is too great a gap to be spanned by analogy.

The first argument is made by Richard Posner, who sees analogical reasoning as unprincipled because it does not move deductively from accepted normative concepts. This kind of objection to analogizing involves the claim that one can move from principles to cases without cases being a logically prior part of those principles. This may work in law, if one subscribes to Posner's economic efficiency theory, which calls for treating all legal issues according to an economic (and therefore a mathematical) calculus. It does not work in morality. The most famous instance of a strictly deductive moral scheme is classic utilitarianism, which is notorious for proposing a unit of calculation — "happiness" — that cannot be calculated without recourse to all the messy (non-quantifiable) moral considerations we have been dealing with since Aristotle.

All moral reasoning is inherently analogical, and all analogical reasoning is inherently case-based. This holds not only for the more obviously case-based appropriations of biblical stories but for appeals to biblical rules and principles as well. One can debate how we should analogize, but I see no good argument showing that we can or should avoid analogizing. The fact that it can be difficult to reason well by analogy is not a reason not to analogize at all.

The second argument against analogizing is also, paradoxically, the best argument in favor of it. If the gap between biblical and modern times is great, then connecting scripture with contemporary life can only be done analogically. However, if the gap is too great, then the analogizing will be strained. In an essay on the role of the New Testament in Christian ethics, Robin Scroggs poses the question whether the gulf between ancient and modern times is so great that, to paraphrase the punch line of an old joke, "you can't get from there to here."[62] In a later essay he calls for giving up the Bible as an authority and using it as a foundational document, in effect honoring it as an indispensable partner in dialogue over ethical and theological matters but not as arbiter.[63]

Scroggs does not deal directly with "analogizing," and he would no

62. Robin Scroggs, "The New Testament and Ethics: How Do We Get from There to Here?" in *Perspectives on the New Testament: Essays in Honor of Frank Stagg*, ed. Charles H. Talbert (Macon, GA: Mercer University Press, 1985), 77-93.

63. Robin Scroggs, "The Bible as Foundational Document," *Interpretation* 49 (1995): 17-30.

doubt agree that any legitimate effort to connect the Bible with contemporary life must be analogical. In terms of our focus, his cautions go to the problem of judging analogies that are extended across time and culture. This is a very serious question. There are two basic hermeneutical responses to the historical-cultural gap between the Bible and the modern world. One is to see the Bible as the historical beginning of Christian tradition and to take tradition, reaching into the present, as the authority from the past that we must consult in constructing our moral views. The second response is to take the Bible as an independent authority alongside tradition. The first of these responses is the traditional Roman Catholic one, the second the traditional Protestant one. The Protestant response is tenable, if at all, only if analogizing can bridge the gap.[64]

Connected with the objection that analogizing to the Bible must span too great a gap is the problem of level of detail discussed above in the analysis of appeals to the exodus. I have pointed out that analogizing spans the historical-cultural gap only with our constructive help, what I have termed "augmentation." The biblical text from which we take a paradigm case fixes a certain direction and set of boundaries but requires a completion of meaning, an augmentation by which we flesh out the paradigm case so that it can speak to our problem case. We reconstruct the details of the case in its ancient social setting. This process of reconstruction usually leaves room for more than one plausible construal of the text, owing to the limits of our historical knowledge and in many cases also to the underdetermination of the text in its original rhetorical setting. If we are to analogize to the biblical text, we must also assimilate the case to patterns that make sense in our time and place and speak to our issues. The very act of analogizing is constructive, not simply analytic, the more so when the analogizing is across history and culture.

If analogizing across history and culture is constructive, one might conclude that this kind of analogizing is simply illegitimate. The idea of "construction" may suggest that we smuggle key elements of our problem case into our biblical paradigm case and then disingenuously claim that the biblical paradigm governs the problem case. Whether this hap-

---

64. The recognition that analogizing across time and space needs our constructive help moves Protestant appeal to scripture somewhat closer to the Catholic side. Tradition can help Protestants discover analogical connections between the ancient text and a contemporary moral issue.

pens must be judged on a case-to-case basis. The concern is obviously justified.

A paradox of analogizing is its power to show meaningful relationships between ostensibly different things. Accepting this paradox and trying to work judiciously with it can help keep debates about the use of the Bible in Christian ethics from getting stuck in the impasse between the historicists who repeatedly argue that "you can't get from there to here" and biblicists who make facile connections between the Bible and contemporary life. In avoiding this impasse, however, judicious analogizers should listen carefully to the historicists, and all others who are keenly attentive to difference. And perhaps biblicists have something to teach as well — an openness to plain-sense similarity and a concern that moral reasoning not get bogged down in hairsplitting.

The problem of drawing the line of judgment between analogizing and distinguishing also involves a question of consistency. If similarity can be principled but not deductive, it is likely that people will show different degrees of tolerance for what counts as sufficiently similar. Not only that, the same person or group may show greater tolerance when analogizing and distinguishing on one moral issue than on another. This seems plausible, but how could we measure it? For example, I may have the impression that Joe is prepared to extend the exodus story to cover almost anything he regards as oppressive but that he operates with a much higher standard of sufficient likeness when it comes to bringing contemporary sexual practices or identities under the rule(s) against homoerotic behavior in Leviticus and Romans 1. For Joe, the contemporary phenomenon of sexual relations between adults who know themselves as having a homosexual or bisexual orientation is something entirely different from anything the biblical writers contemplated under "a man lying with a man" or "a woman lying with a woman." Is Joe consistent in the way he analogizes? Does he show greater freedom in extending the paradigm of the exodus to situations that do not involve literal chattel slavery than he does in extending the rule against homoerotic practice to cases that involve literal homoerotic behavior understood differently (and socially constructed differently) than in ancient times? How would we show consistency or inconsistency? By adding up points of similarity and dissimilarity? That won't work because similarities and dissimilarities have to be assessed for significance, not just counted. All we can do is compare our perhaps only intuitive senses of threshold levels of significant likeness or unlikeness. Debate about questions of consistency can at least sharpen and discipline our judgment in likening and distinguishing.

The rule of analogy holds that *analogical reasoning is an appropriate and necessary method for applying scripture to contemporary moral issues.* It is important to consider how this formulation stands up in view of the objections to analogizing discussed above and in preceding sections of this chapter. The problems with analogizing cast some doubt on whether it is an appropriate mode of appeal to scripture. If we draw that conclusion, however, it may entail that no moral appeal to the Bible is appropriate. That entailment would be present if we agreed that all appeal to scripture is *necessarily* analogical (the second element of the rule). I have argued vigorously that analogizing is inescapable in moral appeal to scripture. In my judgment, the only assault on the rule of analogy that might convincingly be made is an assault on its appropriateness, specifically, the charge that analogizing lacks sufficient methodological controls to serve as a suitable method of argument. I hope my treatment of analogizing in the earlier parts of this chapter shows that there can be no moral thinking without analogizing, that analogical *reasoning* is what brings discipline to moral reflection, and that this kind of reasoning is inherently principled. The question is whether analogical reasoning can remain reasonable and principled when the paradigm cases are historically and culturally distant from the problem cases, which is the hermeneutical situation in analogizing to scripture. It seems wise to avoid a blanket answer to this question. We can take the problem seriously by reserving judgment for particular instances of analogizing where we can make individual assessments.

THREE

The Rule of Countercultural Witness

There is a presumption in favor of according greater weight to countercultural tendencies in scripture that express the voice of the powerless and the marginalized than to those tendencies that echo the dominant voices of the culture.

It is widely held that where a biblical teaching about a practice differs from the predominant view in the surrounding culture, the difference may be taken as a sign of an especially significant biblical value or principle that should be accorded special weight in the construction of biblical theology and ethics. Much of the old Biblical Theology program proceeded on this premise. Moreover, the conviction still persists that the most authentic witness to the divine in scripture is to be found in what is distinctive in comparison to the cultural environment in which the scripture texts were formed.[1] This gives special hermeneutical precedence to voices in scripture supporting such values or causes as nonviolence, gender equality, economic rights for the poor, and the end of slavery.

1. A similar assumption has governed much of modern efforts to reconstruct the historical Jesus. The "criterion of dissimilarity" reflects the assumption that the Jesus who speaks authentically for God is, must be, a Jesus who *stands out* from his cultural matrix as a critical, prophetic voice.

90

I use the term "countercultural" for those tendencies in the text that go against the dominant norms and values of their home culture or environment. These contrast with tendencies in the text that are affiliative toward the dominant culture, reflecting and reinforcing the dominant norms and values. By "tendencies" I mean very broadly any of the rhetorical means by which the Bible tacitly or expressly assumes, reinforces, or asserts a moral position.

Theological and Hermeneutical Warrants

Presumably, those who use the rule of countercultural witness do not all agree about the theological warrants for this approach or about exactly what kind of authority belongs to the countercultural voice in scripture. Nor are these warrants very often discussed. Nevertheless, it is possible to sketch three widely-held theological tenets that, together, give the rule its appeal. First, the revelation of God is against all ideology. Divine revelation is not against culture per se (there being no witness without a cultural form) but against those cultural institutions that serve the interests of the powerful in ways that harm the powerless (or less powerful). Hence, authentic witness to divine revelation characteristically takes a form that is at odds with dominant ideology. Second, the Bible is a locus of authentic countercultural witness; scripture itself has taught the church that God is vindicator of the oppressed. Third, scripture is not to be equated with revelation; the Bible is an indispensable but imperfect human witness to divine revelation. As a human witness, the Bible also carries within itself codes of oppression; it, too, is a bearer of ideology.

These three assumptions give countercultural tendencies in scripture a special significance. By their logic, a countercultural tendency or voice is a likely sign of an emancipatory protest against ideology. I use the term "ideology" in the following traditional sense: a ruling value system in a society that (1) people take for granted and (2) serves the interests of the powerful at the expense of the less powerful.[2] A countercultural tendency is not by definition anti-ideological; the countercultural voice is a likely

---

2. The term "ideology" is also used in other senses, such as any system of values that favors the interests of one group over those of other groups. On the whole question, see Jorge Larrain, *The Concept of Ideology* (Athens, GA: The University of Georgia Press, 1979).

place of resistance to embedded cultural value systems that serve the powerful to the detriment of the weak.

To say that countercultural voices or tendencies should be given special weight means that they have a presumptively greater claim on Christians than do culturally-affiliating tendencies. The rule works as follows. Where A and B accord authority (weight) to the Bible and where A argues to B that X in scripture "merely reflects the dominant culture of the time," A wants B to infer that X should be given little weight as a witness to divine revelation according to the following tacit logic: (i) divine revelation is inherently anti-ideological; therefore (ii) authentic witness to divine revelation is anti-ideological; for that reason, (iii) authentic witness is typically countercultural in form. Alternatively, where A argues to B that Y in scripture "goes against dominant cultural values," A wants B to infer that Y has a presumptively greater claim than X as a witness to divine revelation.

In addition to general theological warrants for the rule of countercultural witness, there is also a more specifically hermeneutical warrant for the rule. At least some who use the rule do so on the basis of what has been termed the epistemological privilege of the oppressed. This idea has been particularly influential in Latin American Liberation theology. The concept of an epistemological advantage of the oppressed also figures in black theology and feminist theology. From these sources the concept has exerted a more general influence on modern theology.[3]

In Latin American theology, the use of the concept of the epistemological privilege of the oppressed has been shaped by Dietrich Bonhoeffer's notion of the "view from below." In "After Ten Years," probably written shortly before his imprisonment by the Nazis, Bonhoeffer wrote:

> We have for once learnt to see the great events of world history from below, from the perspective of the outcast, the suspects, the maltreated, the powerless, the oppressed, the reviled — in short, from the perspective of those who suffer. . . . We have to learn that personal suffering is a more

3. See the excellent discussions in Daniel S. Schipani, *Religious Education Encounters Liberation Theology* (Birmingham, AL: Religious Education Press, 1988), 210-60; also idem, *Conscientization and Creativity: Paulo Freire and Christian Education* (Lanham, MD: University Press of America, 1984).

effective key, a more rewarding principle for exploring the world in thought and action than personal good fortune.[4]

Inspired by Bonhoeffer's theological conception of the "view from below," Gustavo Gutiérrez develops a theological method which he terms "teología desde el reverso de la historia" ("theology from the backside/underside of history").[5] This is theology from the perspective of "history's absent ones," the poor.[6]

The contention that the oppressed have a privileged location for discerning the truth takes a variety of forms, from the very strong claim that valid ethical knowledge can be had only by those who carry out the struggle for liberation from the place and perspective of the oppressed to the softer claim that one cannot adequately understand the situation of the poor, the marginalized, the powerless, without incorporating the view from below.

The concept of the epistemological privilege of the oppressed argues for giving special weight to those voices in scripture that advocate for the socially powerless or marginalized. In theological terms, these voices have a greater claim than culturally-affiliating voices to speak for the God who in Jesus Christ joined with the powerless, the slaves, the outcasts. In view of this, I have phrased the rule as follows. "There is a presumption in favor of according greater weight to countercultural tendencies in scripture that express the voice of the powerless and the marginalized than to those tendencies that echo the dominant voices of the culture." The advantage of this form of the rule is that it avoids implying that everything countercultural is presumptively good, everything culturally normative is presumptively bad. Instead, it focuses on those regions of the cultural symbol system where there is most likely to be ideological distortion.

---

4. Dietrich Bonhoeffer, *Letters and Papers from Prison*, enlarged edition, ed. Eberhard Bethge (New York: Macmillan, 1972), 17.

5. This becomes the title of one of Gutiérrez's books: *Teología desde el reverso de la historia* (Lima: Centro de Estudios y Publicaciones, 1977), which can also be found in English as Part IV of Gutiérrez, *The Power of the Poor in History*, trans. Robert R. Barr (Maryknoll, NY: Orbis, 1983).

6. Gutiérrez, *Power of the Poor*, 201-02. See further, Osvaldo Luis Mottessi, "A Historically Mediated *Pastoral* of Liberation: Gustavo Gutiérrez's Pilgrimage Toward Socialism" (Ph.D. diss.; Emory University, 1985), 218-24.

History and Examples of the Rule

The Biblical Theology Movement: Uniqueness against Environment

The history-of-religions school sought to understand the Bible by comparing it to its religious environment. This comparison revealed both continuities and discontinuities between biblical religion and surrounding religions. For example, Hermann Gunkel discovered deep similarities between the Israelite and Babylonian creation myths, but he also noted that the Israelite stories have a distinctive character all their own. From this Gunkel drew certain theological conclusions. One can speak of God's revelation "in a special way" in the Israelite creation stories,[7] and Genesis 1 is a high point of divine revelation in history.[8] Nevertheless, the theologian should not underestimate the value of the other religious traditions, including the Babylonian Marduk myth from which the Israelites borrowed.[9]

A later generation would use the history-of-religions approach in a very different spirit. The Biblical Theology Movement of the 1930s-50s tended to define authentic biblical faith by contrasting the Bible with its environment.[10] One finds this in the claim that there is a distinctive Hebrew mentality (contrasted with the Greek way of thinking) and that at the heart of Israelite faith are unique elements: monotheism, the "aniconic" nature of God, and a non-mythological, historical understanding of the world.[11] Within biblical studies as a whole, claims for the originality and

7. Hermann Gunkel, *Schöpfung und Chaos in Urzeit und Endzeit: Eine religionsgeschichtliche Untersuchung über Gen 1 und Ap Joh 12* (Göttingen: Vandenhoeck und Ruprecht, 1895), VI. On Gunkel's theological judgments about the nature of divine revelation in the light of his history-of-religions work, see Werner Klatt, *Hermann Gunkel: Zu seiner Theologie der Religionsgeschichte und zur Entstehung der formgeschichtlichen Methode* (Göttingen: Vandenhoeck & Ruprecht, 1969), 74-77.

8. *Schöpfung und Chaos*, 118.

9. *Schöpfung und Chaos*, 118.

10. See Brevard S. Childs, *Biblical Theology in Crisis* (Philadelphia: Westminster Press, 1970), 44-50.

11. Childs, *Biblical Theology in Crisis*, 48. A characteristic assumption of much Biblical Theology has been that Israelite religion and Christian faith have unique qualities, which constitute the essence of biblical faith. See for example Walter Eichrodt's proposal that the task of Biblical Theology is to "examine the content for faith of a particular relationship with God, a relationship which has always to be seen as a dynamic process, expressing itself

uniqueness of the Bible extended well beyond the Biblical Theology Movement itself.[12] Generally, these claims were attuned to and also reflected the prevailing ethos of neoorthodoxy.

Brevard Childs observes that in the writings of G. Ernest Wright, the contrast of Israelite religion with the faiths of surrounding cultures "was developed into a hard-hitting, impressive new form of apologetic for Biblical religion."[13] But even where the use of environmental contrast was not hammering or overtly apologetic, "uniqueness," "originality," and "distinctiveness" served as implicit theological criteria, providing both credentials for biblical religion and markers of the central core of divine revelation. That is, it was inherent to the Biblical Theology Movement's use of the history-of-religions methods and findings that the argument for originality admits continuities with the environment. Not everything in scripture was "unique." But the tendency was to see elements of uniqueness or distinctiveness as constituting the heart of biblical faith, the most reliable signs of divine revelation.

Countercultural and Minority Voices

The Biblical Theology Movement is said to have collapsed in the 1960s, and certainly that conclusion is correct for the "movement" as a general theological project with which many biblical scholars self-consciously identified themselves. Nevertheless, some of the most basic theological

---

in history in many ways, and fluctuating between periods of rich and profound insight and periods of stunting and impoverishment, but which for all that exhibits a marvelous consistency in fundamental features which marks it out from its religious environment as an entity *sui generis.*" Walter Eichrodt, *Theology of the Old Testament,* vol. 1, trans. J. A. Baker (Philadelphia: Westminster Press, 1961; London: SCM Press, 1961), 517. In another context, Eichrodt speaks even more expansively of "uniqueness [of Israelite religion] over against the religious environment — that is, over against the typology of the history of religion generally" (Walter Eichrodt, "Does Old Testament Theology Still Have Independent Significance within Old Testament Scholarship?" in *The Flowering of Old Testament Theology,* ed. Ben C. Ollenburger, Elmer A. Martens, and Gerhard F. Hasel [Winona Lake, IN: Eisenbrauns, 1992], 37). G. Ernest Wright spoke in similar formulations, describing Israelite faith as "an utterly unique and radical departure from all contemporary pagan religions" (G. Ernest Wright, *The God Who Acts: Biblical Theology as Recital* [London: SCM Press, 1952], 19).

12. Childs, *Biblical Theology in Crisis,* 49-50.
13. Childs, *Biblical Theology in Crisis,* 49.

approaches of the movement persist (with modification) in theological interpretation of scripture today. One of these is the assumption that environmental contrast stands closer to divine revelation than does environmental continuity. This idea has become extremely problematic in the light of the cumulative evidence of history-of-religions research.[14] Nevertheless, the following examples of this claim illustrate not only the continuing appeal of the approach but also the significant ways in which it has been recast.

One significant recasting is the reconception of what "environment" really means. Environment is the context in which ideological forces are at work in culture. Hence, the environment is not simply the ancient Near Eastern "background" but Israel (or the church) in a social setting where interests compete and dominant groups oppress less powerful groups.[15] Ideological criticism seeks to expose in both texts and communities of interpretation those ideas about the social order that express and reinforce the interests of a dominant group at the expense of some other group(s) or class(es) in society.[16] Under this kind of analysis, the categories "countercultural," "ideological resistance," and "revolution" represent new biblical-theological conceptions of "environmental discontinuity" and "distinctiveness." Distinctiveness is now dissent from the dominant cultural values, values of the wider environment that may also have been dominant in Israel or in the early Christian movement.

In *Theology of the Old Testament*, Walter Brueggemann observes that there are both iconic and aniconic tendencies in Israelite religion.[17] By iconic he means consolidating tendencies based on a need for social order and typically involving a commitment to the status quo; the purity/holiness interests are generally iconic in orientation. By aniconic Brueggemann has in view socially transformative, liberative tendencies based on

14. See Patrick D. Miller, Jr., "God and the Gods: History of Religion as an Approach and Context for Bible and Theology," *Affirmations* 1/5 (1973): 37-62.

15. Norman Gottwald has been pioneering in advancing this conception of the environmental setting of ancient Israel. See his now classic study, *The Tribes of Yahweh: A Sociology of the Religion of Liberated Israel, 1250-1050 B.C.E.* (Maryknoll, NY: Orbis Books, 1979).

16. These two basic definitions of ideology do not exhaust the possibilities for defining the concept, but I think they fairly represent the most common uses of the term in theological circles.

17. Walter Brueggemann, *Theology of the Old Testament: Testimony, Dispute, Advocacy* (Minneapolis: Augsburg Fortress Press, 1997), 71-72.

"restlessness in every social situation and circumstance."[18] The Old Testament witnesses to both the iconic and the aniconic.

The aniconic-prophetic side of Israelite religion marks it out from its environment, says Brueggemann. Although there are antecedents to Israelite faith, "it is clear," he contends, "that in something like 'the Mosaic revolution' Yahweh burst into world history as a theological *novum*."[19] The "main force" of this revolution "is to establish justice as the core focus of Yahweh's life in the world and Israel's life with Yahweh."[20] Moreover, "[f]rom the outset, Yahweh is known to be a God committed to the establishment of concrete, sociopolitical justice in a world of massive power organized against injustice."[21] Yahweh is pledged above all to distributive justice, in contrast to the dominant ethos of the wider environment, notably the Greek preoccupation with order.[22] In its witness on behalf of distributive justice, the Old Testament goes against the dominant ideology of its time and poses a challenge in our own time, offering an alternative to "the dominant metanarrative to technological, military consumerism."[23]

I take Brueggemann's use of the terms "distinctiveness," "*novum*," "revolutionary character," "aniconic," and so forth as an implicit *argument* that the social-justice witness of the Hebrew Bible has a special claim on the church, presenting itself as a more authentic reflection of God's intent than voices in the Hebrew Bible that support or accept the status quo.

In a similar vein, Bruce Birch distinguishes between Old Testament teachings that grow out of Israel's transforming experience with God and those that "reflect Israel's unexamined participation in widespread social practice."[24] Birch offers, as a specific example, a distinction made by Paul Hanson between two sets of laws, one common to Mesopotamia and designed to uphold a stratified society, the other a Yahwistic humanitarian corpus reflecting in its motive clauses the specific Israelite experience of Yahweh. Birch comments, "In the contrast between these two bodies of law we can see Israel inevitably affected by the social practices of surrounding

---

18. Brueggemann, *Theology of the Old Testament*, 72.

19. Brueggemann, *Theology of the Old Testament*, 735.

20. Brueggemann, *Theology of the Old Testament*, 735.

21. Brueggemann, *Theology of the Old Testament*, 736.

22. Brueggemann, *Theology of the Old Testament*, 736-39.

23. Brueggemann, *Theology of the Old Testament*, 741.

24. Bruce C. Birch, *Let Justice Roll Down: The Old Testament, Ethics, and Christian Life* (Louisville, KY: Westminster/John Knox, 1991), 43.

culture, but placing those practices in tension with patterns of societal relationship which grow specifically out of the uniqueness of Israel's God
and experience in relation to God."[25]

A more specific example of using "countercultural" as a hermeneutical
criterion is William Holladay's treatment of the theme of gender in Jeremiah 31:22. In the first and last chapters of his excellent book on Old Testament theology, *Long Ago God Spoke,*[26] Holladay explores the question of
how modern Christians can hear God's word in scripture, given the Bible's
historical distance from us and the diversity of its teachings, which sometimes amount to contradiction. In his examination of the status and roles
of women in the Old Testament, Holladay asks "why the pre-exilic prophets, who stood out so sturdily against the prevailing assumptions of their
culture in matters of social justice, seem never to have questioned a society
in which there was male domination."[27] He answers that in ancient Israel,
the male/female hierarchy was seen as rooted in the created order. The
prophets' blind eye to patriarchy owes to the fact that the prophetic critique was based on the perception that Israel had violated God's will as expressed in the covenant and in creation, creation being understood as the
basis of patriarchy. Nevertheless, a countervailing note appears in Jeremiah's vision of a new creation in which the role of the female would be re-
versed. Holladay comments that the prophets' "acceptance of the priority
of male over female is not surprising. . . . What is surprising is the ability of
Jeremiah, in this curious verse [Jer. 31:22], to envision what had not there-
tofore been envisioned."[28]

Holladay's discussion is instructive for how the principle I have formulated as the rule of countercultural witness functions as part of
hermeneutical presuppositions shared by author/speaker and reader/
hearer. The audience must share the view that characterizing the prophets
as "countercultural" is both accurate and *significant.* The expression
"stood out sturdily against the prevailing assumptions of their culture in
matters of social justice" is the kind of interpretive statement that could
not be made until the twentieth century. It assumes a modern concept of
"culture" and trades on the value invested in countercultural protest in our

25. Birch, *Let Justice Roll Down,* 161.
26. William L. Holladay, *Long Ago God Spoke: How Christians May Hear the Old Testament Today* (Minneapolis: Augsburg Fortress Press, 1995).
27. Holladay, *Long Ago God Spoke,* 282.
28. Holladay, *Long Ago God Spoke,* 282.

age of liberation. I do not say any of this as a criticism of Holladay, as if I thought his language betrayed objective historical description. To see the past as significant, to move from explanation to understanding, we must use interpretive categories that have significance for us. Holladay's interpretation of the prophets does this. Readers who agree with Holladay's characterization of the prophets as bucking "the prevailing assumptions of their culture" will also hear Holladay's comments about Jeremiah as an implicit argument of the following sort: when Jeremiah challenges hierarchical gender codes, his witness thereby carries a mark of authenticity as a true insight into the divine will, because it flows from the prophetic countercultural breakthrough that is most closely in tune with God's breakthrough in social history.

Feminist Interpretation of the Bible

The operation of the rule of countercultural witness is especially evident in some forms of feminist hermeneutics, specifically, those that claim the Bible as an authority for the church but recognize that the Bible contains codes of patriarchal oppression.

Carolyn Osiek has provided a helpful typology of feminist approaches to the Bible. She distinguishes five basic types: rejectionist, loyalist, revisionist, sublimationist, and liberationist.[29] The revisionist hermeneutic concedes that the Judeo-Christian tradition has been cast in a biblical mold that is "male-dominated, androcentric, and discriminatory" but contends that these characteristics are "separable from and thus not intrinsic to" the biblical witness.[30] In the revisionist approach, "the chauvinistic-misogynist texts are explained by a combination of exegetical method and interpretation of the influence of cultural context."[31] The idea that certain elements in scripture can be explained away as "cultural" is sometimes based on claims of cultural relativity,[32] but here it is clearly not cultural relativity that is be-

---

29. Carolyn Osiek, "The Feminist and the Bible: Hermeneutical Alternatives," in *Feminist Perspectives on Biblical Scholarship*, ed. Adela Yarbro Collins (Atlanta: Scholars Press, 1985), 97.

30. Osiek, "The Feminist and the Bible," 100.

31. Osiek, "The Feminist and the Bible," 101.

32. Cf. Bernard Adeney: "Each of these areas of law [in the Old Testament] was relative to the specific social structures of Israel. The law helped create and maintain these social

ing invoked. Revisionist feminists are not arguing that patriarchy, as embedded in scripture, was culturally relative to its time and place and can be dismissed by us simply because we live in a different cultural context. They regard patriarchy as a pernicious and all too pan-cultural phenomenon. Moreover, patriarchy is an ideology and therefore is not something to be esteemed under the doctrine of cultural relativism. It appears that the revisionists' contention that voices of women and for women's equality in scripture carry authentic revelatory power against the Bible's otherwise culturally assimilating patriarchalism must depend on one (or both) of the following two assumptions: (1) that God is for the liberation of women from patriarchy and that a criterion for judging which texts or impulses in scripture most closely convey the divine word is the degree to which they promote God's commitment to women's liberation and equality; (2) that divine revelation is inherently countercultural in an anti-ideological way. The first of these two assumptions may be understood as a more specific form of the second. Moreover, the two assumptions have a natural relation in modern theology. The conviction that God takes up the cause of any oppressed group usually involves the corollary assumption that ideology is endemic to the human condition. Revelation in an unredeemed world is therefore to be regarded as inherently countercultural: God stands against all "normative" ways of interpreting and ordering social reality that serve the interests of the most powerful at the expense of the less powerful.

Rosemary Radford Ruether, for example, argues that authentic witness to God's Word within scripture is inherently counter-ideological, challenging organized, structural oppression.[33] This prophetic-liberative

---

structures. Today our social structures are different. Insofar as our societies are not agrarian, monarchial, slave-based, patriarchal, tribal, theocratic, polygamous, Middle Eastern and so on, we will have to develop our own laws to govern ourselves." Bernard T. Adeney, *Strange Virtues: Ethics in a Multicultural World* (Downers Grove, IL: InterVarsity Press, 1995), 91. Of course, this begs the question of what we are to do to the extent that our culture *is* patriarchal or polygamous or slave-based, etc. For example, it appears that Adeney's culturally relativist hermeneutic would have called for acceptance and endorsement of patriarchy and slavery in antebellum America.

33. Ruether's characteristic terms for what I am calling "countercultural" are "iconoclastic" and "prophetic" ("prophetic-messianic," "prophetic-liberating"). When she uses the term "countercultural," it carries a very specific sense and one that is narrower than my usage of the term here. See Ruether, "Goddesses and Witches: Liberation and Countercultural Feminism," *Christian Century* 97 (1980): 842-47.

For an excellent discussion of Ruether's biblical hermeneutic, see Jeffrey S. Siker, *Scrip-*

witness in the Bible provides a general theological norm for the critique of patriarchy.[34] Ruether distinguishes two basic religions in the Bible, a religion of the "sacred canopy" that justifies the status quo (reinforcing prevailing ideologies) and a religion of prophetic protest against the sacred canopy.[35] In scripture this impetus of cultural critique is found in the prophetic-messianic traditions, which speak on behalf of the oppressed. Although there is little prophetic critique against patriarchy in scripture, which is on the whole an overwhelmingly patriarchal book, the effect of the prophetic voice in scripture is to call into question the whole social order. "In sum, it is not some particular statements about women's liberation, but rather the critical pattern of prophetic thought, that is the usable tradition for feminism in the Bible."[36] This in turn allows one to give special weight to the rare biblical texts that do speak directly about women in a liberating, countercultural way.[37]

Some typologies of feminist interpretation of scripture distinguish the revisionist approach (sometimes called retrievalist or neoorthodox) from the liberationist approach.[38] There are good reasons for this, but it is important to see that the revisionist tack is often highly liberationist in its

---

ture and Ethics: Twentieth-Century Portraits (New York and Oxford: Oxford University Press, 1997), 170-202.

34. See, for example, Rosemary Radford Ruether, "A Religion for Women: Sources and Strategies," *Christianity and Crisis* 39 (1979): 307-11; "Feminism and Patriarchal Religion: Principles of Ideological Critique of the Bible," *Journal for the Study of the Old Testament* 22 (1982): 54-66; *Disputed Questions: On Being a Christian* (Nashville: Abingdon, 1982), 29-35 and 90-107; "Religion and Society: Sacred Canopy vs. Prophetic Critique," in *The Future of Liberation Theology: Essays in Honor of Gustavo Gutiérrez*, ed. Mark H. Ellis and Otto Maduro, 172-76 (Maryknoll, NY: Orbis, Books, 1989).

35. Ruether, "Feminism and Patriarchal Religion," 55-56; Ruether, "Religion and Society: Sacred Canopy vs. Prophetic Critique," 172-76.

36. Ruether, "A Religion for Women," 310.

37. See Ruether, *Disputed Questions*, 123-24.

38. See Osiek, "The Feminist and the Bible," 97; Elisabeth Schüssler Fiorenza, *In Memory of Her: A Feminist Theological Reconstruction of Christian Origins*, Tenth Anniversary Edition (New York: Crossroad, 1995), 3-40. David Scholer uses the term "retrievalist" for what Osiek calls revisionist. He characterizes the feminist retrievalist approach to scripture as "seek[ing] to find and expose the countercultural impulses within the text." See David M. Scholer, "Feminist Hermeneutics and Evangelical Biblical Interpretation," *Journal of the Evangelical Theological Society* 30 (1987): 409. Schüssler Fiorenza characterizes Ruether's approach as neoorthodox (*In Memory of Her*, 17) distinguishing it from what she regards as an authentic "feminist critical hermeneutics of liberation" (26-36).

orientation, which is to say that some liberationist approaches are also revisionist.[39] Fundamental to the liberationist approach is the contention that liberation of the oppressed is the basic hermeneutical norm for Christian theology. The Bible is then read according to that norm. In some liberationist interpretations the use of this hermeneutical canon proceeds on the assumption that scripture ought to be granted no authority because it is so thoroughly patriarchal (Schüssler Fiorenza). For other liberationists, scripture carries the limited authority of a classic religious text, bearing within itself a witness, in finite human words, to the divine word. The appropriate way for the community to treat scripture as an authority is to differentiate authentic witnesses to God's liberating word from human ideology in scripture in accord with the general principle of prophetic critique in the Bible itself (Ruether[40]).

Feminist revisionists or retrievalists for whom the Bible is the paramount authority also include evangelicals who acknowledge the patriarchal and even misogynist conditioning of scripture. These feminist evangelical interpreters use a countercultural, "prophetic" principle to relativize patriarchal texts in scripture.[41] For example, David Scholer argues for using a prophetic hermeneutic that recognizes theological affirmations such as Gal. 3:28 as central and normative and judges patriarchal

39. Ruether's retrievalist approach is very much in the spirit of Latin American liberationist hermeneutics (as she affirms). See, for example, Ruether, *Disputed Questions*, 90-107. Scholer identifies seven types of feminist hermeneutics and notes that "most practitioners of feminist hermeneutics engage in many of [the types] at the same time" ("Feminist Hermeneutics and Evangelical Biblical Interpretation," 408).

40. For an excellent summary of Ruether's conception of revelation (the divine word manifested in human words), see Siker, *Scripture and Ethics*, 190-91.

41. In addition to David Scholer, discussed below, other evangelical feminists or egalitarians also give special weight to the countercultural dimensions in the biblical witness regarding the role of women. See, for example, Paul K. Jewett, *Man as Male and Female: A Study in Sexual Relationships from a Theological Point of View* (Grand Rapids: Eerdmans, 1975). Jewett sees Gal. 3:28 as a "breakthrough" (*Man as Male and Female*, 144) — a breakthrough to which Paul is not fully faithful because of his "historical limitations," the continuing grip on Paul of dominant cultural assumptions from Paul's background about the proper order of male and female (139).

See also J. Richard Middleton and Brian J. Walsh, *Truth Is Stranger Than It Used to Be: Biblical Faith in a Postmodern Age* (Downers Grove, IL: InterVarsity Press, 1995). Middleton and Walsh argue for attending to "counterideological resources" in scripture "for inner-biblical correction," counterideological resources that they find above all in "minority voices of resistance and dissent" in the Bible (*Truth Is Stranger Than It Used to Be*, 180).

and misogynist texts as "limited."[42] Patriarchal scripture texts "should be interpreted from a particular vantage point — the dual commitments to the equal dignity and equality of men and women and to Scriptural authority."[43] I understand this to mean that even patriarchal texts, when understood with historical-contextual sensitivity, can contain a valuable word for the church but that this word is not to be identified with the patriarchal or misogynist content of these texts.[44]

As the preceding discussion shows, the rule of countercultural witness might just as aptly be termed the rule of prophetic, liberative, or aniconic witness. Countercultural means protest against the dominant culture. Hence, the judgment that a voice in scripture is countercultural depends on the perception that it challenges ideology, protests against something oppressive. Consider an example from J. I. H. McDonald's analytic survey of the use of the Bible in Christian ethics. In his discussion of how to deal hermeneutically with patriarchal teaching about women, McDonald comments as follows:

> The biblical writers . . . are not always true to their highest insights, and exercise power in patriarchal fashion. This becomes a negative marker, a red signal as it were. It denotes a point at which cultural presuppositions have not yet been challenged — or challenged adequately — by the gospel.[45]

In making this assessment, McDonald assumes that "the call for justice for the oppressed and the victims of discrimination [is] central to the Bible and

42. See Scholer, "Feminist Hermeneutics and Evangelical Biblical Interpretation," 412-20.

43. Scholer, "Feminist Hermeneutics and Evangelical Biblical Interpretation," 419.

44. In private correspondence, Scholer affirms that this is an accurate description of his position. A more conservative use of the rule of countercultural interpretation is found in Grant Osborne. In an article on hermeneutics and issues of gender, Osborne sets forth seven principles of interpretation, two of which run as follows: "Teaching that transcends the cultural biases of the author will be normative" and "If a command is wholly tied to a cultural situation that is not timeless in itself, it will probably be a temporary application and not an eternal norm." Osborne uses these principles to show that scripture sanctions the ordination of women but not the equal "headship" of man and wife in the household context. See Grant R. Osborne, "Hermeneutics and Women in the Church," *Journal of the Evangelical Theological Society* 20 (1977): 337-40.

45. J. I. H. McDonald, *Biblical Interpretation and Christian Ethics* (Cambridge: Cambridge University Press, 1993), 214.

affirmed by Christ."[46] Hence, it appears that the insight that patriarchy is oppressive, together with the assumption that God opposes dominant oppressive culture in the name of justice, leads McDonald to see certain texts — such as Gal. 3:28 — as expressing the core of the gospel and embodying the highest insights of the biblical writers. The vast majority of biblical writers did not see patriarchy as oppressive, but McDonald, like Ruether, appeals to the general prophetic stand against oppression as a basis for opposing, in the name of scripture, patriarchy as a form of oppression.

Using the rule of countercultural witness calls for giving greater weight to countercultural tendencies in scripture than to those that reflect the dominant culture ethos of their time and place. Since countercultural is a relative term, I have sharpened its sense to mean "opposing something oppressive in the dominant culture." This sharpening, however, raises the question whether the rule of countercultural witness assumes the *authority* of scripture in any traditional sense or simply asserts a canon-within-the-canon. For if one knows in advance what is oppressive and if arguing from scripture against oppression requires assent from one's audience about what counts as oppressive, then it is not clear how scripture warrants Christian social ethics under the rule of countercultural witness. I will consider possible rejoinders to this criticism at the end of this chapter.

Trajectories

Sometimes the idea of a prophetic, countercultural tendency in scripture is linked with the notion of progressive development. For example, some have claimed that the biblical witness on the question of slavery shows a generally progressive development in a more and more liberative direction. A theology of progressive revelation or progressive moral understanding provides an argument for treating the progression itself, with its implied endpoint, as having greater claim than any point along the way. The implied endpoint thus serves as a kind of utopian ideal by which to judge social reality past or present. In this way, trajectories have an anti-ideological, countercultural aspect to them.

The idea that biblical theology and biblical ethics should be constructed by attending to progressive development or trajectories of the tra-

46. McDonald, *Biblical Interpretation and Christian Ethics,* 214.

dition has been with biblical theology since its inception. In a 1787 address widely regarded as the beginning of biblical theology, Johann Philipp Gabler conceived the Bible as exhibiting stages of rational development in which ideas move from the particular to the universal. Gabler proposed that with the aid of "universal concepts" one can tease out the eternal from the merely accidental and provisional within the Bible's developmental history.[47] In the nineteenth century, Johann K. W. Vatke advanced a Hegelian interpretation of the development of Israelite tradition.[48] Notions of quasi-Hegelian evolution through tensions and contradictions persisted into the twentieth century. Ernst Troeltsch described the history-of-religions school as viewing "the entire territory of Christian life and thought as a gradual unfolding of an immanent impelling power or fundamental ideal, realizing itself in historical Christianity."[49]

More recently, Hartmut Gese has argued that the formation of Israelite tradition exhibits an unfolding process leading toward a goal in which preceding stages are not annulled but sublated, a process "leading through all the stages of human existence in the historical process."[50] According to

47. Johann Philipp Gabler, "An Oration on the Proper Distinction between Biblical and Dogmatic Theology and the Specific Objectives of Each," trans. John Sandys-Wunsch and Laurence Eldridge, *The Scottish Journal of Theology* 33 (1980): 133-44. On Gabler's conception, see also Christian Hartlich and Walter Sachs, *Der Ursprung des Mythosbegriffes in der modernen Bibelwissenschaft* (Tübingen: J. C. B. Mohr [Paul Siebeck], 1952), 46.

48. Johann K. W. Vatke, *Die biblische Theologie wissenschaftlich dargestellt*, vol. 1, *Die Religion des Alten Testaments nach den kanonishen Büchern entwickelt* (Berlin: Bethge, 1835). Vatke planned to publish four more volumes but ecclesio-political opposition to his ideas prevented him. See Ben C. Ollenburger, "From Timeless Ideas to the Essence of Religion: Old Testament Theology before 1930," in *The Flowering of Old Testament Theology: A Reader in Twentieth-Century Old Testament Theology, 1930-1990*, ed. Ben C. Ollenburger et al. (Winona Lake, IN: Eisenbrauns, 1992), 10-12.

49. Ernst Troeltsch, "The Dogmatics of the 'Religionsgeschichtliche Schule,'" *American Journal of Theology* 17 (1913): 11. See also Willy Staerk, "Religionsgeschichte und Religionsphilosophie in ihrer Bedeutung für die biblische Theologie des Alten Testaments," *Zeitschrift für Theologie und Kirche* 31 (1923): 289-300. For Staerk, Old Testament theology means establishing the fundamental origins of the authentic religious moment in Israel (which, Staerk argues, is to be found in the religious experience of Moses) and showing the logic of its development or unfolding through history. Ben Ollenburger observes that this is just the sort of biblical-theological program that Eichrodt took up (Ben C. Ollenburger, "From Timeless Ideas to the Essence of Religion," in *The Flowering of Old Testament Theology*, 16).

50. Hartmut Gese, "Tradition and Biblical Theology," in *Tradition and Theology in the Old Testament*, ed. Douglas A. Knight (Philadelphia: Fortress, 1977), 405.

Gese, "It is the secret of Israel to have been shown this path all the way to the inclusion of the whole world. . . ."[51] To take another example, Gerhard Hasel calls for an Old Testament theology that "bring[s] together the longitudinal themes and motifs and concepts" which "will allow for the presentation of their growth, progression, and expansion throughout the flow of Old Testament times."[52]

Ideas about progressive development are also found in conceptions of the relation between the Testaments. Gerhard von Rad argued that Israelite tradition developed dialectically through a typological hermeneutic of readaptation, also characteristic of the New Testament.[53] Especially notable is von Rad's conception of the evolutionary development of Israel's understanding of God as promisor. Israel's response to disconfirmed prophecies was to treat them as deferred and to reclaim them through dialectical enhancement for the future. Through this process, Israel "swelled Yahweh's promises to an infinity . . . placing absolutely no limit on God's power yet to fulfill."[54] Claus Westermann puts the relationship between the Testaments this way: "The history of God's people in the Old Testament leads away from power toward salvation on the basis of forgiveness. The new people of God can no longer preserve its existence by means of victories over other peoples, but rather only through its existence *for* the rest of humanity, as was already suggested by the servant songs in Deutero-Isaiah. . . . In the history recounted by the Old Testament we can thus see a movement toward a goal which points to what the New Testament says about Christ."[55]

None of these scholars has suggested that the progressive unfolding of theological/religious or ethical understandings in the biblical tradition is unilinear. And some, including Vatke in the early nineteenth century,[56] have recognized that the discernment of what counts as progression is not

---

51. Gese, "Tradition and Biblical Theology," 405. Evidently, the unfolding dynamic does not express itself in a concrete unilinear development in the tradition, which "does not represent a series of individual stages in the material and formal evolution of truth" (396).

52. Gerhard F. Hasel, "The Future of Old Testament Theology: Prospects and Trends," in *The Flowering of Old Testament Theology*, 383.

53. Gerhard von Rad, *Theology of the Old Testament*, vol. 2, *The Theology of Israel's Prophetic Traditions*, trans. D. M. G. Stalker (New York: Harper & Row, 1965), 319-409.

54. Von Rad, *Theology of the Old Testament*, 2:320.

55. Claus Westermann, *Elements of Old Testament Theology*, trans. Douglas W. Scott (Atlanta: John Knox, 1982), 230-31.

56. See Ollenburger, "From Timeless Ideas to the Essence of Religion," 11.

an objective, rationalistic exercise carried out from some standpoint above history but is a relative judgment made from a particular historical location. Nor is the notion of progressive evolution always the dominant mode of evaluation. Many developmental schemes include special places for certain privileged beginnings — the notion of a generative Israelite credo, the celebration of preexilic Israelite theology as focused on God's free and dynamic saving activity in history (absent any creation theology and timeless "orders of creation"), the playing off of early Israelite religion against a late so-called deterioration into legalistic "Judaism," primitive Christianity against "early Catholicism," the original Jesus movement against the Gospels, the authentic Paul against the Pastorals, and so on. What is deemed "original" casts its spell over otherwise evolutionary ways of understanding revelation (or testimony to revelation) in history.

If we were to formulate a hermeneutical rule to express the hermeneutic of progressive developmentalism, it might run as follows: Where a developmental tendency is discernable in the biblical tradition (historically or canonically conceived), it is legitimate to extrapolate from that trajectory an endpoint signifying a value or principle as more fundamentally normative than any stage along the trajectory. This rule, however, has much against it. Again and again, historical-critical demonstration of particularity and heterogeneity in the tradition has undermined claims about progressive development. For example, the claim that the status and rights of women moved along a steadily expanding trajectory in ancient Israel has been pretty roundly discredited. If anything, there is a trajectory in the opposite direction, away from egalitarianism.[57] Yet it is difficult to imagine anyone (and I know of no one) who uses the developmentalist hermeneutic to argue for female subordination. Progressivist hermeneutics is always tied to some value scheme that determines what counts as "progress." Only in such a larger axiological framework can the moral argument from development carry force.

Brueggemann probably voices the consensus judgment when, speaking of the Hebrew scriptures, he says that the biblical witness admits no progressive developmental scheme but is pluralistic, reflecting a conflict of positions at every point. According to Brueggemann, the canon itself does not resolve the many disputes that have marked Israel's history; it bears

---

57. See Carol Meyers, *Discovering Eve: Ancient Israelite Women in Context* (New York and Oxford: Oxford University Press, 1988).

witness to and preserves them in tension with each other.[58] Nevertheless, Brueggemann is willing to speak of "trajectories" within this pluralism: conflicting trajectories of liberation and of consolidation.[59] "Trajectory" in *this* conception is a *continuity* between different historical moments of the tradition, as attested in the biblical literature.

Brueggemann's use of the term "trajectory" also suggests something else, whether he intends it or not. A "trajectory" is an arc. Once we establish the direction of a trajectory, we can pinpoint its final destination in advance. Hence, although Brueggemann speaks of "continuities," the metaphor of trajectory suggests an arc with an endpoint, like a rocket going up out of the stream of the tradition and pointing to a destination beyond the tradition. This metaphor suggests that what Brueggemann terms the liberationist tradition may in each of its moments imply trajectories that are implicitly utopian. Even though the tradition itself does not display unilinear progress or even much *progress* at all, it suggests a *direction* that is progressive. The very term "liberating," as Brueggemann applies it to the Mosaic movement and all the subsequent tradition that movement generates, suggests that each moment of this tradition stands for something more than any of its immediate aims: that it stands for liberation in the best and fullest sense, even if the ancient liberationists had only a very limited understanding of what liberation ought finally to mean.

Similar to Brueggemann's idea of a trajectory as a continuity in the tradition is Paul Hanson's description of the task of biblical theology as tracing "the purposeful movement that it discerns unfolding through the writings of Scripture and that it regards as an essential source of our knowledge of God's will. . . ."[60] This means discovering "the transcendent dynamic of Scripture as one that unfolds precisely within the tensions and polarities represented by the divergent biblical traditions."[61] Hanson ap-

58. Brueggemann, *Theology of the Old Testament,* 63-64.
59. Brueggemann, *Theology of the Old Testament,* 72-74. See also Brueggemann, "Trajectories in Old Testament Literature and the Sociology of Ancient Israel," *Journal of Biblical Literature* 98 (1979): 161-85.
60. Paul D. Hanson, *The People Called: The Growth of Community in the Bible* (San Francisco: Harper & Row, 1986), 531.
61. Hanson, *The People Called,* 532. See further, Hanson, "The Theological Significance of Contradiction within the Book of the Covenant," in *Canon and Authority: Essays in Old Testament Religion and Theology,* ed. George W. Coats and Burke O. Long (Philadelphia: Fortress Press, 1977), 110-31.

parently has in view not so much *progressive* unfolding as the persistence through time of a core revelation that resists, even as it stands side by side with, contrary traditions. A non-progressive, unifying dynamic is discernable in this persistent assertion and reassertion of the core witness in Israel's original confession, the testimony that God has special compassion for the weak, the poor, and the oppressed, for slaves, widows, orphans, and other vulnerable persons and groups.[62]

Finally, mention should be made of Gerd Theissen's evolutionary approach to biblical faith.[63] In Theissen's vision, authentic witnesses to God in scripture are those that go against the principle of selection that drives biological and sociobiological evolution. In the faith of Israel and in the life and teaching of Jesus we meet anti-evolutionary breakthroughs that make possible a different evolution — an evolution against selection and on behalf of altruistic inclusion and protection of the weak. These breakthroughs might be called countercultural inasmuch as they challenge the sociobiological status quo, those mechanisms of social control that establish and promote the inherent selfishness of sociobiological history. However, Theissen sees culture itself as "generally . . . a process that reduces selection."[64] Hence, the prophetic breakthroughs of true witness to God are not properly "countercultural" in Theissen's sense of the term "culture."

Concluding Assessment

The rule of countercultural witness depends on two basic theological judgments: (1) that the Bible is a human witness to the divine word in which God's revelation is communicated but also distorted and (2) that God is against ideology, that is, opposed to those cultural norms, values, institutions, etc. that serve the interests of the more powerful at the expense of the less powerful. These two judgments support the following two inferences: (1) that one of the ways in which the Bible faithfully communicates the divine revelation is by witnessing to God's protest against ideology and (2) that one of the ways in which the Bible distorts the divine revelation is

---

62. See Hanson, "Significance of Contradiction."

63. Gerd Theissen, *Biblical Faith: An Evolutionary Approach* (London: SCM Press; Philadelphia: Fortress Press, 1985).

64. Theissen, *Biblical Faith*, 49.

through ideological distortion. The rule of countercultural witness discriminates between ideological assimilation and counter-ideological protest in scripture. The rule accords special weight to those voices in scripture that advocate for the socially powerless or marginalized against dominant cultural value systems. The rule presumes that these marginalized voices have a greater claim than culturally-affiliating voices to speak for the God made known in Jesus Christ who, in order to save both oppressed and oppressor, joined with the outcasts, the suspects, the maltreated, the powerless, the weak.

The rule of countercultural witness does not presume that everything countercultural is good and everything culturally normative is bad. It focuses culture as a vehicle of asymmetrical power relations. Nevertheless, some may judge the rule to be flawed in its presumption that every countercultural interest or value of the disenfranchised is morally good. For example, polygamy as once taught and practiced in North America by the Church of the Latter Day Saints is a countercultural value espoused by what was at least then a marginalized group. (The outlawing of the practice by Mormon church law has helped change the social status of Mormons in relation to the mainstream.) Should we therefore treat polygamy as presumptively good simply because it is a countercultural practice defended by the marginalized? This is perhaps not the best example, since polygamy is a form of patriarchy, and patriarchy has long been a dominant cultural value justifying asymmetrical power relations of many kinds.

A better example by which to falsify the rule of countercultural witness might be the claim of the Nation of Islam under Elijah Muhammad that the black race is the original people and is morally and intellectually superior to non-blacks and especially to whites, who are inherently evil.[65] But even this example is problematic inasmuch as this racial claim by black Muslims is a form of "reverse racism" and as such is arguably a way in which the Nation, as a marginalized group, *assimilated* dominant racial ideology by becoming racist itself.[66]

In view of the preceding, we might propose that a genuine falsification of the premise of the rule of countercultural witness must take the follow-

65. For a description of the racial views of classical Black Muslim faith, See C. Eric Lincoln, *The Black Muslims in America*, 3d ed. (Grand Rapids: Eerdmans, 1994; Trenton, N.J.: Africa World Press, 1994).

66. I leave aside here the controverted question whether the Nation of Islam today, under Louis Farrakhan, advocates a racist ideology.

ing form: identify a manifestly unjust or immoral countercultural value of a marginal group where that value is not simply a variation of a culturally dominant ideology. The problem with this test is that the perception of what is "manifestly unjust or immoral" may be incorrect. For example, emancipation and full enfranchisement of African Americans seemed manifestly unjust to many nineteenth-century slaveholders, for whom emancipation signified loss of their "property" and being placed on an equal civil footing with blacks. No doubt those in our time who reject the principle of countercultural witness do so on the basis of what they perceive as manifestly unjust or immoral. For them, the principle is falsified by this or that countercultural value, advocated in our own time, that they reject as being obviously wrong.

The example of moral attacks on slavery and the defense of slavery mounted in response is instructive. We live in an age of liberation, the beginnings of which stretch back to the Enlightenment and the social causes of the Enlightenment on behalf of women's equality, the poor, and slaves. I will focus on the American experience. Most Americans today look back and ask how earlier generations could have thought slavery or patriarchy was morally right. The concept of ideology helps explain why. The histories of those liberation movements that the majority of Americans today affirm (notably, the movements against slavery, for racial equality, for women's equality) strike those Americans who use the concept of ideology as a vindication of the theory of ideology as an explanatory system. This in turn makes them suspicious of any opposition to emancipation movements in their own time.

Most of us do not want to be in our time what those who opposed abolition and women's equality were in their time. Those for whom ideology is a working hermeneutical concept use that concept to map the moral landscape today in order to position themselves against ideology. This hermeneutical approach to social issues is what makes many of them suspicious that racism and sexism are still at work in places where it is claimed that they have been eradicated. This same hermeneutical approach leads at least some of them to embrace more recent countercultural causes, such as the gay and lesbian movements. For them, the principle of countercultural witness, applied to the Bible or to any other text or debate, signifies a predisposition to give greater credence to those with the least power where the debate is a dispute *about those with the least power*. This predisposition is based on (1) historical knowledge of the extreme resistance emancipation movements have faced in history, (2) the judgment that moral knowledge must include the testimony of those whose status or practice is rejected by the dominant voices, and (3) the conviction, or at least the strong suspicion, that those in the best position to do justice to both the dominant perspective and the minority perspective are those in the minority position (the epistemological privilege of the oppressed).

A crucial question is whether potential ideology is ever *generated from below.* By potential ideology, I mean a form of consciousness that is not dominant but, if dominant, would favor the interests of the strong to the detriment of the weak. Adapting Karl Mannheim's correlation of ideology and utopia, I will refer to a humane alternative vision to ideology as "relative utopia" and to potential ideology as "dystopia."[67] Both utopia and dystopia are by definition countercultural. Do the disenfranchised produce dystopia?

The question whether the disenfranchised ever produce dystopia may look like another form of the falsification test considered above. But the issue here is not whether we can identify a "manifest" example of dystopia from below (a test we found to be question-begging) but whether, in a more general way, we have reason to believe that dystopia is produced from below. The rule of countercultural witness is plausible only if its adherents are right to wager that the disenfranchised, to the extent they are able to break through to an alternative vision of the world, never or almost never do so in a form that is both countercultural and dystopian. Put positively, this is to wager that the disenfranchised produce alternative visions that are either (1) variations of the ruling ideology and in that sense not really countercultural, though they may be dystopian (e.g., the reverse racist dream of the Nation of Islam), or (2) genuinely utopian (e.g., Martin Luther King's beloved community). On the basis of this hermeneutical wager, the rule of countercultural witness seems valid. Countercultural voices from below are to be taken as presumptively utopian and not dystopian.

The preceding may have a flaw, however. If we can imagine dystopian

---

67. See Karl Mannheim, *Ideology and Utopia,* trans. L. Wirth and E. Shils (New York: Routledge and Kegan Paul, 1972). Mannheim absorbs the concept of ideology into a general sociology of knowledge. I am using ideology in its more traditional pejorative and value-laden sense, which distinguishes ideological from nonideological forms of consciousness.

visions that are simultaneously alternatives to current social arrangements and *variations* of dominant ideology, we should also consider that the same may apply to utopian visions. To the extent that advocates of utopian visions make their case from dominant traditions (including a revered past), they show their visions to be in some sense variations of the dominant tradition. Roland Barthes has remarked on this as the ambiguity of revolution: "Revolution must of necessity borrow, from what it wants to destroy, the very image of what it wants to possess."[68]

I do not regard the paradoxical relation of revolution to the past as fatal to the rule of countercultural witness. Recognizing that there is a paradox or dialectic includes seeing not only genuine continuity with the past but also genuine novelty. Nevertheless, the paradox of revolution is a further caution for any use of the principle of countercultural witness.

A final objection against the rule of countercultural witness is that it is superfluous. We have seen that for some, countercultural witness is a general principle applicable not only to scripture but also to any text or debate. If the rule of countercultural witness depends on a general moral hermeneutic of the oppressed, then it appears that the rule simply repeats what one already knows through ideological critique. In that case, the rule cannot be part of a hermeneutic for *appealing to* scripture; instead, the principle of countercultural witness could only provide a way of validating or invalidating voices in scripture.

I think there is considerable force in the preceding criticism, but it needs qualification. First, every use of the Bible in Christian ethics involves a hermeneutical circle in which moral assumptions based on other sources contribute to how we identify and construe the central message of scripture. Hence, a theory of ideology has a legitimate place in the hermeneutical circle. Moreover, circulating through the hermeneutical circle ought to involve progress in understanding; hence, it is perhaps better to speak of a hermeneutical "spiral."

Second, a strong argument can be made that the principle of countercultural witness by the marginalized is justified by the Bible itself, taken as a whole. Brueggemann makes some pertinent comments in this connection when he discusses what he calls "Israel as Yahweh's partner":

68. Roland Barthes, *Writing Degree Zero*, trans. Annette Lavers and Colin Smith, Preface by Susan Sontag (New York: Hill and Wang, 1968), 87-88.

If we are to identify what is most characteristic and most distinctive in the life and vocation of this partner of Yahweh, it is the remarkable equation of love of God with love of neighbor, which is enacted through the exercise of distributive justice of social goods, social power, and social access to those without leverage; for those without social leverage are entitled to such treatment simply by the fact of their membership in the community. While the case has sometimes been overstated, there is ample ground for the recognition that Israel, as a community under obligation, is indeed a community of social revolution in the world.[69]

Within the hermeneutical spiral, the hermeneutic dialogue between scripture, tradition, and religious experience produces and reinforces for many Christians the perception that the God of scripture stands in protest against oppression. That perception stamps the prophetic protest against "sacred canopy" religion a hermeneutical criterion for identifying the will and activity of God in the world. Moreover, that same criterion also predisposes one to greater trust of countercultural claims in scripture by disenfranchised voices than of culturally-affiliating stances in scripture by enfranchised voices. The church's understanding of the Bible as a whole can appropriately shape the church's hermeneutical approach to the Bible in any of its parts.[70]

The rule of countercultural witness also depends on a view of scripture's authority as derived from Christian experience of scripture as revelatory and life-giving. These are matters for both community and individual judgment. A notable example is Phyllis Trible's critically-reflective feminist witness to the liberative power of the Bible. After her embrace of critical perspectives, she says, the Bible she grew up with — the Bible of "sword drills" and memorization — "continued to make a claim on me," and the absorption of critical approaches did not diminish "my love for it."[71] Trible's lifelong experience of scripture confirms its authority for her; her hermeneutical approach to scripture is a way of honoring that authority in accord with what she sees as scripture's overall redemptive purpose,

---

69. Brueggemann, *Theology of the Old Testament,* 424.

70. This point has often been made. David Kelsey argues it very effectively in *The Uses of Scripture in Recent Theology* (Philadelphia: Fortress Press, 1975), 106-8.

71. Phyllis Trible, "Eve and Miriam: From the Margins to the Center," in Trible et al., *Feminist Approaches to the Bible: Symposium at the Smithsonian Institution, September 24, 1994* (Washington, D.C.: Biblical Archeology Society, 1995), 6.

which includes for her the redemption of scripture from bondage to patriarchy.[72]

Taken as a whole, my assessment of the rule of countercultural witness leads to the following two judgments about the rule. First, it depends on the cogency of the concept of ideology. Second, if we grant that the concept of ideology is valid and provides a basis for the rule, the rule merits at most presumptive, not final or absolute, force. Presumptive force makes the rule controlling unless and until sufficiently countervailing reasons are adduced against its application in a particular instance.

72. Trible, "Eve and Miriam," 8.

FOUR

The Rule of Nonscientific Scope

Scientific (or "empirical") knowledge stands outside the scope of scripture.

The Bible contains both momentous and trivial instances of scientifically outmoded empirical knowledge. To take a weighty example, the temporal and cosmological aspects of much early Christian eschatology is untenable within the modern scientific worldview. An inconsequential example is the Gospel saying, "The eye is the lamp of the body . . . ," which assumes that the eye is a source of light.[1]

It is widely acknowledged that where modern scientific knowledge contradicts ancient biblical assumptions about empirical reality, the church ought not to assert those ancient assumptions in the teeth of scientific evidence. Thus, for example, although ancient and medieval Chris-

---

1. Matt. 6:22-23. On ancient theories of vision, including the idea that the eye contains its own light or receives light from within, see Hans Dieter Betz, *The Sermon on the Mount: A Commentary on the Sermon on the Mount, including the Sermon on the Plain (Matthew 5:3– 7:27 and Luke 6:20-49)*, ed. Adela Yarbro Collins (Minneapolis: Fortress Press, 1995), 442-49. For evidence in ancient Judaism that the eye was thought to be a source of light, see W. D. Davies and Dale C. Allison, Jr., *A Critical and Exegetical Commentary on the Gospel according to Matthew*, vol. 1, *Introduction and Commentary on Matthew I–VII* (Edinburgh: T. & T. Clark, 1988), 635-36.

116

tians treated Genesis 1 as providing an authoritative cosmology, today many Christians do not look to the creation accounts for cosmological guidance. Likewise, when it comes to other parts of scripture, many Christians seek to appropriate the theological meaning of scripture without submitting themselves to the ancient views of the physical world asserted or assumed by the Bible. New Testament eschatology can be theologically true without being empirically true; the metaphor about the "eye" can be spiritually true without being literally true.

In the domain of ethics, the conflict between ancient empirical assumptions and modern science is sometimes treated under the concept of cross-cultural "relevance." The term "relevance" can be misleading, as if the problem were simply that some biblical moral teachings concern matters that have no real analogue in modern cultures. Victor Paul Furnish speaks of two problems of relevance in connecting Paul's teaching with modern practice. One is that the more Paul's instruction is tailored to a particular situation, the less directly relevant it is likely to be to other situations.[2] The other is that some things are no longer relevant to us because we know that they rest on mistaken empirical assumptions. Thus, moral instruction based on the expectation of an imminent end of the world "cannot possibly be relevant in a world that no longer lives with that kind of expectation, and whose very existence shows that Paul was mistaken."[3] The biblical writers, Furnish observes, "generally presuppose beliefs about the physical world, human beings, and social relationships that we can no longer presuppose."[4] The gap between antiquity and modernity is in part a matter of scientific supersession.

---

2. Victor Paul Furnish, *The Moral Teaching of Paul: Selected Issues,* 2d ed. (Nashville, TN: Abingdon, 1985), 16-17.

3. Furnish, *The Moral Teaching of Paul,* 19.

4. Victor Paul Furnish, "The Bible and Homosexuality: Reading the Texts in Context," in Jeffrey S. Siker, ed., *Homosexuality in the Church: Both Sides of the Debate* (Louisville, KY: Westminster/John Knox, 1994), 31. See also Furnish, *The Moral Teaching of Paul,* 79-80. Furnish has in view ancient understandings of homosexual desire and practice in the light of modern knowledge, provisional as it still is, about sexual identity and the origins of sexual orientation.

The Bible in the Modern[5] World

Two developments in the early modern world impelled certain seventeenth-century European Christians to define the scope of scripture in relation to "scientific knowledge." One was the rise of global European exploration, which brought startling information back to Europe from "new world" discoveries. In his fascinating study of early modernity, Anthony Grafton observes that prior to the sixteenth century, educated Europeans assumed that knowledge of the world was to be found in ancient books: "the Bible, the philosophical, historical, and literary works of the Greeks and Romans; and a few modern works of unusually high authority."[6] By the mid-seventeenth century, however, the travel reports brought back to Europe by European explorers had exploded this assumption. An exchange between the North American Iroquois and seventeenth-century "new world" explorer Louis Hennepin illustrates the challenge of the new discoveries for learning based on old-world books. Hennepin explained to the Iroquois that Europeans "know all things through written documents," to which the Iroquois responded by asking, "Before you came to the lands where we live, did you rightly know that we were here?" Hennepin admitted that Europeans had not known, to which the Iroquois replied, "Then you don't know all things through books, and they didn't tell you everything."[7] The discovery of lands and peoples, whole worlds, about which

5. Throughout this chapter, I use the term "modern" for the period stretching from roughly the seventeenth century through the present. In so doing I am treating postmodernity as part of the evolution of modernity, and I am ignoring the important continuities between the Middle Ages and the early modern period. Although important lines of development can be drawn between the Middle Ages and early modernity and although some useful contrasts can be made between modernity and postmodernity, these continuities and contrasts are not generally germane to my discussion, which focuses on the epochal knowledge gap between ancient times and modern/postmodern times. Nevertheless, I speak briefly to the issue of postmodern philosophy of science at the end of this chapter.

6. Anthony Grafton, *New Worlds, Ancient Texts: The Power of Tradition and the Shock of Discovery* (Cambridge, MA: Harvard University Press, 1992), 2.

7. From the dust jacket of Grafton, *New Worlds, Ancient Texts*. A seventeenth-century translation of Hennepin's work has "knew all by Scripture." See Father Louis Hennepin, *A New Discovery of a Vast Country in America*, vol. 2 (Chicago: A. C. McClurg, 1903; reprint of 1698 London ed.), 536. I have not consulted the original French but this difference between the two translations no doubt turns on how to construe the French word *écriture* — as "writing" ("written documents") or as "scripture" (meaning the Bible).

the authoritative classical texts knew nothing, shook Western confidence that an adequate understanding of the universe could be derived from the study of ancient books.

A second development, the rise of what we now call modern science, also eroded confidence in ancient learning. The conceptual frameworks by which we understand the empirical world, including important aspects of human history, have altered our perception of the nature of the Bible. Unlike premodern Jews and Christians, most moderns do not assume that the Bible and ancient classical texts provide a reliable guide to empirical knowledge. Today it is a Christian commonplace to say that scripture is not a book of science, which means not simply that the Bible is silent on vast areas of scientific knowledge but also that where the Bible does speak or make assumptions about such things as cosmology, human and natural history, biology, etc., it does not provide a reliable scientific voice. One says that the Bible speaks in the language of its time(s) and place(s), that is, in a premodern voice and therefore in prescientific idioms. Moreover, the dominant modern Christian view is that the Bible as scripture is authoritative in spiritual matters (theology and ethics), not empirical knowledge.

As I have just described it, this modern view involves an equation of scientific knowledge with empirical knowledge. Empirical knowledge is knowledge of a state or event *as determined by natural and/or human causes.* By this definition of "empirical," that God exists and that God does such and such are not empirical facts because they do not have to do with natural or human cause-effect relationships.[8] Moreover, the statement that a certain action is morally good does not assert an empirical fact (except on theories of values that transform values into empirical statements, as in emotivism), although the statement that so-and-so holds a certain action to be morally good asserts an empirical fact.

The Bible makes fact-assertions that do not fit the modern distinction between the theological and the empirical. For example, the description of creation in Genesis 1 has God acting in the material world. At the literal level, some aspects of these statements are open to empirical investigation; others are not. That *God* acts is not an empirical claim; that stars are

---

8. Cf. Langdon Gilkey on the classic modern (neo-orthodox) distinction between theology and science, *Religion and the Scientific Future: Reflections on Myth, Science, and Theology* (New York: Harper & Row, 1970), 23-25.

formed at a certain point in the sequence of creation involves a kind of empirical claim — the sort of claim that leads a modern person to conclude that the creation story is not empirically true as a description of the formation of the universe and of life on earth. On the other hand, the mode of language and the "philosophical" assumptions informing the story are so different from those of a modern scientific account that it is also fair to say that the two kinds of account — the biblical and the modern scientific — are incommensurable. Hence, I use the term "quasi-fact" for any assertion that has God as actor in the empirical domain. The qualifier "quasi" means that to speak of God acting in the world is to use the term "act" in a sense that resembles but is also very unlike other kinds of action in the world. Specifically, one cannot investigate, scientifically, the implied cause-effect relation in any statement about God acting in the world because the "cause" in this kind of statement is not empirical.

The human sciences are empirical in the broad sense of the term. Nevertheless, some human science disciplines are also properly concerned with establishing nonempirical truths. Examples are moral philosophy and law. It is not necessary here to decide whether these and like disciplines are true or pure sciences. The term "science" can be used broadly (corresponding to the German *Wissenschaft*). Here it suffices to say that the exclusion of scientific questions from the scope of scripture refers to the empirical sciences and also to the human sciences to the extent that the human sciences seek to establish empirical knowledge.

For some Christians, the exclusion of scientific knowledge from the scope of scripture means that, strictly speaking, the Bible makes no empirical assertions (see the comment about incommensurability above); for others it means that empirical assertions or assumptions do appear in the Bible but that these stand outside the purpose of scripture and thus do not carry the weight of scriptural authority; for still others the rule of scope means that only certain kinds of empirical assertions (or certain ways of taking scripture as making empirical claims) stand outside the scope of scripture. This chapter examines these different views and elaborates the rule of scope by exploring its history and warrants.

The History and Nature of the Exclusion
of Scientific Knowledge from the Scope of Scripture

Since the emergence of the modern scientific disciplines, the history of science has become generally progressive. Scientific knowledge advances in a process that is irreversible. Conceptual frameworks that have been abandoned do not become viable at some later point. This means that earlier scientific knowledge is inferior to later scientific knowledge. Moreover, later scientific knowledge is superior not simply in the cumulative sense of an increase in information; it is also superior in the conceptual frameworks that make sense of information and generate it.

In scientific change, especially across those epochal gaps that Thomas Kuhn calls paradigm shifts, past and present are disjunctive.[9] This is certainly the case between ancient science and modern science. Ancient and modern science are related in a hierarchy of inferior to superior where the superior does not include but supersedes the inferior in a disjunctive way. This means that ancient science cannot be conceived as standing in a relation of prototype (much less archetype) to modern science. Modern science does not build on ancient science, and there is no way to make ancient conceptual frameworks fit modern scientific ones.

The preceding must be qualified for the human sciences. Some of the human sciences, notably philosophy, continue to draw inspiration from ancient thinkers. A philosopher can be a neo-Aristotelian in a meaningful sense (notably, in the sphere of ethics); a modern physicist (qua physicist) cannot be. Thus, the ancient classical heritage continues to serve as a foundation for some of the human sciences.[10] Nevertheless, insofar as the human sciences establish empirical knowledge, their superiority to ancient science is discontinuous.

---

9. See Thomas S. Kuhn, *The Structure of Scientific Revolutions,* 2d ed. (Chicago: University of Chicago Press, 1970), 43-51. Kuhn uses the term "incommensurable" to describe the gaps between successive paradigms (112, 198).

10. Hilary Putnam observes that "when the notion of 'progress' first began to be discussed in the seventeenth century, the progressivists clinched their case with the claim that 'Newton knew more than Aristotle.' No one could argue convincingly that Shakespeare is a better dramatist than any of the ancient tragedians, or a better poet than Homer; but it seemed undeniable that the scientist Newton had made a real and undeniable advance upon knowledge over the scientist Aristotle." See Hilary Putnam, *Reason, Truth, and History* (Cambridge: Cambridge University Press, 1981), 176.

The disjunctive superiority of modern science to ancient empirical knowledge poses a challenge to the authority of scripture where scripture makes empirical claims or assumptions. Christian intellectuals of the seventeenth century met this challenge by arguing that the Bible does not intend to be a book of science.[11] It was seventeenth-century philosophers (scientists)[12] who first developed this new conception of the scope of scripture. Johannes Kepler argued against those who looked to the "teaching of the saints" for guidance in "natural matters." According to Kepler, "in theology the authorities [Scripture as elucidated by the theologians] have decisive importance, but in philosophy [science] the decisive importance attaches to calculations."[13] In the words of Galileo, "the authority of Holy Scripture is directed mainly towards convincing men of such conceptions and principles which, because they transcend all human thought, cannot find belief through science or any means other than through the revelation of the Holy Spirit."[14]

A more complicated view eventually emerged as Christian intellectuals sought to work out the implications of distinguishing theology from science. Klaus Scholder sums up one effort to mediate between Cartesian philosophy and biblical authority, setting forth its four basic presuppositions:

1. The unqualified authority of scripture in all theological questions where it makes clear and unequivocal statements on them. 2. The certainty and reliability of philosophical knowledge in the sphere of natural matters and its right to examine all things freely and critically in that sphere. 3. The separation in principle between theology and philosophy as two ways of knowledge based on different principles and working with different materials. 4. The freedom of philosophical and theological statements from contradiction.[15]

Christoph Wittich was evidently the first *theologian* to defend and elaborate the distinction between theology and science for understanding the

11. See Klaus Scholder, *The Birth of Modern Critical Theology: Origins and Problems of Biblical Criticism in the Seventeenth Century,* trans. John Bowden (Philadelphia: Trinity Press International, 1990).

12. In the seventeenth century, "science" was a branch of philosophy and "scientists" were still called philosophers.

13. Kepler, as quoted in Scholder, *Birth of Modern Critical Theology,* 57.

14. Galileo as quoted in Scholder, *Birth of Modern Critical Theology,* 60.

15. Scholder, *Birth of Modern Critical Theology,* 124.

scope of scripture. The scope of scripture, Wittich maintained, is "to convey what is to be believed, not erroneous thoughts about natural matters."[16] It is therefore contrary to the nature and purpose of scripture to seek to harmonize it with science/philosophy as if scripture treated the subject of natural things. "Scripture often speaks of natural things according to the view of the people . . . not in accordance with the exact truth."[17] Hence, one ought not to confuse theology and science as is done "by those who make us a Mosaic or a Christian physics and want to develop the intrinsic connection and the nature of things from scripture."[18] These statements show that Wittich advocated an accomodationist view, according to which the Holy Spirit speaks in scripture through the prescientific conceptions of ordinary ancient people in order to lead them to spiritual, not scientific, truth. The scope of scripture is to conduct us to salvation.[19]

Many Christians today take an approach to scripture that is similar to Wittich's (although not necessarily accommodationist). A typical assertion is that scripture is authoritative not on all subjects but specifically for "matters of faith and practice." An assumption of this view is that reliable knowledge about empirical facts stands outside the scope of scripture. As a limiting principle, the rule of scope does not touch the question of *the way* in which scripture speaks authoritatively on matters lying *within* its purpose.

Distinguishing a nonscientific scope of scripture was a theological judgment meant to preserve the authority of scripture. In Greek, *scopos* means "target." The term was used as a hermeneutical concept from Reformation times, having antecedents in patristic interpretation of scripture.[20]

16. Christoph Wittich as quoted in Scholder, *Birth of Modern Critical Theology,* 176, n. 75.

17. Wittich as quoted in Scholder, *Birth of Modern Critical Theology,* 124-25.

18. Wittich as quoted in Scholder, *Birth of Modern Critical Theology,* 126.

19. A similar position is found in John Wesley. For Wesley, scripture is "sufficient" not for all forms of knowledge but specifically for matters of faith and practice. Outside this scope, it is not scripture but reason and experience that carry authority. See Scott J. Jones, *John Wesley's Conception and Use of Scripture* (Nashville, TN: Kingswood Books, 1995), 37-41 and 65-80.

20. See Gerald T. Sheppard, "Between Reformation and Modern Commentary: The Perception of the Scope of Biblical Books," in William Perkins, *A Commentary on Galatians,* ed. Gerald T. Sheppard, with introductory essays by Brevard S. Childs, Gerald T. Sheppard, and John H. Augustine (New York: The Pilgrim Press, 1989), xlviii-lxxvii. For the meaning of *scopos* in patristic usage, see G. W. H. Lampe, *A Patristic Greek Lexicon* (Oxford: Clarendon, 1961), s.v., *skopos.*

One application of the concept to the Bible is the scope of a particular writing or passage of scripture, that is, its focus and aim. This is at least one meaning of "scope" *(scopos)* in Calvin.[21] Likewise, Johann August Ernesti defines the scope as the overall design of the writer, to be gathered from express statements in the work as a whole (*Institutio Interpretis,* 1761).[22] This is ordinary scope — scope as a concept of general hermeneutics. Ascertaining the overall design provides a guide to the interpretation of particular passages. The scope functions in the hermeneutical circle at the point where the whole determines the part.

A second application of scope is the design, focus, and aim of *scripture* as a whole.[23] Where the ordinary sense of scope means the purpose of the human writer in this or that biblical book, scriptural scope traditionally refers to the divine purpose, what God intends to communicate and accomplish with scripture.[24] Scope of scripture refers to the proper subject matter and aim of the Bible as *sacred text or canon* and as *a whole.* Scope of scripture is thus a hermeneutical concept by which the church construes the nature and purpose of the Bible as bearer of God's word.

The concept of the scope of scripture had both a positive and a negative application in the sixteenth and seventeenth centuries. In its positive use, it offered a guide to right interpretation.[25] In its negative use, it marked the

21. See, e.g., Calvin, *Ioannis Calvini opera quae supersunt omnia,* ed. W. Baum, E. Cunitz, and E. Reuss, vol. 10 (Braunschweig: C. A. Schwetschke and Son, 1871), 403.

22. Johann August Ernesti, *Elementary Principles of Interpretation,* 3d ed., trans. Moses Stuart (Andover: Gould & Newman, 1938), 44-45.

23. See Sheppard, "Between Reformation and Modern Commentary," lix-lxviii. This use of the concept stems from the post-Reformation English commentators and remained a working hermeneutical category until the end of the nineteenth century.

24. With the advent of post-intentionalist theories of textual meaning, however, the idea of a scope of scripture has become conceivable as an implicit quality of scripture as a whole, apart from questions of specific divine or human intentions behind individual statements in scripture. It is possible to interpret Brevard Childs' canonical approach as entailing some such non-intentionalist model of scripture. Paul Ricoeur's theory of textual meaning (and "surplus of meaning") also offers a hermeneutic framework for positing a scope of scripture on a non-intentionalist basis. The debate over intentionalism, however, need not be pursued further here.

25. One aspect of the scope is the aim of scripture in a particular substantive sense, akin to that of the analogy of faith. Writing in 1818, Thomas Horne described the scope as "the soul or spirit of a book" (as quoted in Sheppard, "Between Reformation and Modern Commentary," lxv). Another aspect of the scope is the idea that the Bible displays a design,

border of scriptural authority. As I have noted, Christoph Wittich construed the scope of scripture as a limiting concept, maintaining that scripture's purpose is to teach matters of faith, not knowledge of natural things.

The scope of scripture as a limiting concept rests on a combination of external and internal judgments. Several New Testament passages speak explicitly of the nature and purpose of scripture: 2 Tim. 3:16-17; 1 Cor. 10:11; Rom. 15:4; Matt. 22:34-40. These texts share the view that scripture has a focused purpose, namely, to promote a right knowledge of God and a right way of living with God and neighbor. The New Testament's use of scripture indicates that the four passages just mentioned represent the predominant view of the early church: the purpose of scripture is instruction in the faith (promised and fulfilled in Jesus Christ) and in the way of life belonging to that faith.

By itself, however, this early Christian conception of scripture's scope is *not* necessarily *limiting*, since early Christians could have affirmed the idea of a scope of scripture and nevertheless believed that a secondary surplus of intelligence exists in scripture beyond scripture's central purpose. It is in fact highly unlikely that scope was conceived as a limiting concept during or after the period of the formation of the Christian Bible (from roughly the second through the fourth centuries), since the dominant hermeneutic environment imbued sacred texts with inexhaustible meaning on virtually any subject. This view of the Bible appears to have been held by Jews and Christians from ancient times until at least the seventeenth century. James Kugel notes four assumptions characteristic of all ancient interpretation (Jewish and Christian) that contributed to the view that scripture is omnisignificant: (1) the Bible is a cryptic document (it means more and other than what it appears to mean); (2) the Bible is universally relevant and contemporary; (3) the Bible is perfect and perfectly harmonious; and (4) all scripture is divinely authorized.[26] The notion of the perfection of scripture and its cryptic nature led to the view that every detail in scripture is loaded with meaning. Interpreters with a philosophical bent used this hermeneutical presupposition as a basis for arguing that the best of Greek philosophy owed originally to Moses and could be discovered, in

---

overall and in its parts. Grasping the soul and design of scripture was seen as essential to right interpretation.

26. James L. Kugel, *Traditions of the Bible: A Guide to the Bible as It Was at the Start of the Common Era* (Cambridge, MA: Harvard University Press, 1998), 15-19.

its perfection, in scripture's hidden revelations.[27] In its fullest flowering during the medieval period, the Christian hermeneutic of scriptural omnisignificance saw the Bible as a cryptic mirror of the world. As Paul Ricoeur puts it, "Scripture appears here as an inexhaustible treasure which stimulates thought about everything, which conceals a total interpretation of the world."[28]

With the rise of modernity, however, the implicit potential of scope as a limiting category suggested itself as a way out of the confrontation between the Bible and humanist scholarship, modern science, and the discovery of new worlds unknown to the ancient texts. An accommodationist theory made scope as a limiting concept plausible in the seventeenth century.[29] The Holy Spirit, it was said, accommodated the language of scripture to the thought-patterns of biblical times, it being the task of scripture "not to teach us natural things as they are in themselves but to contemplate them to God's glory and man's blessedness."[30] God "does not explain nature himself nor alter language" but "speaks of himself in human fashion."[31]

To the extent that the accommodationist theory depends on some kind of dictation theory of inspiration, it is no longer persuasive. It seems better to say that the witness of the authors and shapers of scripture is framed in the language and conceptualities of the cultures in which the biblical traditions were produced. The scriptural authority of these witnesses applies to their religious purpose (their scope), not to their assertions about history, geography, science, etc.

27. See John G. Gager, *Moses in Greco-Roman Paganism* (Nashville: Abingdon, 1972), 76-79.

28. "Preface to Bultmann," in *The Conflict of Interpretations: Essays in Hermeneutics*, ed. Don Ihde (Evanston, IL: Northwestern University Press, 1974), 385.

29. The theory of accommodation did not originate in the seventeenth century. Accommodationist theories of scriptural communication were common among the church fathers as a way of dealing with what they regarded as inadequate depictions of God's being and nature in the Bible. See, for example, Novatian, *De Trinitate* 6. The application of a theory of accommodation to matters of cosmology is found at least as early as Aquinas (and probably earlier). See Thomas Aquinas, *Summa Theologiae* Ia.68.3. I owe these two examples to Richard Swinburne, "Meaning in the Bible," in *Religion, Reason, and the Self: Essays in Honour of Hywel D. Lewis*, ed. Stewart R. Sutherland and T. A. Roberts (Cardiff: University of Wales Press, 1989), 24-25.

30. Balthasar Bekker (*Die bezauberte Welt*, 1693) as quoted by Scholder, *Birth of Modern Critical Theology*, 129.

31. Bekker as quoted by Scholder, *Birth of Modern Critical Theology*, 130.

Nevertheless, differentiating the scope of science from the scope of scripture does not answer the question of how to proceed when these two types of knowledge are mixed. It appeared to the seventeenth-century theologians that in some matters theology necessarily assumes truths that belong to the investigative field of science. Amandus Polanus expressed the position of Protestant Orthodoxy as follows: "[Theology] also has to judge on other things by virtue of its greater and more infallible truth; . . . whatever is found in other sciences as being in conflict with theological truth is condemned as utterly false."[32]

The debates of the seventeenth century dealt with matters of cosmology and geography, not ethics. The possibility that the ethical teaching of scripture might rest at points on assumptions as outmoded as ancient cosmology did not become an issue until much later. An influential precursor to this debate in the English-speaking world is probably the influence of the antislavery movement on English and American jurisprudence. At a time when law, like every other subject, was being approached as a historical discipline, growing recognition that slavery, although sanctioned by law since time immemorial, is immoral, helped shape a new conception of law as relative and evolving.[33] The twentieth century witnessed the rise of cultural relativity, which set the intellectual stage for confronting the historical and culturally relative nature not only of law but also of scripture and offered a new way of understanding the apparent acceptance or even affirmance of slavery in scripture.

In modern theology, the judgment that scientific language and theological language belong to different (and perhaps incommensurable) orders of discourse (or different "language games") has alleviated many of the problems associated with so-called mixed types. Special difficulties remain, however, in the sphere of ethics. Questions about right Christian practice do not admit a facile distinction between scientific matters and those belonging properly to theological ethics. Factual claims have an important place in moral reasoning.[34] For example, the question whether women have

---

32. As quoted in Scholder, *Birth of Modern Critical Theology,* 106.

33. See William E. Nelson, "The Impact of the Antislavery Movement on Styles of Judicial Reasoning in Nineteenth Century America," *Harvard Law Review* 87 (1974): 513-66.

34. Hilary Putnam, *Realism with a Human Face,* ed. James Conant (Cambridge, MA: Harvard University Press, 1990), 163-78; Henry David Aiken, "Levels of Moral Discourse," in *Reason and Conduct: New Bearings in Moral Philosophy* (New York: Alfred A. Knopf, 1962), 70-71.

natural capacities, equal to those of men, for exercising reason and serving as leaders in the church and the wider society is in large part an empirical question, to be settled by the disciplines of history (including disciplined investigation of women's experience and self-knowledge), sociology, biology, etc.

In view of the place of factual claims in moral reasoning, doctrines of the exclusion of a scientific scope from the purview of scripture have taken either a strong or a weak form. The strong form is the position that empirical knowledge stands entirely outside the scope of scripture, including facts assumed in scripture's moral claims. The weak form holds that only those empirical matters that are incidental to faith or practice stand outside the scope of scripture.[35]

The weak form confronts three difficulties. First, if scripture presupposes scientific knowledge in its moral teachings, that knowledge must be based on the science of some particular moment in the history of science, a moment eventually to be surpassed in the course of scientific evolution. Thus, if scientific knowledge belongs within the scope of scripture, then some unsurpassable forms of scientific knowledge (even if couched in ancient language and conceptions) would have to be available to the biblical writers to prevent their empirical presuppositions from being superseded. This possibility is incompatible with post-Kuhnian understandings of the nature and development of scientific knowledge, specifically, with the recognition that facts are theory-laden. The biblical writings presuppose the empirical knowledge of the world current in their own day and time — views of creation, cosmos, the natural history of the world, human biology, etc. — that have been superseded by (and are disjunctive with) modern knowledge.

35. The weak form of the rule of nonempirical scope was advocated by many American evangelicals following the rise of neo-evangelicalism in the 1940s and 1950s as a part of a general view that runs more or less as follows: where the Bible's teaching about any (or at least essential) matters of faith and practice includes empirical claims, those claims do belong within the scope of scripture, although they are typically couched in the language of the times. A classic statement is Bernard Ramm, *The Christian View of Science and Scripture* (Grand Rapids: Eerdmans, 1954). Ramm does not, however, discuss the empirical implications in the moral teaching of scripture but concentrates on issues of cosmology. He does say at one point that "[t]he theological, the ethical, and the practical are so conjoined in the Bible with the statements about Nature or Creation that it is impossible to separate them, and to impugn one is to impugn the other" (33).

A second challenge to the weak form of the rule of nonempirical scope is theological. Rudolf Bultmann argued that if empirical knowledge stands within the scope of scripture, then scripture's call to faith entails a summons to *assent* to biblical cosmology and other biblical assumptions about the natural world. In that case, however, biblical faith requires something different from us today than it did from the Bible's original audiences, audiences for whom the biblical cosmology was simply part of their received worldview. That is, the original addressees of the kerygma were not summoned to *believe in* (put their trust in the purported truth of) ancient cosmology; they simply took that cosmology for granted. For us, however, the inclusion of ancient empirical knowledge in the scope of scripture poses a demand for believing assent. That, Bultmann observes, creates a false offense, a stumbling block that has nothing to do with the authentic offense of the cross.[36]

Finally, a consistent application of the weak form of the rule of scope would require that one accept in a factual sense the *cosmological* ideas found in the Bible since cosmological assertions and assumptions appear not only in trivial but also in momentous biblical teachings, such as the creation story in Genesis 1. Of course, one might argue that the creation story contains a cosmology in a nonscientific sense and therefore should not be treated as in any sense a scientific account.[37] However, the weak form of the rule of scope assumes that biblical assumptions or assertions

36. See Rudolf Bultmann, "New Testament and Mythology: The Mythological Element in the Message of the New Testament and the Problem of Its Re-interpretation," in *Kerygma and Myth: A Theological Debate,* vol. 1, ed. Hans Werner Bartsch, trans. Reginald Fuller (New York: Harper & Row, 1961), 3-4; Walter Schmithals, *An Introduction to the Theology of Rudolf Bultmann,* trans. John Bowden (Minneapolis: Augsburg Publishing House, 1968), 255-56.

37. I have mentioned this possibility above as the view that the creation story and a modern scientific account of the formation of the known universe are incommensurable. Claus Westermann argues that the creation story in Gen. 1 deliberately avoids being any kind of scientific account by using a variety of competing ways of describing creation. The Priestly writer allows for a pluralism of views about the "how" of creation in order to assert the fundamental mystery of creation. Moreover, Westermann thinks that the entire controversy between faith and science (beginning in the sixteenth century) has been misplaced. See Claus Westermann, *Genesis 1–11: A Continental Commentary,* trans. John J. Scullion, SJ (Minneapolis: Fortress Press, 1994), 173-74, 176. However, Westermann's conception of the Bible's relation to science does not vindicate (and is not meant to vindicate) the weak form of the rule of nonscientific scope. Westermann means to reject any use of the Bible for scientific knowledge.

of historical or natural facts are to be treated as empirically true; the rule differentiates only between facts that are relevant for faith and practice and those that are not. This explains why most interpretations of Genesis 1 by those who hold to the weak form of the rule of scope involve efforts to harmonize biblical cosmology and modern science.[38] In the end, the weak form of the rule of scope does not permit consistent affirmation of the relative superiority of modern scientific understandings of the universe over ancient cosmology and hence does not deal satisfactorily with the conflict between the Bible and science.

If the weak form is untenable, the strong form has its own difficulties. In matters of the human sciences there are cases where it is very difficult to distinguish purely empirical aspects within our moral knowledge. For example, does a particular biblical teaching about human nature fall into the category of the empirical? Or are judgments about the nature of the human being not reducible to purely empirical investigation? The essays in a recent collection devoted to the question "Is there a human nature?" make use of insights from Aristotle to Augustine to Arendt.[39] It is probably fair to say that for all but the purist behaviorists, ancient knowledge can be as valuable as modern knowledge when it comes to defining and making sense of human nature.[40] The very notion of the "classic," which has become such an important concept these days, depends on this assumption.

If we adopt the view that knowledge of the nature of humanity is not a purely empirical matter, then biblical teaching about "human nature" presents us with a mixed type in which separating out the empirical from the nonempirical judgments is difficult and probably at some points artificial. Consequently, applying the strong form of the rule to ethical teach-

---

38. A notable example is Bernard Ramm, *The Christian View of Science and Scripture.* Ramm achieves this harmony by distinguishing scientific language and conceptuality from biblical language about empirical matters. The biblical language, Ramm says, is popular, phenomenal (related to appearances), untheorized, and cast in ancient cultural terms (66-70). He then seeks to show that biblical language, thus understood, does not conflict with modern science.

39. Leroy S. Romer, ed., *Is There a Human Nature?* (Notre Dame, IN: University of Notre Dame Press, 1997).

40. An extremely forceful and eloquent defense of this view has recently been made by Martha C. Nussbaum, *Love's Knowledge: Essays on Philosophy and Literature* (New York and Oxford: Oxford University Press, 1990).

ings in scripture may at times strip the text of elements that cannot be eliminated without distorting the text.

Related to the preceding is the problem of faith and history. Do *historical* assertions stand within the scope of scripture? Three possible answers to this question are especially worth considering. One is that some or all assertions about history do stand within the scope of scripture. The weak form of the rule of scope figures here as claiming that all historical matters that are asserted or assumed by scripture and are germane to faith and practice belong within the scope of scripture. A second view is that certain fundamental historical assertions stand within the scope of scripture but require modern historical vindication in order to carry weight. This is the view of the stream of Biblical Theology associated with G. Ernest Wright, who sought to vindicate the major historical claims of biblical faith through the use of history and archeology. A third view holds that history stands within the scope of scripture but that questions about the *empirical truth* of history in the Bible do not. I take this to be Rudolf Bultmann's position. Remarkably, it appears that Karl Barth also entertained a version of this view, at least as a theoretical possibility.[41] My impression is that many today negotiate the relation between faith and history by seeking a tensive position between the second and third types. Thus, for example, Ernst Käsemann sought to show that while faith is not dependent on history, it is properly informed by history. Hence, for Käsemann, reconstructions of the historical Jesus do matter for faith even though faith is not ultimately dependent on them.[42]

The question of history bears on ethics when the historical Jesus, for example, is appropriated as the criterion of Christian faith and practice. When the witness of the New Testament is seen as being about the public Jesus of history, history becomes in some way or other a part of the scope of scripture. Applying the strong form of the rule seems arbitrarily to eliminate elements of public history that are intimately bound up with the gospel message. Hence, those who reject the Bultmannian stance on faith and

41. In an exchange with Paul Tillich about revelation and history, Barth commented that "if all is myth, the myth nevertheless also describes the revelation as inseparably bound to an 'empirical fact.'" See Karl Barth, "Von der Paradoxie des 'positiven Paradoxes': Antworten und Fragen an Paul Tillich," in *Anfänge der dialektischen Theologie*, part 1, 2d ed., ed. Jürgen Moltmann (Munich: Chr. Kaiser Verlag, 1966), 185.

42. See Ernst Käsemann, "The Problem of the Historical Jesus," in *Essays on New Testament Themes*, trans. W. J. Montague (Philadelphia: Fortress Press, 1982).

131

history but who otherwise affirm the strong form of the rule of scope may do best to apply the strong form cautiously, holding that some empirical (or semi-empirical) matters (such as certain aspects of history in the biblical witness) are germane to faith and practice and stand within the scope of scripture. But this creates a problem of consistency analogous to that confronted by advocates of the weak form of the rule.

Empirical Facts and Moral Values

The rule of the nonempirical scope of scripture makes a form of the distinction between facts and values. The scope of scripture includes values but not empirical facts. To explain this more precisely, it is necessary to distinguish some of the issues that the fact-value dichotomy has come to symbolize.

In a set of influential essays, Max Weber marked off those things susceptible of empirical demonstration — things that are the proper objects of empirical science — from subjects of evaluation (normative judgments) that lie outside the scientific domain (in which he included sociology and economics). The empirical sciences, Weber argued, cannot establish the "ends" of practical activity; they can only show the best means to achieve chosen ends.[43] Something very close to this was probably also the view of that important father of modern science, René Descartes.[44]

Weber's view provided a strong impetus to the notion of science as "value-free." As applied to scientific method, "value-free" is often taken to

43. Max Weber, *The Methodology of the Social Sciences,* trans. and ed. Edward A. Shils and Henry A. Finch (Glencoe, IL: The Free Press, 1949).

44. There are two definitions of the soul in Descartes: the soul as comprehended by scientific reason *(res cogitans)* and the mind-body composite (the unity of *res cogitans* and *res extensa*), the seat of passions and desires, known by sensation and imagination. The latter soul is the subject of moral action, the bearer of free will and of moral virtues; human purpose resides with it. Science cannot know this composite soul, but it can serve the interests of this soul. Therefore, science can serve ethics, but ethics falls outside the scope of scientific method. I am indebted to my brother, Joseph Cosgrove, for drawing my attention to these distinctions in Descartes. On the whole matter, see Richard Kennington, "The 'Teaching of Nature' in Descartes' Soul Doctrine," *Review of Metaphysics* 26 (1977): 86-117; on method in Descartes, see Joseph K. Cosgrove, "Technology, Philosophy, and the Mastery of Nature" (Ph.D. diss.; Washington, D.C.: Catholic University of America, 1996), 12-55 (with concluding comments on method and ethics).

mean free from prejudice, from moral evaluation, and from ideology. Nevertheless, much recent sociology of science (including ideological critiques of science from disciplines such as feminism and culture studies) is at pains to show that all forms of knowledge (and all methods of knowing) are inherently ideological or are at least so entrenched in ideology that the way out of politically-biased knowledge remains only a future possibility (perhaps a utopian one). Proponents of these views typically affirm an inescapable connection between science and values, arguing either nihilistically that the values embedded in science are mere ciphers for power interests or that science must be revolutionized so that it embodies good (liberating, egalitarian, etc.) moral values.

By some accounts, logical positivism has defended an even broader form of the claim that science is value-free than Weber did, holding that science (when rightly practiced) is free of all values and not just ideological or moral ones. The positivist theory of the disjunction between facts and values sees science as rational and objective, values as nonrational and subjective. The association of values with subjectivity and lack of logical rigor stigmatizes value judgments as inferior to scientific judgments. The more recent perception that scientific rationality includes informal induction and non-positivist justifications ("explanation") has recast this hierarchy. For some this means that there is no such thing as rationality/objectivity, for others that rationality is broader than positivism allows and that subjectivity is not the polar opposite of objectivity but is rather an aspect of rationality.[45]

The rule of the nonempirical scope of scripture takes a position on only one aspect of the debate about facts and values. By asserting that science and not scripture is the proper arbiter over empirical facts, it holds that moral knowledge stands outside the scope of science and that empirical knowledge stands outside the scope of scripture. But the rule does not assume that science is free from all values. The sciences as social institutions are influenced by all sorts of values, including moral ones. Moreover, the justificatory criteria of science entail certain cognitive values.[46]

---

45. A notable and influential example is Michael Polanyi, *Personal Knowledge: Towards a Post-Critical Philosophy* (Chicago: University of Chicago Press, 1958). Polanyi sees the participation of the knower in what is known as part of the essential structure of knowing. This does not make understanding "subjective"; the participation of the knower is part of objective knowledge.

46. See Hilary Putnam, *Reason, Truth, and History,* 127-49.

The rule of nonempirical scope does not take any stand on the types of rationality that are at work in science and moral knowledge or how subjectivity and objectivity figure in the different methods of science and moral understanding. These are important questions, but the rule of nonempirical scope can accommodate different answers to them.

Moral judgments include both moral and empirical-factual assumptions. Hence, to understand the moral content of scripture, one must identify both the moral and the empirical-factual assumptions on which scripture's moral judgments rest. One must also grasp the logical interrelation between these two types of assumptions in a given moral judgment. This kind of analysis permits one to see how a scriptural moral judgment would have to change (given its own moral assumptions), if a different set of empirical facts were assumed. In discussing the rule of purpose (chapter one), I showed that moral assertions can be analyzed to show their logical presuppositional (inferential) structure. The formalization of the justifications for moral rules produces a hierarchy of informal syllogisms, each of which contains at least one major premise normative. This kind of analysis has wide application to moral assertions, including those that are not rules, strictly speaking. In moral logic, major premise normatives combine with major and minor premise fact statements, some of which may be empirical facts.

The moral scope of scripture (as a hermeneutical category) is its moral teaching independent of its empirical assumptions. One cannot predict in advance that it will always be possible to identify and distinguish moral and empirical assumptions within biblical moral judgments. One has to work case by case. Nevertheless, to the extent that such distinctions can be made, the hermeneutical procedure implied by the rule of scope is to construct fresh moral arguments from the scriptural logic by replacing biblical assumptions of empirical fact with the best available current empirical knowledge.

Empirical Assumptions in Biblical Moral Discourse

Factual judgments figure in biblical moral discourse in the conceptual frameworks that inform the terms of moral assertion and in the express and tacit assumptions that go into the data, warrants, and backing behind biblical moral positions. The following examples reveal different ways in which empirical assumptions operate in biblical morality. Some of these examples also serve as occasions to illustrate the method of reframing the logic of biblical morality on the basis of modern empirical knowledge.

Dietary Laws

The dietary regulations given in Lev. 11 and Deut. 14 remain a contested field of interpretation.[47] No theory of their underlying logic fully accounts for all their detail, although some explanations are clearly more powerful than others. Among the most compelling interpretations are those in the tradition inaugurated by Mary Douglas in her famous study, *Purity and Danger.*[48] According to this approach, the dietary laws depend at least to some degree on empirical assumptions about the order of the world. We do not know exactly what rationale underlies the distinctions between clean and unclean animals, but it is likely that it involved an empirical judgment about what is natural and what is unnatural.[49] In saying this, I do not mean to suggest that the rationale was solely empirical. Any moral conception of what is "natural" in the sense of the proper order of the creation is more than a mere factual interpretation. At the same time some kinds of factual judgments, or quasi-facts, are involved, analogous to the way someone today who claims that homosexuality is "unnatural" typically has in mind some conception of empirical facts (or quasi-facts) understood within a particular moral framework (e.g., that people are biologically heterosexual and incline to homosexuality only by a perverse moral choice).

47. For overviews of scholarship on the dietary regulations, see Walter Kornfeld, "Die Unreinen Tiere im Alten Testament," in *Wissenschaft im Dienste des Glaubens: Festschrift für ABT Dr. Hermann Peichl,* ed. J. Kisser et al. (Vienna: Catholic Academy of Vienna, 1965), 11-27; Edwin Firmage, "Zoology," *Anchor Bible Dictionary,* 6 vols. (New York: Doubleday, 1992), 6:1124-25.

48. Mary Douglas, *Purity and Danger: An Analysis of Concepts of Pollution and Taboo* (London: Routledge & Kegan Paul, 1966). See also *Reading Leviticus: A Conversation with Mary Douglas,* ed. John F. A. Sawyer (Sheffield: Sheffield Academic Press, 1996).

49. I think John Barton is correct when he argues that, although ancient Hebrew has no terms for "natural" and "unnatural," the rationale behind the dietary laws involves some such conception. See John Barton, *Ethics and the Old Testament* (Harrisburg, PA: Trinity Press International, 1998), 71.

Wisdom Ethics in Ecclesiastes

Wisdom teaching, found not only in the so-called wisdom literature of the Old Testament but also in (and underlying) many other parts of Hebrew scripture, is based generally on a conception of cosmic order. Wisdom is a kind of prudential consequentialist ethic based on traditions of collective knowledge about how the world works.[50] Although moral consequences were often understood in terms of divine intervention, there are also examples where wisdom assumes an intrinsic connection between act and consequence (e.g., Prov. 26:27 and 28:10),[51] as well as many instances where success in living is tied to practical knowledge of good etiquette and prudence.[52] Hence, from our perspective, much of this ancient wisdom is cultural knowledge. A close look shows that it mostly reflects upper-class culture.

A difficult question is whether (or to what degree) the sages thought that their teaching rested on an original divine act of creation establishing an unchanging moral order (or ongoing divine maintenance of order).[53] It is easy for us to see that a good deal of the ancient wisdom teaching is local knowledge applicable only to particular cultural conditions and classes. But did the sages regard their teaching with any comparable perception of what we would call cultural relativity? Or did they see as universal what we see as limited and historically contingent?

Ecclesiastes (Qoheleth) offers an interesting example of how ancient empirical assumptions operate in the wisdom of a sage (or school) whose teaching not only makes universal claims but continues to resonate powerfully beyond its original setting and assumptions. The sage asserts that

50. See the pioneering work of H. H. Schmid, *Wesen und Geschichte der Weisheit: Eine Untersuchung zur altorientalischen Weisheitsliteratur* (Berlin: Alfred Töpelmann, 1966). Other valuable treatments are Gerhard von Rad, *Wisdom in Israel* (Nashville and New York: Abingdon Press, 1972); James L. Crenshaw, *Old Testament Wisdom: An Introduction* (Atlanta: John Knox, 1981); and Joseph Blenkinsopp, *Wisdom and Law in the Old Testament: The Ordering of Life in Israel and Early Judaism* (Oxford: Oxford University Press, 1995). An excellent survey, with extensive bibliography, is James L. Crenshaw, "The Wisdom Literature," in *The Hebrew Bible and Its Modern Interpreters,* ed. Douglas A. Knight and Gene M. Tucker (Minneapolis: Fortress Press, 1985; Atlanta: Scholars Press, 1985), 369-407.

51. See Blenkinsopp, *Wisdom and Law in the Old Testament,* 47.

52. Blenkinsopp, *Wisdom and Law in the Old Testament,* 29-31.

53. On the assumption that an original divine act of creation created a stable moral order, see James L. Crenshaw, *Prophetic Conflict: Its Effects Upon Israelite Religion* (Berlin and New York: Walter de Gruyter, 1971), 116-23.

"there is nothing new under the sun," that "what has been is what will be" (1:9). This assertion is clearly intended in a maximal sense: in all respects, cosmological and social, the world does not change. The tedious, unchanging movement of the sun, wind, and waters is isomorphic with the unchanging course of society. Human forgetfulness gives an "illusion of novelty"[54] in history, when there is no novelty and never will be. Interpreting this claim requires a judgment about what counts as change. No doubt Qoheleth did not mean that there are no changes. Presumably, the only form of change that exists for him is variation on what is basically the same and therefore does not count as real change.

Qoheleth draws certain moral implications from his premise about invariability. One is his judgment that the best a man can do with his life (the implied reader is male) is to keep the commandments of God and take pleasure in whatever gifts God bestows, as opposed to (among other things) organizing with others for social transformation.[55] The assumption that the entire cosmic order (including the social order) is fixed is not the only ground for quietism in Ecclesiastes, but it is an important ground.

Qoheleth's theory that the cosmic-social order does not change and is not susceptible to alteration by human effort is untenable in the light of modern knowledge. We now recognize that "human forgetfulness" (absence of reliable historical knowledge) is far less responsible for illusions of novelty than for illusions of sameness. The rule of scope calls for engaging the witness of Ecclesiastes on different assumptions about history and social change, assumptions that may lead us from the same concerns that Qoheleth voices about social injustice to different conclusions about the possibilities for social justice.

Factual Grounds of Social Ethics

A dominant interpretation of the difference between prophecy and apocalyptic in ancient Israel holds that prophecy looks for social justice in history, understanding that God works for justice through human agency

54. James L. Crenshaw, "Ecclesiastes," in *Harper's Bible Commentary*, ed. James L. Mays (San Francisco: Harper & Row, 1988), 521.

55. On the socioeconomic context of Qoheleth, see C. L. Seow, *Ecclesiastes: A New Translation with Introduction and Commentary*, Anchor Bible (New York: Doubleday, 1997), 21-36. On Qoheleth's social quietism, see Seow, 58.

(immanent sociopolitical forces), whereas apocalyptic looks for a new creation beyond history brought about by divine intervention apart from human agency. According to Paul Hanson, apocalyptic arose in ancient Israel because people lost confidence in historical possibilities.[56] We may call the apocalyptic understanding of history quasi-factual because it entails assumptions about what human beings are capable of and also about how God works in history.

Deeper than specifically apocalyptic or prophetic conceptions of history is a common view of history and society that prophets and apocalyptic seers share. The ancient understanding of history assumes flux but no fundamental structural social change. (We have already noted an extreme version of this perspective in Ecclesiastes.) One finds pockets of optimism in the ancient world about growth in knowledge, but these have almost nothing to do with social betterment through changes in social structure. There are reform movements but no revolutions in antiquity.[57] Radical visions of society were not translated into social ethics. They were relegated to some primordial age[58] and served purposes other than social activism. Neither Cynics, nor Epicureans, nor Stoics sought to implement any of their radical social ethics.[59]

The absence of revolutionary thought, reinforced by the apocalyptic cast of early Christianity, is a grounding presupposition of New Testament social ethics. Paul, for example, preaches that in Christ "there is neither . . .

56. Paul D. Hanson, *The Dawn of Apocalyptic* (Philadelphia: Fortress Press, 1975), 11-12.

57. Robert Nisbet has challenged the views of Bury and others that the very notion of progress is modern. In *History of the Idea of Progress* (New York: Basic Books, 1980), Nisbet appeals to recent scholarship showing that many ancient thinkers not only had some idea of social development and of growth in knowledge and technology through past time but that they also projected future progress (pp. 10-46). How much of this thinking was part of the worldview of the early church is impossible to determine. In any case, ancient speculations about alternative forms of society did not drive any social revolutions in antiquity.

58. See M. I. Finley, "Utopianism Ancient and Modern," in *The Use and Abuse of History* (New York: Viking Press, 1975), 181.

59. See Wayne A. Meeks, *The Moral World of the First Christians* (Philadelphia: Westminster Press, 1991), 34, 55, 60-61. Finley attributes the absence of an idea of social progress in antiquity to the extremely limited economic possibilities of ancient agrarian society (poor resources, low level of technology, no avenue for growth other than conquest) and the fact that people regarded social inequality as natural and immutable. What little practical "utopian" thinking existed tended to be extremely modest in scale. See Finley, "Utopianism Ancient and Modern," 190.

138

slave nor free, male nor female" (Gal. 3:28), but he does not see this as a warrant for a new social ethic. At most, he is prepared to accept a limited eschatological anticipation of the end of the male/female distinction in the practice of the Christian churches. It is customary to explain this as a consequence of Paul's expectation of the imminent return of Christ and also by observing that Christians lacked political leverage and therefore could not have imagined influencing the structures of their society.[60] Behind these reasons is also the deeper static view of history, the sheer inconceivability of a change of social relations between men and women and between slaves and masters.[61]

In Gal. 6:10, Paul says, "So then, whenever we have an opportunity, let us work for the good of all, and especially for those of the family of faith." The qualifier, "whenever we have opportunity," assumes the sorts of constraints described above. By contrast, in an era and social setting (e.g., North America) where the church has an established and protected social status, where Christians have far more social and economic power than the ancient church did, where Christians operate on different assumptions than Paul did about the nature of history and about possibilities for social change, where the church has opportunities for cooperation with other groups, social agencies, and so forth to influence society (opportunities unthinkable in Paul's day), "working for the good of all" naturally acquires a different meaning than it carried in Paul's time.

---

60. See Wayne Merritt, for example: "Paul, to be sure, is a child of his age and the arena of direct social control open to him and his contemporaries in an era of Hellenistic monarchy and empire is none other than that of the family, and voluntary, religious and professional associations of which the church, itself, provided Paul with his most direct access to social power. Paul's attitude toward social change, therefore, needs re-thinking from precisely this point of view; namely, how is Paul's work and message related to social change given the identifiable means of social change in the ancient world. Moreover, the cul de sac of Paul's apocalyptic vision of the approaching end of the world as an *inhibition* toward social change needs to be seen as precisely that — a cul de sac that serves the interests of the status quo." H. Wayne Merritt, "Paul and the Individual: A Study in Pauline Anthropology," *Journal of the Interdenominational Theological Center* 17/1 (Fall 1990): 42.

61. Relations between Jews and gentiles are a notable exception in Paul. Paul is able to see the distinctions between Jews and gentiles as historically contingent and therefore alterable. He traces this insight to revelation (assuming that Paul has the end of the Jew/gentile distinction in mind as part of the revelation he refers to in Gal. 1:11-12). He also points to scripture, where he finds a story in which historical contingency governs the status and relations of Jews and gentiles (see Gal. 3:15-18).

Appropriating New Testament moral teachings on social ethics within their scope means discerning their significance beyond the factual assumptions that inform the concrete moral vision of the New Testament writers. Loosed from ancient socio-empirical assumptions, New Testament social ethics can present a socially radical face, susceptible to an activist interpretation. Tied to its original socio-empirical assumptions, the New Testament presents a quietist social ethic.

Engaging the Powers

Ethical action in the New Testament also involves what Walter Wink calls "engaging the powers."[62] Wink makes the following salient observations about early Christian understanding of the forces that determine human existence. "These Powers are both heavenly and earthly, divine and human, spiritual and political, invisible and structural."[63] The Powers "do not . . . have a separate, spiritual existence."[64] Rather, they exist in embodied form. Thus, for example, "demons can become manifest only through concretion in material reality."[65] Wink interprets this ancient conception of the powers by using the structural metaphors of "inner" and "outer." "The Powers are simultaneously the outer and inner aspects of one and the same indivisible concretion of power."[66] Accordingly, the New Testament writers can use the same power language to refer to human rulers, supernatural beings (angels and demons), or to both simultaneously, without concern for distinguishing forms and types of power. The transhuman powers are understood as embodying and manifesting themselves through this-worldly reality. Hence, the language of power is almost seamless.

From a modern perspective, the ancient language of power is mythical. Ancient Jews and Christians thought of angels and demons as crea-

---

62. See Walter Wink's trilogy: *Naming the Powers: The Language of Power in the New Testament* (Philadelphia: Fortress, 1984); *Unmasking the Powers: The Invisible Forces That Determine Human Existence* (Philadelphia: Fortress, 1986); *Engaging the Powers: Discernment and Resistance in a World of Domination* (Minneapolis: Augsburg Fortress, 1992).

63. Wink, *Naming the Powers*, 100.

64. Wink, *Naming the Powers*, 105.

65. Wink, *Naming the Powers*, 106.

66. Wink, *Naming the Powers*, 107.

tures possessing self-consciousness and intention and inhabiting not only the earth (in various forms and ways) but also heaven or the heavenly places. The heavenly places were conceived as literally and absolutely above the earth. The orientation of religion to the heavenly was not, however, "otherworldly" in the modern sense. First of all, ancient religion looked to the heavenlies as the immediate *source* of powers that determine life on earth. Second, ancient religion did not conceive of the heavenlies as altogether "off the map" of the perceptible world inhabited by human beings. The heavenlies were not a wholly different order, another universe without continuity with earthly reality. Ancients looked up at the sky and saw the beginnings of the heavenlies touching the earthly sphere. They regarded the stars, with their apparent eternal existence and perfection of motion, as heavenly bodies composed of a different kind of material substance than anything found on earth; yet the stars were observable and belonged to the same spatial world as human beings. Ancient people located the storehouses of rain, snow, and hail in the heavenlies. They thought of human beings ascending into the heavenlies by going "up" and of heavenly beings descending into earthly reality by coming "down."

Wink emphasizes that although the New Testament language of power belongs, from a modern point of view, to a mythical conception of reality, it nonetheless describes something real. We should recognize that the myth, with its peculiar language, has a special epistemological value. Myth says more than we can otherwise know. Its symbolism is indispensable.[67]

Interpreting New Testament teaching about the powers within the scope of scripture means that we do not accept the factual cosmology of the New Testament conception. However, since the powers language involves quasi-facts (the activity of the divine), it is not appropriate simply to reject the ancient cosmology as empirically wrong. Wink calls for transposing the mythical into another key, which he achieves by treating the language of the powers as symbolic.[68] The symbol describes something that is real and which cannot be known except through symbolic language. The powers incarnate individuals, groups, and institutions. These individuals, groups, or institutions *are* powers and at the same time are also only

---

67. Wink, *Naming the Powers*, 142-43.

68. Wink, *Naming the Powers*, 104 and 142. Thus, demons are "the name given that real but invisible spirit of destructiveness and fragmentation that rends persons, communities, and nations" (107).

the outward manifestation of a spiritual reality that cannot be compre-hended in ordinary "scientific" terms.[69]

The Unity and Equal Standing of Humankind in Acts

In his sermon on Mars Hill, the Paul of Acts tells the Athenians that "from one ancestor he [God] made all nations to inhabit the whole earth" (Acts 17:26). The purpose of this claim is to argue that all human beings are chil-dren of God called to the same universal salvation. Implicit is the Lukan concern to affirm the equal standing of all peoples (Jews and gentiles) be-fore God. In the American debate on slavery and in the prophetic Chris-tian witness for racial equality, Acts 17:26 has often been appealed to and paired with Peter's assertion in Acts 10:34-35: "I truly understand that God shows no partiality, but in every nation anyone who fears him and does what is right is acceptable to him." These two have served as scriptural slogans for the unity and equality of all peoples.[70]

In the pre-Darwinian uses of the "one blood" saying, the biblical story of the creation of humankind was interpreted via Acts 17:26 as literally factual. This is evident from related debates about the identity and history of the "races" descending from the three sons of Noah (Shem, Ham, and Japheth). During this period, the Bible was still being treated by many Christians as a source of reliable empirical knowledge about human ori-gins and ethnological history. Today, however, use of Acts 17:26 is likely to

69. For a different but in significant ways complementary approach, see Paul Tillich, "The Demonic: A Contribution to the Interpretation of History," in *The Interpretation of History* (New York: Scribner, 1936). Although Wink criticizes Bultmann's demythologizing program as dispensing with myth once it has been interpreted, Bultmann's existential inter-pretation of mythical language strikes me as being hermeneutically similar to Wink's sym-bolic interpretation. In each case one is looking for a modern language that does justice to the truth of the original mythical language.

70. Both Acts 17:26 and Acts 10:34-35 were biblical slogans of the nineteenth-century abolition movement. For example, Nathaniel Paul joined together both texts in asserting that the abolition of slavery "is certain, because that God who has made of one blood all na-tions of men, and who is said to be no respecter of persons, has so decreed." See Herbert Aptheker, *A Documentary History of the Negro People in the United States*, vol. 1, *From Colo-nial Times through the Civil War* (New York: Carol Publishing Group, 1990), 87. The two passages have remained well-known and oft-cited words of scripture throughout African-American Christian history.

be filtered through post-Darwinian assumptions.[71] Christians of a wide range of theological tendencies reinterpret the empirical-factual assumptions of Acts 17:26 (regarding a single human ancestor) by substituting a modern scientific view of the unity and equality of the so-called "races" (various human populations) or taking the text on a purely theological level. Probably most of us "modernize" this text without even realizing we're doing so. We appeal to it in moral contexts as theological argument against racism but do not rely on it for scientific knowledge about the origin of human populations.

Sexual Ethics

In his editorial conclusion to a particularly fine collection of articles on the Bible and homosexuality, David Balch observes that a major fault line between contributors emerged in differences over the status of science in hermeneutical judgments. As he puts it, "our ecclesiastical debates do not concern simply Paul's ethics and ours, but Paul's *science and* ethics and our science and ethics."[72] The same goes for the use of other biblical sources (e.g., Leviticus) in debates about human sexuality. Balch's point is not that contemporary science can settle questions of sexual ethics but that ethical positions (ancient or modern) are informed by theory-laden empirical assumptions. These have to be taken into account, and judgments about the scope of scripture for contemporary practice must face honestly the operation of theory-laden scientific assumptions in the way biblical teaching about sexuality is cast in scripture (notably in Leviticus and Romans).

The Question of Women's Status and Authority in 1 Tim. 2:8-15

The rule of scope has special relevance for scriptural teaching about the status and rights of women. Genesis 2-3 has played a significant role in Christian teaching about gender difference. An example of New Testament ap-

71. Of course, there are still many Christians, of various cultural heritages, who reject or only selectively accept modern theories of evolution.

72. David L. Balch, "Concluding Observations by the Editor, Including a Comparison of Christian with Jewish Interpretation," in David L. Balch, ed., *Homosexuality, Science, and the "Plain Sense" of Scripture* (Grand Rapids: Eerdmans, 2000), 300.

peal to Genesis 2-3 as a basis for distinguishing the proper roles of men and women is 1 Tim. 2:8-15. Verse 12 presents a command: "I permit no woman to teach or to have authority over a man; she is to keep silent."[73] The appeal to Genesis 2-3 in 1 Timothy reflects standard ancient exegesis of these Genesis texts from the Second Temple period and after.[74] The view that Eve was to blame for the expulsion from the Garden carried the following meaning during the Hellenistic period: women are more passional than men and are therefore a threat to the proper ordering of the passions by reason, a faculty which women lack (or possess imperfectly). Because women are more passional and lack full reasoning powers, they are more easily deceived than men. Hence, women must come under the ordering power of male reason so that they do not threaten the social order. These ideas are spelled out most explicitly by Philo, who probably represents educated opinion in his day, even though his misogyny was more extreme than most.[75]

The prevailing view of antiquity that women are by nature intellectually inferior to men and more passional than rational entails factual claims that modern science (as well as modern experience) has shown to be empirically false. There is no evidence that females have a lesser capacity for rationality than males. The few cognitive differences between men and women that have been identified are modest. Maccoby and Jacklin found that girls have greater verbal ability than boys, while boys have greater mathematical and visual-spatial ability than girls,[76] but these differences

---

73. The word translated here "have authority" is the uncommon verb *authentein*, which may carry the meaning "lord it over." Taking the term in this way does not affect the sense of the passage, since the rationale adduced from the creation stories shows that for this author a woman having any authority over a man would count as lording it over him. Some egalitarian evangelicals have argued that this command is intended as a local rule, meant only for the church at Ephesus and only while certain social conditions prevail there. See the bibliographical references in David M. Scholer, "1 Timothy 2:9-15 and the Place of Women in the Church's Ministry," in *Women, Authority, and the Bible,* ed. Alvera Mickelsen (Downers Grove, IL: InterVarsity Press, 1986), 194n. 4. While I am not persuaded by this line of interpretation, it is not necessary to debate the question here.

74. See Kugel, *Traditions of the Bible,* 100-103.

75. On Philo, see Richard A. Baer, Jr., *Philo's Use of the Categories Male and Female* (Leiden: E. J. Brill, 1970). See further, Josephus, *Against Apion* 2.201 (perhaps a Christian interpolation); *Testament of Reuben* 5:1–6:5. See also my discussion of Hellenistic-Jewish assumptions about gender as a possible background to Rom. 1:26-27 (chapter one above).

76. Eleanor Emmons Maccoby and Carol Nagy Jacklin, *The Psychology of Sex Differences* (Stanford, CA: Stanford University Press, 1974), 75-98.

are modest[77] and may owe more to environment than genetics.[78] More important, there is far more statistical variation among individual males or females than between the sexes. Sex is therefore a useless predictor of cognitive abilities.

First Timothy does not spell out the factual assumptions about men and women that guide its interpretation of Genesis 2-3. However, since Genesis 2 and 3 are susceptible to both patriarchal and non-patriarchal interpretations, it is evident that 1 Timothy's very traditional interpretation of these stories depends on the traditional factual assumptions that made this interpretation plausible to first-century people. Reading 1 Tim. 2:8-15 according to the nonscientific scope of scripture calls for discounting these traditional factual assumptions about differences in nature between males and females, with the effect that the whole argument justifying the rule of silence and submission for women collapses. This raises the question of how 1 Tim. 2:8-15 is then to function as part of the witness of scripture. The following are some suggestions for how a hermeneutical rejection of the patriarchal assumptions of 1 Tim. 2:8-15 could lead to an appropriation of this passage on egalitarian assumptions.

In a guide for preachers, Luke Timothy Johnson comments that "[o]ur experience and growth in awareness (a growth abetted by passages such as Paul's 'neither male nor female') no longer allow the perception of women as subordinate to men by nature or divine will nor the perception that they are 'weaker' or more easily 'deceived' than men."[79] The theory of women's inferiority in 1 Timothy and in Genesis itself carries no more validity, says Johnson, than the perception "that it took seven calendar days to create the world."[80] Nevertheless, Johnson urges, 1 Tim. 2:8-15 should still be read in the Christian assembly and listened to in our effort to discern our way in Christ. 1 Tim. 2:8-15, heard in tension with the egalitarian ideal we affirm, is also a positive reminder that we never "perfectly realize the reconciliation that Paul saw as the norm in Christ."[81] The passage can also teach us

---

77. See James A. Doyle and Michele A. Paludi, *Sex and Gender: The Human Experience,* 2d ed. (Dubuque, IA: Wm. C. Brown Publishers, 1991), 107-109.

78. See Anne Fausto-Sterling, *Myths of Gender: Biological Theories about Women and Men* (New York: Basic Books, 1985), 13-60.

79. Luke Timothy Johnson, *1 Timothy, 2 Timothy, Titus,* John Knox Preaching Guides (Atlanta: John Knox, 1987), 73.

80. Johnson, *1 Timothy, 2 Timothy, Titus,* 73.

81. Johnson, *1 Timothy, 2 Timothy, Titus,* 74.

how to recognize the tensions between the given authority structures, norms, and roles of society and the ideal of equality in Christ.[82]

Another approach is a theological reading that rejects the hierarchical gender teaching of 1 Tim. 2:8-15 but listens to what the passage has to say when it is reframed by egalitarian assumptions. As a hermeneutical experiment, we might take 1 Timothy's teachings about men as equally applicable to women, and its teachings about women as equally applicable to men. I have not yet found an explicit example of this approach, but it is a logical option for those who apply the rule of scope to New Testament teachings about household order, and it has affinities with the way Leonhard Goppelt has suggested we should hear the teaching of the household codes (see below).

We may begin with 1 Timothy's teaching that critical moral discernment is decisive for Christian leadership or community order. The NRSV translates 1 Tim. 3:6, which describes qualifications for the role of bishop, "He must not be a recent convert, or he may be puffed up with conceit and fall into the condemnation of the devil." Jouette Bassler observes that the verb *typhōthēnai* (which the NRSV renders as "puffed up with conceit") is probably best translated "to be deluded" or "blinded."[83] This makes good sense in the context. As Bassler points out, a recent convert is more likely to be deceived by false teachings. This shows, despite the impression that might be given by 1 Tim. 2:14 — "Adam was not deceived, but the woman was deceived" — that 1 Timothy does not regard males as invulnerable to deception. Moreover, 2 Timothy, which has so many affinities with 1 Timothy, characterizes the wicked as both deceiving and *deceived* (2 Tim. 3:13). In view of this, we can best understand 1 Timothy's assumption of a gender difference in deception by construing female deception as passive deception and male as active *self*-deception.

A connection between right teaching, moral character, and deception is also evident in the descriptions of the false teachers in 1 Tim. 6:3-5. False teachers are "deluded" (*tetyphōtai*, v. 4)[84] and "depraved in mind" (v. 5). These stock polemical descriptions hold up the opponents as bad examples, implying that one should not become like them, which assumes that

---

82. Johnson, *1 Timothy, 2 Timothy, Titus*, 74.

83. Jouette M. Bassler, *1 Timothy, 2 Timothy, Titus*, Abingdon New Testament Commentaries (Nashville: Abingdon, 1996), 68.

84. The NRSV has "conceited." On the meaning of *tetyphōtai*, see above.

their delusion and depravity are at least in part their own choice. Presumably, Hymenaeus and Alexander are examples of leaders who have been deluded by false teaching and have become opponents (1:20).[85] "By rejecting conscience," they "have suffered shipwreck in the faith" (1:19). Hence, they are morally responsible for their delusion.

The preceding analysis indicates that for 1 Timothy, weakness in moral discernment is not simply a failure of the intellectual faculty. It is also a matter of the will, that is, of moral choice. Moreover, regarded in this light, the implication of 1 Tim. 2:8-15 is that women are passively vulnerable to deception, while men are willingly vulnerable (since they can resist). Both passive deception and self-deception are especially dangerous when the deceived have authority, which is why 1 Timothy is so concerned that church leaders and teachers keep a good conscience. An egalitarian reading translates this hermeneutically as the danger to the church when a man or women in authority is overcome by falsehood or chooses to be self-deceived. The collapse of the gender distinction that differentiates persons who are passively deceived from those who are complicitously deceived relocates these two aspects in the human being as such. The human being is vulnerable to deception, yet also willing to be deceived. The Adam of 1 Timothy now stands for all men and women; so does Eve.

Patriarchy is also found in the household codes (Eph. 5:21–6:9; Col. 3:18–4:1; 1 Pet. 2:18–3:7). An example of how we might listen to these teachings without making patriarchy the key to our hearing is suggested by Leonhard Goppelt's treatment of the codes. Goppelt stresses the common element in the household codes of ordering oneself to the other.[86] This ordering, he argues, is intended to express eschatological obedience to God and not society. Moreover, it places the needs of the other above one's own interests.[87] If one recasts Goppelt's argument along the lines of our analysis of Brueggemann's interpretation of the holiness interests in scripture

---

85. 2 Tim. 2:17 describes Hymenaeus as someone who has "swerved from the truth."

86. Leonhard Goppelt, *Theology of the New Testament*, vol. 2, *The Variety and Unity of the Apostolic Witness to Christ*, trans. John E. Alsup, ed. Jürgen Roloff (Grand Rapids: Eerdmans, 1982), 168-74.

87. Goppelt argues that the *hypo* prefix in the term *hypotassein* did not carry any theological emphasis. The idea of subordination is present in the call for wives to order themselves to their husbands but the theological stress lies elsewhere, specifically, on enlisting oneself in the institutions to which one belongs. See Goppelt, *Theology of the New Testament*, vol. 2, 168-71.

(see chapter three), one could say that the iconic, patriarchal interest should be treated as subordinate to the aniconic, egalitarian interest but not in such a way as to deprive the iconic patriarchal texts of any value. Rather, by giving primary weight to the purpose of these texts (in accord with the hermeneutical rule of purpose) and construing that purpose at a higher level of generality than reinforcement of patriarchy, one can co-ordinate their valid interest in "order through submission" with the countercultural egalitarian vision of the gospel. This is what Goppelt seems to be driving at, a way of giving greater weight to the concern for or-dering oneself to the other for the other's sake than to the traditional obli-gation of subordinates to submit to their superiors. One can do this most effectively by a combination of the rules of scope, purpose, and counter-cultural witness.

Conclusion and Assessment

The rule of the nonempirical scope of scripture was forged through the church's encounter with modernity, particularly the rise of modern sci-ence. The rule takes two forms: a strong form that excludes all empirical matters from the scope of scripture and a weak form that excludes only those that are incidental to faith or practice. My statement of the rule gives the strong form.

I have argued that the weak form of the rule is untenable. The strong form is much more defensible. Nevertheless, applying the strong form also has some difficulties. Some subjects do not lend themselves to neat dis-tinctions between empirical and nonempirical parts or aspects. When it comes to certain matters within the human sciences, we do not assume that modern knowledge is in all respects superior to ancient knowledge. Further, some empirical claims are so central to the biblical witness that strict adherence to a rule of nonempirical scope may appear fundamen-tally at odds with scripture. I have in mind especially a radical exclusion of historical claims and assumptions from the proper scope of scripture, such as one finds in a Bultmannian stance on faith and history.

The rule of the nonempirical scope of scripture assumes a form of the distinction between facts and values. By asserting that science and not scripture is the proper arbiter over empirical facts, the rule holds that moral knowledge stands outside the scope of science and that empirical knowledge stands outside the scope of scripture. Nevertheless, the rule does not thereby assume that science is free from all values. It is compatible with the rule to hold that the sciences, as social institutions, are influenced by all sorts of values, including moral ones, and that the justificatory criteria of science entail, at the very least, certain cognitive values.

Moral judgments include both moral and empirical-factual assumptions. Hence, to understand the moral content of scripture, we must identify both the moral and the empirical-factual assumptions on which scripture's moral judgments rest. We must also grasp the logical interrelation between these two types of assumptions in a given moral judgment. This kind of analysis permits us to see how a scriptural moral judgment would have to change (given its own moral assumptions), if a different set of empirical facts were assumed. Thus, the moral scope of scripture (as a hermeneutical category) is its moral teaching transformed on the basis of new empirical assumptions.

The scope of scripture, as a limiting concept, was conceived as a means of preserving biblical authority in the face of modern science. While "scope" as a term of exegesis refers to the purpose, intent, and design of a particular biblical author or text, scope of scripture refers to the proper subject matter and aim of the Bible as *sacred text or canon* and as *a whole.* Scope of scripture is thus a hermeneutical concept by which the church construes the nature and purpose of the Bible as bearer of God's word. Hence, to say that scientific knowledge stands outside the scope of scripture does not mean that the Bible does not make empirical assertions or assumptions; it means that those assertions and assumptions do not belong properly to the teaching office of scripture.

The most potent criticisms of the rule of nonempirical scope are (1) that the rule does violence to scripture, (2) that the rule is an arbitrary and artificial fix for what is really an insurmountable set of problems with biblical authority in our time, and (3) that the rule is overly modernist in its assumptions.

As for the first criticism, the concern is certainly well-placed. To substitute modern empirical assumptions for fact-assumptions in the biblical text as a way of appropriating the text involves a transformation that could be called violence to the text. However, those who affirm the rule of scope see this transformation as a way of honoring the text by avoiding two worse kinds of violence. One is the violence perpetrated on the text by those who claim to find modern factual assumptions in texts that lack those assumptions. Examples are efforts to read Genesis 1 as factually compatible with modern science or attempts to find room for gender equality (or at least absence of patriarchy) in passages like 1 Tim. 2:8-15. These are forms of unacknowledged modernizing that make the Bible out to be something that it is not. The second violence is the refusal to learn from a biblical text because the text assumes things that we reject as empirically false. An example is the dismissal of patriarchal texts as having nothing to teach us. Regarded as an alternative to unacknowledged modernizing and wholesale dismissal, the rule of scope seems both honest and respectful toward the Bible.

The second criticism grows from a reflection on the erosion of biblical authority in the modern era, an erosion that appears to be inexorably progressive. Seen in this light, the rule of scope looks like an arbitrary and artificial stopgap, an intellectually dishonest way of escaping the implications of modern knowledge for biblical authority. Rather than admitting that modern knowledge has undermined biblical authority, the rule of scope claims that the Bible and the modern sciences (including the human sciences) do not conflict because they have different subject matters. This seems *arbitrary* because there is nothing in the Bible itself (or in the thinking of the ancient communities that bequeathed the Bible to us) that suggests this differentiation of subject matters. The rule seems *artificial* because the subject matter of the Bible — notably God's activity in history and moral claims on human beings — appears to mix the theological, ethical, and empirical in ways that do not admit neat differentiation.

The only adequate response to this second criticism is that the way we learn from all premodern sources involves a discounting of the prescientific assumptions of those sources and some separation of those assumptions from the imaginative vision, inspired insight, or reflective reasoning that we otherwise prize as vitally significant for us. We learn from Aristotle's *Nicomachean Ethics* or Aquinas' *Summa* without accepting Aristotle's or Aquinas' scientific views. One can trust that Aristotle has something to teach us about ethics or that Aquinas has something to teach us about being a Christian, without trusting Aristotle or Aquinas as a guide in scientific matters. Likewise, one can trust the Bible for guidance in faith and practice without trusting the Bible as a guide on scientific questions.

This answer to the second criticism is admittedly partial because it does not take up the question of the *nature* of biblical authority, which is presumably not identical with the authority of an Aristotle for modern ethicists or an Aquinas for modern Catholics. Here I will note only that the rule of scope can accommodate a variety of conceptions of biblical authority. I leave aside the question of the precise nature of biblical authority because many other studies treat this question in detail and an adequate discussion requires more space than I can devote to it here.

The third criticism is that the rule of scope is basically modernist and has therefore become outmoded with the advent of postmodernity. The rule may appear overly beholden to modernist assumptions in two crucial respects: (1) that it assumes a modernist, positivistic view of science and (2) that it exudes a corresponding modernist faith in scientific knowledge and progress.

The rule of scope is manifestly a child of the church's engagement with modernity. Hence, the history and fate of modernity must naturally affect any interpretation and use of the rule. This includes taking account of postmodern philosophy of science, which in its most extreme or progressive forms (depending on one's perspective) seems to deny that scientific knowledge is objective, that science makes progress, or that scientific answers are superior to other answers to the same questions. According to this view, modern science is a social construction and as such is merely relative to and not superior to other social constructions of knowledge.[88] This relativist-constructivist view draws inspiration from philosophical comments on science by some leading twentieth-century physicists[89] and

88. The radical relativist-constructivist view in contemporary sociology of science is well represented in, for example, *Handbook of Science and Technology Studies,* ed. Sheila Jasanoff et al. (Thousand Oaks, CA: Sage Publications, 1995). In a colloquium on the subject, Daniel Kleppner cites two examples from the popular press showing the bizarre implications that some have drawn from radical social constructivist accounts of modern science. One is a 1993 essay by John Lukacs in the *New York Times* equating modern science with medieval attempts to weigh the soul, the analogy being justified, Lukacs claimed, because Heisenberg's "uncertainty principle" shows that there is no objectivity at all to "nature" or "matter." The other is an assertion by Stanley Arronowitz that "since physics has discovered the uncertainty principle, it can no longer provide reliable information about the physical world, has lost its claim to objectivity." See Daniel Kleppner, "Physics and Common Sense," in *The Flight from Science and Reason,* ed. Paul R. Gross, Norman Levitt, and Martin W. Lewis (New York: The New York Academy of Sciences, 1997), 126-27.

89. Werner Heisenberg figures prominently here. Consider the following statement: "We can no longer speak of the behavior of the particle independently of the process of observation. As a final consequence, the natural laws formulated mathematically in quantum theory no longer deal with the elementary particles themselves but with our knowledge

from some eminent philosophers of science, notably Thomas Kuhn. Kuhn, however, has rejected the claim that his brand of philosophy of science supports the radical social constructivist position.[90]

The rule of nonscientific scope assumes progress in science but, as formulated, does not take up sides in the debate over whether scientific progress means ever closer approximation to an absolute truth of nature or produces an increasing core of facts.[91] These questions hinge on how one defines truth and how one conceives the relation of the knower to the known. The debate itself, however, cannot evade one of Thomas Kuhn's basic insights, namely, the irreversibility of scientific development. There is no possibility after Einstein of a return to Newton because general relativity makes better sense (and whatever may replace it will make even better sense) than Newtonian mechanics by any scientific definition of "better."[92]

---

about them. Nor is it any longer possible to ask whether or not these particles exist in space and time objectively, since the only processes we can refer to as taking place are those which represent the interplay of particles with some other physical system, e.g., a measuring instrument." Werner Heisenberg, *The Physicist's Conception of Nature*, trans. Arnold J. Pomerans (New York: Harcourt Brace, 1958), 15. Heisenberg is here describing a twentieth-century form of a problem familiar to philosophers since at least Kant's time (and treated by Kant in a far profounder way). Realizing that we do not have direct knowledge of "the particles themselves" (whatever "direct" might mean) and that our traditional ways of understanding objectivity can be misleading does not undermine the mathematical reliability (reliable statistical knowledge) of quantum physics (which Heisenberg himself presupposes).

90. In his 1992 Rothschild Lecture, Kuhn attacked the "strong program" of social constructivism according to which "power and interest are all there are" in science. "What passes for scientific knowledge becomes, then, simply the belief of the winners. I am among those who have found the claims of the strong program absurd: an example of deconstruction gone mad" (as quoted in Stephen Cole, "Voodoo Sociology: Recent Developments in the Sociology of Science," in *The Flight from Science and Reason*, 276).

91. In his earlier book, *The Copernican Revolution*, Kuhn had written as follows: "Each new scientific theory preserves a hard core of the knowledge provided by its predecessor and adds to it. Science progresses by replacing old theories with new" (Thomas S. Kuhn, *The Copernican Revolution: Planetary Astronomy in the Development of Western Thought* [Cambridge, MA: Harvard University Press, 1957], 3). Kuhn's later book, *The Structure of Scientific Revolutions*, does not repudiate this view (although it is sometimes mistakenly read that way) but clarifies the sense in which Kuhn means it. Of course, the metaphor of "core" may be misleading, since what is preserved does not belong to some enduring and increasing center around which everything else is organized.

92. The knowledge that the theory of general relativity provides and generates about the physical universe is far more comprehensive and reliable for such things as carrying out

Scepticism toward modern science is very healthy, including ideological critique and philosophical quarryings of science's epistemological foundations. It is not my aim here to defend any form of modern science against such questioning in order to defend the rule of scope as an intelligible hermeneutical principle. Let the rule fall, if its "modernist" assumptions in fact fail. In the meantime, a cautious and self-critical use of scientific knowledge — including history and the social sciences — is called for in the engagement of scripture under the aegis of the rule.

Modernity is also associated with faith in progress of other sorts, notably social progress. Nothing in the rule of scope requires us to adopt any particular interpretation of historical possibility. Moreover, modernity is as much a quest for knowledge of limits as for the breaking of limits. "To be modern," says Roland Barthes, "is to know what is no longer possible."[93]

---

space flight or devising global navigation systems (to mention just two familiar examples). In the case of both space flight and the Global Positioning System, the prediction of general relativity that gravity (as a function of curved space) affects time has to be taken into account and has been confirmed.

93. "Être moderne c'est savoir ce qui n'est plus possible." Roland Barthes, "Requichot et son corps," in *L'obvie et l'obtus: Essais Critiques III* (Paris: Suil, 1982), 211. My thanks to Prof. Mary Warner Marien of Syracuse University for drawing my attention to this essay.

FIVE

The Rule of Moral-Theological Adjudication

*Moral-theological considerations should guide hermeneutical
choices between conflicting plausible interpretations.*

In a 1979 essay on Paul and anti-Judaism, Lloyd Gaston asserts that if it is
exegetically possible to interpret Paul as Judaism-affirming, then it is also
morally necessary to do so, after Auschwitz.[1] This claim reckons with the
possibility of other plausible interpretations of Paul's theology of Israel; it
further assumes that moral-theological considerations should guide reso-
lutions of the conflict of interpretations.

Some version of a "rule of moral-theological adjudication" is often
tacitly at work in appeals to scripture. Analyzed in rhetorical terms, an appeal to *one* interpretation of scripture when other equally reasonable op-

---

1. This is how I construe the following concluding comments of his article, in view of
his treatment of Paul as a whole. "All of the positive things Paul has to say about the righteousness of God effecting salvation for the Gentiles in Christ need not at all imply anything
negative about Israel and the Torah. Indeed, it may be that Paul, and Paul alone among the
New Testament writers, has no left hand. Although it has only been hinted at here, I believe
that it is possible to interpret Paul in this manner. That it is necessary to do so is the implication of the agonized concern of many in the post-Auschwitz situation. . . ." Lloyd Gaston,
"Paul and the Torah," in *Paul and the Torah* (Vancouver: University of British Columbia
Press, 1987), 34.

tions are available typically functions as follows: the attractiveness of the resultant ethical/theological construction is held out as a kind of silent argument for the exegesis adduced in its support.

It seems plain to biblical scholars that nonspecialists operate with a version of the rule of moral-theological adjudication. Given their own criteria of reasonable interpretation (which is not necessarily what a scholar would count as good exegesis), nonspecialists routinely embrace those reasonable interpretations that appeal to their moral and theological sense. Over the years, I have had many students who treated the appealing quality of a given interpretation as part of the evidence in its favor. Their logic seems to be that a reasonable interpretation that is also appealing (by their own moral and theological lights) must be right, or should be taken as right. They regard the attractive quality of an interpretation as a sign that the interpretation was intended by the biblical author(s) and/or by God. This assumption helps them adjudicate between competing interpretations.

This kind of adjudication is not, however, confined to nonspecialists. Theologians (including biblical scholars with theological interests and motivations) also allow substantive considerations to influence their judgments about which exegetical option to defend. I regard this as a truism, allowing that some theologians and exegetes make it a matter of principle to avoid operating in this way (whether they succeed is another matter). An increasing number of interpreters also recognize that since hermeneutical adjudication is unavoidable, it ought to be principled.[2]

Wilfred Cantwell Smith observes that it was axiomatic for the great medieval interpreters of scripture that one should seek the "best" interpretation.[3] Smith offers the example of Bernard of Clairvaux, whose exegetical practice he describes as follows:

> [Bernard] is quite conscious that the task of human discerning of the meaning often means in effect a choice. The reader is free, one might

---

2. In addition to the literature discussed below, see Charles H. Cosgrove, ed., *The Meanings We Choose: Hermeneutical Ethics and the Conflict of Interpretations* (Sheffield: Sheffield Academic Press, forthcoming).

3. See Wilfred Cantwell Smith, *What Is Scripture? A Comparative Approach* (Minneapolis: Fortress Press, 1993), 32 (speaking of Bernard's hermeneutic as an example of medieval exegesis). See also p. 72 for a similar conclusion about traditional interpretation of the Qur'an.

say, to choose how to interpret an ambiguous passage, except that that freedom is constrained by the vivid awareness that it is at the best possible meaning that one is striving to arrive.[4]

"Best" here refers to the most exalted moral and theological sense. Of course, human notions of what is "best" include not only humane and ennobling values and practices but also oppressive and dehumanizing ones.[5] Nevertheless, acknowledging one's use of criteria of the theologically or morally best reading (as a way of adjudicating between otherwise reasonable interpretations) has the value of exposing one's judgments to scrutiny and criticism. It is a way of taking greater responsibility for one's interpretations.

It should now be clear that the rule — in its explicit and tacit operations — is to be distinguished from the mere fact that all interpretation is more or less subject to the interests of interpreters. The rule assumes this fact and commands that choosing one plausible interpretation over another be guided by substantive norms.

Legal Antecedents and Analogues

The idea that substantive criteria have a proper place in judging between conflicting interpretations of authoritative texts is not new; nor is it peculiar to the interpretation of scripture. Hence, it may be helpful to look at some earlier examples of this approach.

We begin with law, which Schleiermacher in the nineteenth century and Gadamer in the twentieth saw as a particularly illuminating model for understanding interpretation of scripture.[6] In Greek and Roman treatments of legal interpretation, we find consideration of the problem of what to do in cases where a governing legal text is ambiguous. Speaking of this problem, Quintilian comments as follows: "the only questions which confront us will be, sometimes which of the two interpretations is most natural, and always which interpretation is most equitable, and what was the intention of the person who wrote or uttered the words" (*Institutio*

4. Smith, *What Is Scripture?* 32.
5. Smith, *What Is Scripture?* 217.
6. See Hans Georg Gadamer, *Truth and Method,* 2d rev. ed. (New York: Continuum, 1989), 307-11, 324-41.

Oratoria 7.9.15).[7] It follows that when one has no independent knowledge of the intention of the speaker/author and is faced with two equally "natural" interpretations, considerations of equity must be decisive. Moreover, it was widely held that equity should have primacy even in cases where there is no dispute about meaning and applicability. Aristotle defines "equity" *(epieikeia)* this way, as the correction of legal justice in cases where it is defective owing to the universality of law *(Nicomachean Ethics* 5.10). The idea here is that a general rule cannot adequately do justice to all fact situations; hence, equity is necessary as a substantive jurisprudential norm in cases where applying the letter of the law would violate justice. In such a case, the judge decides according to the intent of the law, not its letter.[8]

For purposes here an especially significant debate is whether the norms of justice or equity standing "outside" the letter of the law should be viewed as nevertheless intrinsic to the *law as a whole.* That is, if one construes "the law" not simply as a set of authoritative rules but as a tradition with certain substantive norms or ideals, then the substitution of equity for the letter of the law is itself a form of *legal* justice. This is how Aristotle and Aquinas saw the law.[9] In a similar vein, some modern legal scholars see substantive principles as part of the law and therefore as hermeneutical guides to the interpretation of legal rules.[10] Likewise, one may view scripture as properly interpreted only where it is construed according to certain substantive principles, conceived as intrinsic to scripture itself, taken as a whole.

---

7. *Institutio Oratoria of Quintilian,* trans. H. E. Butler, Loeb Classical Library (Cambridge, MA: Harvard University Press, 1921; London: William Heinemann, 1921), 3:161.

8. A more specific example of a substantive hermeneutical norm is the old Roman principle, also taken over into English law, of interpreting the law "in favor of liberty" *(in favorem libertatis).* See Max Kaser, *Roman Private Law,* 4th ed., trans. Rolf Dannenbring (Pretoria: University of South Africa, 1984), 79, 87-88. The currency of the principle in Anglo-American law as late as the nineteenth century is attested in an 1859 American case involving a slave, in which an Ohio court commented that according to "a rule older than the constitution — older than the Declaration of Independence, older than magna carta — older even than the common law itself — wherever the right of man to his liberty is the subject of question, every doubt is to be resolved in favor of liberty" (Ex Parte Simeon Bushnell v. Ex Parte Charles Langston, 9 Ohio St. 77, 115 [1859]).

9. See Aquinas, *Summa Theologiae* 2a2ae.120, art. 3 (citing Aristotle).

10. See, for example, Ronald Dworkin, "The Model of Rules," *The University of Chicago Law Review* 35 (1967): 14-46 (reprinted in *Taking Rights Seriously* [Cambridge, MA: Harvard University Press, 1977].

The Rule of Love

In Christian history the earliest example of advocacy of a substantive hermeneutical principle may be Jesus' teaching about the two great commandments in Matthew 22:34-40. This is so if Jesus' statement in v. 40 that "on these two commandments [love of God and neighbor] hang all the law and the prophets [all of scripture]" means that the double love commandment expresses the purpose and unity of scripture *and,* in so doing, constitutes a hermeneutical norm: all of scripture should be interpreted and practiced in accord with the double love command.[11]

When we consider Matt. 22:34-40 in light of the conflict over interpretations of the law in which Jesus engages in Matthew 12, for example, it is reasonable to conclude that Jesus' arguments for construing the law as being for the sake of human life (e.g., Matthew 12:1-8, 9-14)[12] follow from his understanding of the purpose of the law as a hermeneutical guide. Admittedly, I am inclined to favor the view that Matt. 22:40 is a hermeneutical pronouncement by the same moral-theological hermeneutic that I attribute to the passage. There is no way out of this circularity; I'm simply being frank about it.

Besides Matthew 22, the most famous early Christian example of the view that certain substantive norms should be used as hermeneutical rules is found in Augustine. In Book 1 of *De Doctrina Christiana,* Augustine identifies the purpose of scripture as love for God and neighbor (1.84-85 [XXXV-XXXVI]).[13] The first implication he draws from this is that a faulty

11. So Günther Bornkamm, "Das Doppelgebot der Liebe," in *Neutestamentliche Studien für Rudolf Bultmann,* 2d ed. (Berlin: Alfred Töpelmann, 1957), 85-93; Birger Gerhardsson, "The Hermeneutic Program in Matthew 22:37-40," in *Jews, Greeks, and Christians,* ed. R. Hammerton-Kelly and Robin Scroggs (Leiden: E. J. Brill, 1976), 129-50; Terence L. Donaldson, "The Law That Hangs (Matthew 22:40): Rabbinic Formulation and Matthean Social World," *Catholic Biblical Quarterly* 57 (1995): 689-709; Klyne R. Snodgrass, "Matthew's Understanding of the Law," *Interpretation* 46 (1992): 368-78; Wolfgang Schrage, *The Ethics of the New Testament,* trans. David E. Green (Philadelphia: Fortress Press, 1988), 148-50. W. D. Davies and Dale Allison dispute the characterization of Matt. 22:40 as hermeneutical. See W. D. Davies and Dale C. Allison, Jr., *A Critical and Exegetical Commentary on the Gospel according to Matthew,* vol. 3, *Commentary on Matthew XIX–XXVIII* (Edinburgh: T. & T. Clark, 1988), 246.

12. To my mind, much (perhaps all) of the legal interpretation found in the Sermon on the Mount makes good sense if we view it as Jesus' way of interpreting the law by the double commandment.

13. I have used the following Latin/English edition: Augustine, *De Doctrina Christiana,* ed. and trans. R. P. H. Green (London: Clarendon Press, 1995).

interpretation that edifies is not pernicious, although the interpreter should be corrected. A second is that the right approach to scripture is to make one's understanding of it aim at love (1.95-96 [XL]).[14] In Book 3 the rule of love appears again, now as an interpretive guide. Augustine counsels that in cases where the literal meaning of a passage of scripture does not promote "good morals" or "true faith," the language must be construed figuratively (3.33 [X]). By "good morals" Augustine has in view "love of God and neighbor."[15] He later puts his advice this way:

> Therefore in dealing with figurative expressions we will observe a rule of this kind: the passage being read should be studied with careful consideration until its interpretation can be connected with the realm of love. If this point is made literally, then no kind of figurative expression need be considered. (*De Doctrina Christiana* 3.54 [XV])

Most of Augustine's examples treat statements in which distinguishing the literal from the non-literal poses no difficulty for the modern interpreter. But occasionally Augustine provides an example that strikes closer to our modern sense of a difficult or ambiguous passage. For example, Augustine observes of the saying, "Give to the merciful and do not support a sinner" (Ecclus. 12:4), that it seems to forbid kindness to the sinner. One should therefore interpret "sinner" as a figure for "sin," so that the sense is "do not support his sin" (*De Doctrina Christiana* 3.57 [XVI]). Augustine endorses this figurative interpretation against the literal meaning on the grounds that the hermeneutical rule of charity favors it.[16]

---

14. "So when someone has learnt that the aim of the commandment is 'love from a pure heart, and good conscience, and genuine faith', he will be ready to relate every interpretation of the holy scriptures to these three things and may approach the task of handling these books with confidence" (*De Doctrina Christiana* 1.95 [XL]).

15. "Good morals have to do with our love of God and our neighbor" (*De Doctrina Christiana* 3.33 [X.14]).

16. Augustine also takes up the problem of passages that admit more than one interpretation, such that the intention of the author cannot be discovered from the words (*De Doctrina Christiana* 3.84-86 [XXVII-XXVIII]). It is not clear whether he sees the double possibility of literal and figurative senses of texts as a species of this. Perhaps he has in view questions of interpretation that cannot be resolved by the rules for distinguishing the literal and the figurative. In cases where the text supports multiple interpretations, one is free to accept all interpretations that find independent support in other parts of scripture (the rule of letting scripture interpret scripture) (*De Doctrina Christiana* 3.86 [XXVIII]; 2.31 [IX];

Closely related to the hermeneutical rule of charity is the rule of faith (3.3 [II]), a widely accepted hermeneutical norm of the patristic age[17] that also remained an important hermeneutical guide throughout the medieval period, in part due to the influence of *De Doctrina Christiana*.[18] In theory the rule of faith is the clear teaching of scripture; in fact it is an orthodox conception of the essential teachings of scripture. Appeal to "unambiguous" passages typically means appeal to the consensus interpretation of the rule of faith in scripture. As a traditional concept, the rule of faith was often understood as embracing matters of practice, including moral practice.[19] This is confirmed by Augustine's statement at the beginning of Book 3 of *De Doctrina Christiana* (3.3 [II]) that he has set forth the rule of faith in Book 1. Central to Book 1 is the double commandment as the purpose of scripture (see above). Hence, the rule of love is part of the rule of faith.[20] For Augustine and his followers, the idea that "love" is a hermeneutical principle rests on the assumption that love is the divine *scopos* of scripture and as such a guide to the best and highest meaning of scripture as intended by God.

The use of love and other general theological concepts as hermeneutical guides is also found in several historic documents of the Reformed tradition. The Second Helvetic Confession of 1566 (framed by Heinrich Bullinger) holds as "orthodox and genuine" those interpretations

---

2.37-38 [XII]; 3.3-4 [II]; 3.83 [XXVI]), taking them as intended by the Holy Spirit, which may differ from the intention of their human authors (3.85 [XXVII]).

17. It is found before Augustine in Irenaeus, *Adv. Haer.* 1.10, and in Tertullian, *De Praescriptione Haereticorum* 13. See further Nils A. Dahl, "Trinitarian Baptismal Creeds and New Testament Christology," in *Jesus the Christ: The Historical Origins of Christological Doctrine,* ed. Donald H. Juel (Minneapolis: Fortress Press, 1991); Georges Florovsky, "The Function of Tradition in the Ancient Church," in *Bible, Church, Tradition: An Eastern Orthodox View* (Belmont, MA: Norland Publishing Company, 1972); R. P. C. Hanson, *Tradition in the Early Church* (Philadelphia: The Westminster Press, 1962), 75-129; Bengt Hägglund, "Die Bedeutung der 'regula fidei' als Grundlage theologischer Aussagen," *Studia Theologica* 12 (1958): 1-44.

18. See Eileen C. Sweeney, "Hugh of St. Victor: Augustinian Tradition of Sacred and Secular Reading Revised," in *Reading and Wisdom: The* De Doctrina Christiana *of Augustine in the Middle Ages,* ed. Edward D. English (Notre Dame and London: University of Notre Dame Press, 1995), 69; Joseph Wawrykow, "Reflections on the Place of the *De doctrina christiana* in High Scholastic Discussions of Theology," *Reading and Wisdom,* 112-114.

19. See Hanson, *Tradition in the Early Church,* 100 (and 76-129 in general).

20. Wawrykow comes to the same conclusion ("Reflections on the Place of the *De doctrina christiana* in High Scholastic Discussions of Theology," 112).

of scripture that "agree with the rule of faith and love, and contribute much to the glory of God and man's salvation" (5.010).[21] The Synod of Berne (1528) speaks as follows: "But where something is brought before us by our pastors or others, which brings us closer to Christ, and in accordance with God's Word is more conducive to mutual friendship and Christian love than the interpretation now presented, we will gladly accept it. . . ."[22] The Scots Confession (1560) asserts, "We dare not receive or admit any interpretation which is contrary to any principal point of our faith, or to any other plain text of Scripture, or to the rule of love" (3.18).[23] A recent example comes from the 1983 consensus statement, "Presbyterian Understanding and Use of Scripture":

> The fundamental expression of God's will is the twofold commandment to love God and neighbor, and all interpretations are to be judged by the question whether they offer and support the love given and commanded by God. When interpretations do not meet this criterion, it must be asked whether the text has been used correctly in the light of the whole of Scripture and its subject.
>
> Any interpretation of Scripture is wrong that separates or sets in opposition love for God and love for fellow human beings, including both love expressed in individual relations and in human community (social justice). No interpretation is correct that leads to or supports contempt for any individual or group of persons either within or outside of the church. Such results from the interpretation of Scripture plainly indicate that the rule of love has not been honored. This rule reminds us forcefully that as the rule of faith and life, Scripture is to be interpreted not just to discover what we are to think or what benefits we receive from God in Christ, but to discover how we are to live.[24]

---

21. As quoted by "Presbyterian Understanding and Use of Scripture," Position Statement adopted by the 123rd General Assembly (1983) of the Presbyterian Church in the United States (Louisville, KY: The Office of the General Assembly, 1992), 20.

22. As quoted by "Presbyterian Understanding and Use of Scripture" (1983), 20.

23. As quoted by "Presbyterian Understanding and Use of Scripture" (1983), 20.

24. "Presbyterian Understanding and Use of Scripture" (1983), 19-20.

Contemporary Trends within Critical Scholarship

At the beginning of this chapter, I referred to an argument by Lloyd Gaston to the effect that if it is exegetically possible to interpret Paul in a Judaism-affirming way, then it is morally necessary to do so. The preceding survey shows that this kind of argument stands within a classical hermeneutical tradition. With the rise of modern historical-critical studies, this tradition of moral-hermeneutical interpretation came under suspicion and attack, along with other nonhistorical interpretive principles of the premodern church, for example, the rule of faith and the rule of scripture. Principles of this sort were seen as a technique for importing foreign ideas into the text. Historical criticism required that the Bible be interpreted (1) "like any other book," (2) in its original discrete parts (not as a whole), and (3) according to an authorial-intent model of textual meaning.[25] However, contemporary trends in philosophical hermeneutics, literary criticism, and biblical theology have changed this picture, allowing for an accommodation of older hermeneutical rules within new critical frameworks.

Contemporary Advocacy of a Rule of Moral-Theological Adjudication

The following survey looks at contemporary advocacy of a rule of moral-theological adjudication. I have not included every thinker or tradition in which advocacy of a rule of moral-theological adjudication has a place. The survey seeks to be representative, not comprehensive.[26]

25. For an instructive survey, see Edgar Krentz, *The Historical-Critical Method* (Philadelphia: Fortress Press, 1975).

26. I would like to mention here a few others, not included below, who have proposed a hermeneutic of moral-theological adjudication or something analogous to it. Willard Swartley advocates love as a hermeneutical norm. Willard M. Swartley, *Slavery, Sabbath, War, and Women: Case Issues in Biblical Interpretation* (Scottdale, PA, and Waterloo, Ontario: Herald Press, 1983), 203-4. Richard Hays summarizes his hermeneutical approach to New Testament ethics as follows: "The community that seeks to be shaped by Scripture must in the end claim responsibility for adjudicating between good and bad readings. In this book I have proposed one way to do this: we must ask whether any given interpretation is consonant with the fundamental plot of the biblical story as identified by the images of community, cross, and new creation." Richard B. Hays, *The Moral Vision of the New Testament: Community, Cross, New Creation: A Contemporary Introduction to New Testament Ethics* (San

Liberationist Hermeneutics

Various forms of liberation theology (including feminist theology) have provoked the question of the "ethics of interpretation."[27] Sometimes the claim is that patriarchy, racism, classism, and so forth have produced an ideological distortion of the text that liberationist hermeneutics clears away. This is revolutionary exegesis in a traditional scientific mode, combining historical criticism with ideological critique.[28] Sometimes the claim is that all theology and interpretation of scripture is inescapably "subjective" or ideological in the soft, relativist sense that we all interpret out of particular sociocultural perspectives. In that case, it is argued, a liberationist reading should not be subjected to the standard of so-called objective scientific norms, which are merely a guise for maintaining the status quo.[29]

Francisco: HarperSanFrancisco, 1996), 304. Hays characterizes the guiding focal images of "community, cross, and new creation" as having a function "analogous to the Rule of Faith" (195). See also Daniel Boyarin's comments about the ethics of interpretive "starting points" in his study *A Radical Jew: Paul and the Politics of Identity* (Berkeley: University of California Press, 1994), 5-6.

Mention should also be made of Stephen E. Fowl and L. Gregory Jones, *Reading in Communion: Scripture and Ethics in Christian Life* (Grand Rapids: Eerdmans, 1991), and Stephen E. Fowl, *Engaging Scripture: A Model for Theological Interpretation* (Malden, MA and Oxford, UK: Blackwell, 1998). Both books argue that impasses in interpretation cannot be settled by method alone and that the proper approach to the formulation and resolution of interpretive questions is for the church to be a community of character. Hence, interpretation involves ethical judgment, which in turn depends on community-shaped character and practical wisdom. See also David M. Scholer, "The Authority of the Bible and Private Interpretation: A Dilemma of Baptist Freedom," *Baptists in the Balance: The Tension between Freedom and Responsibility*, ed. Everett C. Goodwin (Valley Forge, PA: Judson Press, 1997), 174-93.

27. See Elisabeth Schüssler Fiorenza, "The Ethics of Interpretation: De-Centering Biblical Scholarship," *Journal of Biblical Literature* 107 (1988): 3-17; Daniel Patte, *Ethics of Biblical Interpretation: A Reevaluation* (Louisville, KY: Westminster/John Knox Press, 1995).

28. Much early Latin American liberation theology was done in this mode. The feminist biblical scholarship of Elisabeth Schüssler Fiorenza stands in the same tradition.

29. Michael LaFargue sees this kind of claim (which he doesn't like) as typical of contemporary theological interpretation of scripture. His description is polemical: "The contemporary scene, dominated as it is by a plurality of contending viewpoints, fosters a style of discourse in which the merely rhetorical furthering of one's favored cause prevails. . . . One treats one's own allegiances, as well as those of others, as something ultimately irrational and arbitrary, not really susceptible to critical examination (even self-examination) and substantive discussion. In this situation, the allegedly indeterminate, 'polysemic' character

This is a form of postmodern liberationist hermeneutics in which the non-relativist convictions of a liberation ethic stand in uneasy tension with the assumption that hermeneutics has no critical-objective element. Sometimes the claim is that the ideological conditioning of interpretation requires ideological critique and analysis through which one tests the set of commitments and perspectives that will guide interpretation. This is postpositivist liberationist hermeneutics in which ideological criticism takes place through the encounter with other perspectives and experiences, thus producing what might be called "dialogical objectivity" — the ability to subject one's own view to critical analysis based on the knowledge and experiential witness of others.[30] The claims of the preceding three forms of liberationist hermeneutics are sometimes made explicitly, but often they are implicit aspects of liberationist rhetoric. In particular, the third type of claim, which sees interpretation of scripture as properly guided by ideological critique and commitment, creates the intellectual conditions in which an ethics of hermeneutical adjudication makes sense and becomes a necessary condition of responsible use of scripture.

Werner Jeanrond Reading Paul Ricoeur

Werner Jeanrond treats hermeneutical ethics and the conflict of interpretations in the course of his analysis of the work of Paul Ricoeur. Jeanrond observes that almost everything Ricoeur says about texts leads to the unspoken question, "Where," in the plurality of readings, "are the possibilities and limitations of appropriation?"[31] Jeanrond finds no explicit answer to this question in Ricoeur. While Ricoeur affirms "text identity" and ac-

---

of the biblical text, and the necessity of a 'fusion of horizons,' easily become welcome excuses neither to take the otherness of the biblical text seriously nor to submit oneself to its challenges." Michael LaFargue, "Are Texts Indeterminate? Derrida, Barth, and the Role of the Biblical Scholar," *Harvard Theological Review* 81 (1988): 357.

30. I would place Juan Luis Segundo in this category. See in particular *Liberation of Theology,* trans. John Drury (Maryknoll, NY: Orbis, 1976). In philosophy, the most persuasive advocate of this sort of critical dialogical hermeneutics is Jürgen Habermas. See, for example, *Moral Consciousness and Communicative Action,* trans. Christian Lenhardt and Shierry Weber Nicholsen, introduction by Thomas McCarthy (Cambridge, MA: The MIT Press, 1996).

31. Werner G. Jeanrond, *Texts and Interpretation as Categories of Theological Thinking,* trans. Thomas J. Wilson (New York: Crossroad, 1988), 62.

knowledges the inescapability of a "pluralism of readings," he never addresses the relation between these two.[32] Jeanrond sees this as a problem of the ethics of interpretation and proposes a set of criteria for negotiating "reading pluralism and reader responsibility."[33]Jeanrond stresses that interpretation involves "choice" of the genre by which we read the text. He calls this a "reading style" based on "a selection and modification of available reading genres."[34] Ethically responsible reading of the Bible calls for "theological reading genres and reading functions."[35]

Choice of Method: Phyllis Trible

Jeanrond's discussion of the possibilities and limitations of appropriating biblical texts focuses on interpretive responsibility at the level of choice of method. A similar approach is taken by Phyllis Trible in her groundbreaking work, *God and the Rhetoric of Sexuality*.[36] Trible observes that texts can be interpreted by "many acceptable methodologies"[37] and that the use of any given method typically produces multiple interpretations of the same passage by different interpreters because they are guided by different interests.[38] This does not mean that all interpretations are equally valid; both the form and content of the text limit the possibilities for interpretation.[39] In summary, the interests of interpreters provide hermeneutical clues from outside scripture to the relation between the text and the world; one's chosen method provides further clues; the text itself also provides clues in its form and content.[40] Interpretation involves a correlation of these different sets of clues.

Trible announces her own chosen clues for the study of "God and the rhetoric of sexuality" as follows:

32. Jeanrond, *Texts and Interpretation*, 62-63. Jeanrond contends that Ricoeur's model must be extended so that "[t]ext identity and pluralism of readings" can be grasped as "elements in a dialectic" (63).

33. Jeanrond, *Texts and Interpretation*, 120-28.

34. Jeanrond, *Texts and Interpretation*, 125.

35. Jeanrond, *Texts and Interpretation*, 128.

36. Phyllis Trible, *God and the Rhetoric of Sexuality* (Philadelphia: Fortress Press, 1978).

37. Trible, *God and the Rhetoric of Sexuality*, 8.

38. Trible, *God and the Rhetoric of Sexuality*, 11.

39. Trible, *God and the Rhetoric of Sexuality*, 11.

40. Trible, *God and the Rhetoric of Sexuality*, 1-12.

Within scripture, my topical clue is a text: the image of God male and female. To interpret this topic, my methodological clue is rhetorical criticism. Outside scripture, my hermeneutical clue is an issue: feminism as a critique of culture.[41]

At the beginning of her analysis of Genesis 2–3, she explains that her purpose is not to defend the biblical narrative against traditional patriarchal and misogynist interpretations but to offer an alternative reading using a different method, a literary method that offers insights that traditional perspectives miss.[42] Her chosen hermeneutical clue (feminism) leads her to choose a method (from the many appropriate methods) that brings out egalitarian dimensions of the text that traditional androcentric interpretations conceal. This choice is a moral-theological decision, and the many interpretive decisions about the details of the text by which Trible builds up her alternative picture of Genesis 2–3 are, accordingly, as much moral-theological as literary judgments.

The preceding is one way to construe Trible's hermeneutical comments in the light of her interpretive practice in *God and the Rhetoric of Sexuality*. But it does not do justice to everything she says about her approach. In one place, Trible asserts that traditional patriarchal interpretations of Genesis 2–3 "violate the rhetoric of the story" and "fail to respect the integrity of this work as an interlocking structure of words and motifs with its own intrinsic value and meaning."[43] This sounds like a traditional historical-critical claim to be offering a better method and a better exegetical result, and it stands in tension with Trible's acknowledgment that even the same method can support different interpretive results. Perhaps the apparently contradictory assertions Trible makes about method can be reconciled, but I think there is a genuine tension here.

41. Trible, *God and the Rhetoric of Sexuality*, 23.

42. Trible, *God and the Rhetoric of Sexuality*, 74. Trible understands the kind of rhetorical criticism she applies to the Genesis narratives as a form of literary criticism (8). In an illuminating study, Susan Lanser points out that a historical-contextual model of textual meaning (used in a way consistent with speech-act theory) supports traditional patriarchal interpretations of Genesis 2–3, while a literary-formal approach (like Trible's) casts the text in a non-patriarchal (or at least less patriarchal) light. Choice of theory of language predetermines the exegetical possibilities. See Susan S. Lanser, "(Feminist) Criticism in the Garden: Inferring Genesis 2–3," *Semeia* 41 (1988): 67-84.

43. Trible, *God and the Rhetoric of Sexuality*, 73.

The tension is also noted by David Rutledge. According to Rutledge, Trible argues that "the Garden of Eden narrative is by no means intrinsically sexist,"[44] but Rutledge suggests that perhaps Trible does not mean to represent her interpretation as demonstrating "'a complete thematic unity'." Perhaps "she is simply working through some of the redemptive possibilities suggested by what she sees as the 'depatriarchalizing' principle [in the text]."[45] Rutledge himself, writing in 1996, is unequivocally committed to the idea that texts support multiple, contradictory readings; Trible, writing in 1978, is not.

The methodological tension in *God and the Rhetoric of Sexuality* seems to reflect the ambivalence of biblical scholarship in the last quarter of the twentieth century. On one hand there has been increasing recognition that the old historical ideal of "one correct answer" to any question about the meaning of the text fails to do justice to the nature of texts. On the other hand there has remained the tendency to argue for one's own interpretation as if it were the one correct (or historically most probable) answer to the interpretive question at hand. Looking back, one can regard *God and the Rhetoric of Sexuality* as a step toward a hermeneutic of moral-theological adjudication.

Scripture Criticism: Daniel Patte

Daniel Patte has recently called for "scriptural criticism" in which interpreters confront the conflict of interpretations and "take responsibility" for their own choices of method and their own interpretive judgments.[46]

According to Patte, the traditional assumption of biblical scholarship

44. David Rutledge, *Reading Marginally: Feminism, Deconstruction and the Bible* (Leiden: E. J. Brill, 1996), 32.

45. Rutledge, *Reading Marginally*, 40. Anne Gardner comments that "Trible says she 'does not propose to defend the narrative' against [the traditional patriarchal reading] but in fact does just that in her analysis of Genesis 2–3 as a literary study." See Anne Gardner, "Genesis 2:4b–3: A Mythological Paradigm of Sexual Equality or of the Religious History of Pre-Exilic Israel?" *Scottish Journal of Theology* 43 (1990): 5.

46. Daniel Patte, *The Challenge of Discipleship: A Critical Study of the Sermon on the Mount as Scripture* (Harrisburg, PA: Trinity Press International, 1999), xv-xix; *Discipleship according to the Sermon on the Mount: Four Legitimate Readings, Four Plausible Views of Discipleship, and Their Relative Values* (Valley Forge, PA: Trinity Press International, 1996); *Ethics of Biblical Interpretation: A Reevaluation*.

that the proper object of interpretation is a single correct meaning misconceives the nature of the text and the nature of interpretation. There is no one best interpretation because biblical texts are multidimensional and admit multiple legitimate interpretations.[47] Moreover, a plausible interpretation assumes some context of the interpreter in which the text makes practical sense; believers' situations vary and therefore multiple possibilities for plausible interpretation arise.[48]

Patte's model of interpretation vindicates non-scholarly "faith-interpretations" against the pretension of critical biblical scholarship to be the sole arbiter over the meaning of the text.[49] By "faith-interpretations" Patte means interpretations that are "primarily concerned to discern what the biblical text teaches believers for and about their lives."[50] Faith-interpretations, as one kind of "interested" interpretation, are the appropriate way to read the Bible as scripture for the Christian community.

In every faith-interpretation of scripture, it is the transformative power of one dimension of the text, not the whole text, that confronts believers. Focusing on one dimension to the exclusion of others involves choice by the interpreter. Interpretive choice entails responsibility: being accountable for one's faith-interpretations.[51] This accountability in turn requires critical awareness of the multidimensionality of the biblical text, an understanding of other viable interpretations and their rationales, and a grasp of what theological and ethical issues are at stake in one's interpretive choices.

Interpretive choice entails three critical judgments: legitimacy judgments, epistemological judgments, and value judgments.[52] Legitimacy judgments have to do with the textual warrants for a given interpretation: how textual features do or do not support a given interpretation.[53] Epistemological judgments mean conceptualizing a theme of the text in terms of a particular present context. An interpretation is plausible only

47. Patte, *Discipleship according to the Sermon on the Mount*, 27.

48. Patte, *The Challenge of Discipleship*, 16-18, 49-52, 65-66.

49. See, e.g., Patte, *Discipleship accoding to the Sermon on the Mount*, 3, 7, 10, 13; also Patte, *The Ethics of Biblical Interpretation*, 17-36. On the distinction between "legitimate" and "plausible" in Patte's terminology, see below.

50. Patte, *The Challenge of Discipleship*, 6.

51. Patte, *The Challenge of Discipleship*, 3-4.

52. Patte, *Discipleship according to the Sermon on the Mount*, 17-18.

53. Patte, *Discipleship according to the Sermon on the Mount*, 21-22.

if it makes sense in a particular cultural context.[54] Value judgments are assessments of the relative merit of different interpretations for a particular context in the light of ethical considerations about the practical effects of one's interpretation.[55] Patte uses the terms "legitimate," "plausible," and "most valuable" as shorthand for these three kinds of judgments.[56]

Legitimacy, plausibility, and value judgments are at work not only in particular interpretations but also in the very way we opt for critical approaches and conceptualize the roles of the Bible and the reader in the interpretive process. Patte's call is for interpreters to become aware of how these judgments figure in their construal of scripture and to subject these judgments to criticism.[57]

For Patte, the role of critical biblical studies is not "to produce new interpretations" but to assess and establish the text-based warrants of faith-interpretations.[58] That is, critical biblical studies have an important role to play in legitimacy judgments. In fact, although it has not been widely acknowledged, a sociological analysis of critical biblical studies reveals that it has always had as one of its main goals "to establish the legitimacy and plausibility of 'certain' faith-interpretations."[59] It is time now for biblical scholarship to acknowledge the viability of other faith-interpretations (outside the circle of what Western theological academe has prized as the best faith-interpretations). This requires that Western biblical scholars acknowledge the way in which their own social location influences their interpretations. Patte therefore refers to his approach as

---

54. Patte, *Discipleship according to the Sermon on the Mount,* 18-19, 20-21. In *The Challenge of Discipleship,* Patte contends that an interpretation of the teaching of the text for believers is not "plausible" if it is not new, that is, if it simply repeats what they already know (29, 140-43). This assumes that scripture functions properly in interpretation when it has a transformative effect. It may be, however, that Patte underestimates the importance of what might be termed the "epideictic" function of scripture: its power to make "compelling" what we already know. On the other hand, to grasp something afresh in a way that is compelling for practical life is in one sense to discover something new in the text (or to confront the text "anew"). (In private correspondence Patte affirms that he wishes to include seeing the familiar afresh in a transformative way as a valid form of plausibility.)

55. Patte, *Discipleship according to the Sermon on the Mount,* 19-20.

56. Patte, *Discipleship according to the Sermon on the Mount,* 13-14.

57. Patte, *Discipleship according to the Sermon on the Mount,* chapter one.

58. Patte, *The Challenge of Discipleship,* 44.

59. Patte, *The Challenge of Discipleship,* 6.

"androcritical."[60] In so doing he acknowledges and seeks to be accountable for approaching the text from a male Euro-American perspective. The androcritical approach differs from traditional critical biblical studies in that it acknowledges not only its legitimacy judgments but also its epistemological and value judgments.

For the scholar, recognizing the viability of faith-interpretations other than one's own also means acknowledging the legitimacy and plausibility of non-scholarly pragmatic readings. Moreover, in Patte's estimation, it is non-scholarly readers and interpretive communities who are the chief font of legitimate and plausible faith-interpretations. Non-scholarly readers "reach practical conclusions about the teaching of the text for believers today that are readily comparable to those implied by the diverse scholarly interpretations."[61] Further, when non-scholarly conclusions about the teaching of the text find no echo in scholarly interpretations, Patte believes that they "call the attention of scholars to a dimension of the text that has been neglected."[62] Hence, Patte is "ready to claim that most practical interpretations are basically legitimate and plausible, even though they might need refinements."[63] This does not mean that faith-interpretations are typically free from inaccuracies in what they allege about the text. The text-based warrants for faith-based interpretations are often fanciful or question-begging. One task of critical study is to establish such faith-interpretations by supplying them with solid text-based warrants.[64]

A further role of critical biblical studies is to mine the history of interpretation in order to present the many possible legitimate interpretations and set forth their text-based warrants.[65] In this way believers discover that

---

60. Patte, *Ethics of Interpretation*, 1-16; *Discipleship according to the Sermon on the Mount*, 11-17.

61. Patte, *The Challenge of Discipleship*, 17.

62. Patte, *The Challenge of Discipleship*, 17.

63. Patte, *The Challenge of Discipleship*, 17. In *Discipleship according to the Sermon on the Mount*, Patte comments, "Thus, I want to insist that, until proven otherwise, any authentic *pro me/nobis* interpretation — which 'authentically' reflects how the text affects a given interpreter in a concrete situation — should be viewed as basically legitimate . . ." (23).

64. Patte, *Discipleship according to the Sermon on the Mount*, 23.

65. This is one of the aims of the Society of Biblical Literature seminar, "Romans through History and Cultures," under the leadership of Patte and others. See the first volume of essays drawn from this seminar: Daniel Patte and Cristina Grenholm, eds., *Reading Israel in Romans: Legitimacy and Plausibility of Divergent Interpretations*, Romans Through History and Cultures Series (Philadelphia: Trinity Press International, 2000).

their own faith-interpretations are not the only legitimate ones. Thus, critical biblical studies help believers confront the plurality of plausible interpretations and to take responsibility for the interpretations they choose.[66]

Although Patte does not say so explicitly, a close examination suggests that interpreters confront three different kinds of interpretive choices: (1) choices between logically incompatible alternatives, (2) choices between "perceptually" incompatible alternatives,[67] and (3) choices between practically incompatible alternatives (where practicality has to do with both feasibility and relevance). Choosing between these alternatives is a matter of finding the "most valuable" interpretation for one's own context. This most valuable interpretation must be contextually plausible and it must have a foundation in the text. Hence, any interpretation must be tested for epistemological-contextual fit and textual legitimacy. Moreover, confronting the plurality of legitimate and plausible interpretations challenges believers to reconsider whether their own interpretations really are the most valuable for their respective contexts.

Canonical Adjudication: Charles Cosgrove

Similar to Patte's program (but somewhat differently focused) is a proposal that I put forward in a 1996 article and further developed in a subsequent book.[68] I contend that for any question we put to scripture, there is typically a range of plausible (reasonable) answers that can be demonstrated through rigorous use of methods suited to answer the question we are asking.[69] This state of interpretive affairs holds for the biblical traditions at any point or level of their history. Language is inherently ambigu-

---

66. Patte, *The Challenge of Discipleship*, 10, 13.

67. Patte uses figure/ground studies in perception as a metaphorical model for how different interpretive frames amount to mutually excluding ways of seeing the text. See *The Challenge of Discipleship*, 18-20, 55-56, 96-97.

68. Charles H. Cosgrove, "Rhetorical Suspense in Romans: A Study in Polyvalence and Hermeneutical Election," *Journal of Biblical Literature* 115 (1996): 271-87; *Elusive Israel: The Puzzle of Election in Romans* (Louisville, KY: Westminster/John Knox Press, 1997). See also my essay, "The Justification of the Other: An Interpretation of Rom. 1:18–4:25," in *Society of Biblical Literature 1992 Seminar Papers*, ed. Eugene H. Lovering (Atlanta: Scholars Press, 1992).

69. I use the term "plausible" in the sense that Patte uses the term "legitimate." He reserves the term "plausible" for meaningfulness/relevance for the interpreter's own situation.

ous, especially in complex forms. This is true not only of language out of socio-rhetorical context ("distantiated," to use Paul Ricoeur's term) but of language in context. Some measure of virtually all utterance is underdetermined by the interaction between language system and rhetorical situation. At whatever level of the history of the tradition, the tradition almost invariably admits more than one reasonable interpretation.[70]

The reworking of biblical traditions in oral and textual form, involving ultimately their incorporation into a scripture corpus, enlarges this underdetermination by multiplying the possibilities for interpretation. Scripture presents a huge semantic potential as an intertextual field by virtue of the fact that the church conceives its collection of sacred writings as constituting a whole, a "book." The presence of otherwise disparate writings in the same canonical corpus produces canonical effects. The various parts of scripture "co-determine" one another. This allows for many different kinds of interpretive construction because it involves a high degree of interpretive supplementation to make the connections. There are always multiple reasonable ways for construing a single passage of scripture, for construing a passage of scripture within the larger context of scripture, and for construing various parts of scripture into larger wholes (or for construing "scripture as a whole"). The interplay of textual polyvalence and codetermination at these different levels of interpretation makes us "co-responsible" with scripture for the meaning of scripture we appropriate for Christian faith and life.[71]

In describing textual polyvalence as a range of plausible meanings, I have in mind *incompatible* meanings (*competing* answers to a given interpretive question). There are of course other ways in which texts are polyvalent. Texts are polyvalent because we can ask an unlimited number of *different* questions of them. They are also polyvalent because we can extend their meaning as *significance* to innumerable new human situa-

---

70. In *Elusive Israel* (chapters 1 and 2) I seek to show that the identity of (true) Israel is underdetermined by Romans.

71. In *Elusive Israel* I describe co-responsibility under the heading of "co-deliberation." One way to interpret Rom. 9-11 is to see Paul using the ancient rhetorical device of co-deliberation (*communicatio*) and suspense (*sustentatio*). According to this interpretation, Paul's argument is structured explicitly and implicitly to invite co-deliberation by his hearers. Moreover, because his final resolution/disclosure in ch. 11 is ambiguous, the codeliberation in effect goes on (perhaps against his intent) and becomes a permanent part of the rhetoric of Romans for us. See *Elusive Israel*, 26-38.

tions. In addition to these kinds of polyvalence, however, is a logically prior form: in every hermeneutical situation a conflict of interpretations arises because we confront forced choices between more or less equally reasonable ways to construe scripture in response to the question we are asking.

I use the terms "reasonable" and "plausible" interchangeably. A plausible interpretation is not simply a "possible" one. Plausibility here means *comparable* in strength, where strength is a probability judgment based on careful analysis of evidence and a rigorous application of method.[72] The fact of multiple reasonable interpretations makes texts "indeterminate" or "underdetermined." In the case of most texts, including biblical texts, indeterminacy means limited semantic openness. One can speak of "bounded indeterminacy." Texts admit multiple interpretations, but they also limit interpretation.[73]

The church has a responsibility to define and acknowledge the full range of plausible interpretations for a given scripture text (in response to a given interpretive question). This is important for at least two reasons. First, some pernicious readings of scripture are plausible, and the church has a moral responsibility to say so. The church should be honest and admit that pernicious readings can be as reasonable as humane readings, where both depend on a fair application of the same methods.[74] A good example is the debate over whether this or that New Testament writing is anti-Jewish. The church has a long history of seeing various forms of anti-Jewishness as integral parts of the scriptural witness. Today many Christians are reexamining scripture and the history of interpretation in order to test and reject the traditional theological bases for anti-Jewishness. In the process, the church is discovering alternative plausible ways to read scripture. Lloyd Gaston's Judaism-affirming interpretation of Paul is a notable example. Nevertheless, it would be a mistake to fall back into exegetical positivism here, when at many points (I do not say at every point) older anti-Jewish interpretations remain plausible alongside newer competing ones. Christians must be honest about the semantic openness of scripture to conflicting interpretations

72. Cosgrove, *Elusive Israel*, 21-25.

73. Although he does not, as far as I know, use the term "bounded indeterminacy," this is basically the view argued by Umberto Eco in *Interpretation and Overinterpretation*, with Richard Rorty, Jonathan Culler, and Christine Brooke-Rose, ed. Stefan Collini (Cambridge: Cambridge University Press, 1992).

74. See Cosgrove, *Elusive Israel*, 97-100.

and about the moral-theological responsibility this places on Christians for the interpretive choices they defend.

Interpretive choice requires adjudication, principled deliberation toward a decision about which interpretation is valid for the church's faith and life. As a moral-theological act, adjudication means choosing the interpretation that best conforms to the purpose of scripture set forth in Matthew 22:34-40 as the rule of love.[75] The two great commandments can be seen as mutually interpreting each other. In Matthew, the command to love one's neighbor seems to be treated as a hermeneutical key to love of God;[76] in a different situation, it might be more important to stress love of God as a hermeneutical key to love of neighbor. Ultimately, the two commandments belong together as a guide to the interpretation of scripture.

The criteria of exegetical reasonableness and the double love commandment as a norm of hermeneutical adjudication are both matters of fallible judgment, shaped by a shared community sense and subject to debate. Reasonableness is a matter of judging which methods are suitable for answering the questions we pose to the text and using those methods with logical rigor and evenhandedness.

If we interpret scripture by the rule of love, our conception of love should also be informed by scripture and filled out by love's central paradigm in the New Testament, the love of God in Christ.[77] At the same time, learning about love from scripture does not take place apart from our having a knowledge and experience of love outside scripture. Indeed, it is typical of scripture, when it commands love, to assume that we know what love is — or can learn what it is (see Matt. 7:12).

As an example of canonical adjudication, I examine the question of the identity of Israel in Romans. Elect Israel in Romans has been plausibly interpreted as the church (spiritual as opposed to literal, fleshly Israel), an elect remnant within fleshly Israel (that blends into the church

---

75. Cosgrove, *Elusive Israel*, 43-45.

76. I see this, for example, in the way the scripture word "I desire mercy and not sacrifice" is used by Jesus in Matthew 12:1-8 to interpret the sabbath law, which was seen by some of his contemporaries as placing obedience to God above human needs.

77. Richard Hays makes this point effectively in *The Moral Vision of the New Testament*, 200-203. Hays rejects the common view that love is a unifying theme of New Testament ethics. He argues that the basic coherence of New Testament ethics is best grasped through the integration of the themes "community, cross, and new creation." Insofar as love is a pivotal theme, it is defined by community, cross, and new creation in a distinctive way.

as the new people of God), or the Jewish people as a whole. I choose the third of these defensible alternatives, construing "elect Israel" as literally the Jewish people, whose identity is grounded in and maintained by the Torah. The election of the Jewish people as Israel includes God's love of Israel in its "fleshly" particularity (not simply as a part of universal, abstract "humanity"). God cherishes the Jewish people in their concrete social identity(ies), formed by unrepeatable experiences and memories. The election of Israel also entails a call, a vocation to bring the light of God's merciful justice, witnessed to in the Torah, to the world. The divine impartiality of God, expressed in the universalism of Paul's gospel, can accommodate this idea of the election of the Jewish people as Israel, if "Israel" can also be taken as a symbol and applied metaphorically to other peoples. In this sense every people has the "right to be Israel," but that "right" has a very specific and limited meaning here. First of all, it depends on the affirmation that the Jewish people are Israel and that the name Israel can be applied to others only *metaphorically*. This permits no "expropriation" of the identity of Israel. Second, the meaning of Israel in its metaphorical application to others is the following: Israel is a people cherished by God in their particularity and social concreteness and charged with a vocation of justice to the world, in which they recognize that God loves all peoples in ways that are analogous to how God loves them.

I assert my interpretation of Israel in Romans against (1) any interpretations that attribute a purely spiritual meaning to (true) Israel, thus denying that the Jewish people are true Israel, and (2) any interpretations that affirm the election of the Jewish people as Israel in a way that excludes a similar election for other peoples.[78] Both of these interpretations can be reasonably defended on exegetical grounds. Nevertheless, both have implications that I reject on moral-theological grounds, including incompatibility with the double love commandment as I construe it within the context of scripture as a whole. In arguing in this way, I acknowledge that I am co-responsible for the meaning of Israel in Romans. Keeping within what I take to be the constraints on plausible interpretation of Paul, I have made a

---

78. In defending my interpretation at a canonical level, I draw attention to the suggestions in Amos 9:7 and Isaiah 19:19-25 that God has also elected other peoples. These clues from the prophets shape my negotiation of Paul's teaching about divine impartiality and divine election in Romans. See *Elusive Israel*, 82-86.

moral-theological judgment about what the identity and vocation of Israel ought to be.[79]

Freedom and Responsibility in the Interpretation of Narrative Texts: Robert Tannehill

A final example of advocacy of the rule of moral-theological adjudication appears in an article by Robert Tannehill on freedom and responsibility in interpretation.[80] Tannehill observes that biblical texts "grant us more freedom [of interpretation] than we commonly recognize," a freedom that "we can and should use responsibly."[81] Responsible interpretation means looking "to find in sacred texts, whenever possible, a benefit for humanity (including the benefit of promoting harmony with God)."[82] Using examples from Luke, Tannehill goes on to describe various ways in which biblical texts — and in particular narrative texts — are open to multiple interpretations.[83] Biblical literature often uses evocative language designed to stimulate the imagination of the hearer; narratives have gaps that hearers

---

79. One reviewer has complained that by extending the identity of Israel to peoples other than Israel I am, unwittingly, opening the door to pernicious nationalism, while, at the same time, undermining the right of the Jewish people to be exclusively Israel. Perhaps I should not have used the provocative expression "right to be Israel." In any case, I remain committed to the view that we do best to honor the identity of the Jewish people as Israel in the twofold sense I have set forth, applying it literally to the Jewish people and metaphorically to others. As I make clear in my book, I define this twofold sense by synthesizing the views of Daniel Boyarin, Jonathan Boyarin, and Immanuel Levinas, Jewish thinkers who have made profound contributions to contemporary understandings of what Israel means (and can mean). I intend my own construal of the meaning of "Israel" in Romans to disallow any expropriation of the identity Israel from the Jewish people, to oppose any form of nationalism that denies the equal value of other peoples, and to protect against a universalism that, in rejecting particularity, in effect tacitly universalizes the particularity of one group. The sense in which other peoples may be metaphorically "Israel" is (1) as valued by God in their concrete particularity (Boyarin and Boyarin) and (2) as charged with a vocation to serve the cause of mercy and justice for all nations (Levinas). See *Elusive Israel*, 65-90.

80. Robert C. Tannehill, "Freedom and Responsibility in Scripture Interpretation, with Application to Luke," in *Literary Studies in Luke-Acts,* ed. Richard P. Thompson and Thomas E. Philips (Macon GA: Mercer University Press, 1998), 265-78.

81. Tannehill, "Freedom and Responsibility," 266.

82. Tannehill, "Freedom and Responsibility," 266.

83. Tannehill, "Freedom and Responsibility," 266-77.

are expected to fill in; characters are sketched in ways that allow for different interpretations of their motivations, qualities, roles, and growth or transformation through experience; multiple possibilities present themselves for making meaningful connections between narrative units; tradition history offers up multiple contexts in which to interpret a given unit of tradition; judgments about the "center of Scripture" affect how we construe its parts.

Tannehill proposes that the double love commandment of Matt. 22:34-40 should function as a hermeneutical principle in our exercise of freedom and responsibility in interpretation.[84] Applying this principle will lead us to one of two judgments about a given scripture text: (1) that the text can be understood in a beneficial way, even if it can also be interpreted in an oppressive way; (2) that the text does not promote love of God or neighbor and must not be appropriated as a guide for Christian life.[85] In cases where a beneficial interpretation can be demonstrated as one of the genuine possibilities, that interpretation should be chosen for Christian use. Tannehill emphasizes that "[t]he choice to read Scripture as an invitation to love God and neighbor is a religious and ethical decision, as are other options for deciding what is central in Scripture."[86]

Conclusion and Assessment

The rule of moral-theological adjudication assumes that the conflict of interpretations cannot be resolved through exegetical methods alone; it takes the fact of interpretive freedom for granted. A first objection to the rule is that it is really not a rule at all but only a description of a state of affairs. We do, necessarily, interpret from our own "horizon." In terms of the rule of moral-theological adjudication, one might say that we necessarily interpret from the horizon of our own moral and theological convictions. The rule is accordingly more like a law of nature than a hermeneutical prescription.

The preceding objection overlooks an important feature of interpretation and also misconstrues the nature of the rule of adjudication. While it

---

84. Tannehill, "Freedom and Responsibility," 276-77.
85. Tannehill, "Freedom and Responsibility," 277.
86. Tannehill, "Freedom and Responsibility," 277.

is true that we always interpret from our own perspective, it does not follow that we are so locked into that perspective that we cannot recognize
how the object of our interpretation differs from us, challenges us. Moreover, we are able to recognize that *interpretations* often differ and do so
reasonably and meaningfully (or, in Patte's terminology, "legitimately" and
"plausibly"). The point of the rule of moral-theological adjudication is not
to state what is obvious and unavoidable but to command that we take responsibility for our constructive part in interpretation by (a) being cogni-
zant of the range of interpretations, (b) acknowledging that in any interpretive situation there is typically more than one plausible interpretation,
(c) identifying and using moral and theological criteria for judging between competing interpretations, (d) submitting the moral-theological rationales for our interpretive choices to scrutiny and criticism.

A second objection to the rule is that it rests on a bad theory of interpretation. Although the rule is compatible with a variety of views about
the nature and goals of interpretation, it is at odds with some hermeneutic
theories. E. D. Hirsch's account of textual meaning is one of the most powerful challengers.

Hirsch has defended as compellingly as anyone I know the view that
the purpose of a text is to communicate the verbal meaning of its au-
thor(s) and that the proper and only coherent goal of interpretation is that
verbal meaning.[87] For Hirsch, the first rule of the ethics of interpretation is
to seek authorial intent and in this way to honor the rights of authors to
have their words understood as they intend.[88] Beyond this duty lies another reason for seeking the verbal meaning of the author. We are interested in classic texts because we believe that they have something to teach
us; we do not (or should not) want to discover our "own" meanings in
texts, since then we would learn nothing.[89] Hence, the intentionalist model
is the only theory of textual meaning that proposes a worthy goal of interpretation.

87. E. D. Hirsch, Jr., *Validity in Interpretation* (New Haven, CT: Yale University Press, 1967); "Counterfactuals in Interpretation," in *Interpreting Law and Literature: A Hermeneutic Reader,* ed. Sanford Levinson and Steven Mailloux (Evanston, IL: Northwestern University Press, 1988), 55-68; "Three Dimensions of Hermeneutics" in *The Aims of Interpretation* (Chicago and London: The University of Chicago Press, 1976).

88. See, for example, Hirsch, "Three Dimensions of Hermeneutics," 90-92.

89. In *Validity in Interpretation,* Hirsch describes this defense of authorial meaning as the traditional one (25-26).

The Hirschian model and ethic of interpretation suggests that we should deal with the conflict of interpretations as follows. First, we should continue always to seek the most probable intent of the author(s). Second, where we confront equally probable but incompatible interpretations, we ought not to choose one over another but should simply admit that the state of interpretation does not permit us to make a choice. At a hermeneutical level, this implies that where interpretive probability is not secure, we cannot in good conscience appropriate the text.

One response to the Hirschian challenge is that the church through the centuries has never operated by these limits on interpretation. Interpretation of scripture has always been contested and probability judgments (according to whatever method in whatever era) have never been sufficient in themselves to resolve interpretive debates intellectually.

The question Hirsch raises does not go away, however. What is it we think we are getting from (or doing with) scripture when we choose between interpretations on other than probabilistic judgments about author meaning? The theory that "linguistic signs can somehow speak their own meaning" (apart from the communicative intent of their human authors), Hirsch says, is "a mystical idea that has never been persuasively defended."[90] My answer to this is that linguistic signs do not speak their own meaning by themselves. They speak with the help of interpreters. When interpreters help meaning come into focus, they also multiply possibilities for meaning. The question is whether the perception that textual meaning is co-determined by text and interpreter undermines the force of appeal to the text as warrant (which is what the five hermeneutical rules of this study are about). This is a fair and serious concern. The full intelligibility of the rule of moral-theological adjudication requires a theory of scriptural authority that accounts for the constructive and adjudicative role of the interpreter (or interpretive community). Short of providing a full theorization of their approach, however, those who affirm the authority of scripture and acknowledge that exegetical method alone cannot resolve many significant conflicts of interpretation have good grounds for using a rule of moral-theological adjudication and taking responsibility for their hermeneutical appropriation of scripture. To do otherwise would require (a) eschewing virtually all appeal to scripture as warrant for Christian practice or (b) adopting the vain pretense that rigorous ap-

---

90. Hirsch, *Validity in Interpretation*, 23.

plication of this or that exegetical method can settle all (or almost all) exegetical disputes.

Another criticism of the rule of moral-theological adjudication is that it takes us no further toward resolution of conflicts of interpretation than any other interpretive principle does. This criticism has force in two respects. First, no moral-theological norm, whether a single principle or a more complex rule of faith and life, can be applied in a logically deductive way, leading to unambiguous conclusions.[91] For example, adjudicating a conflict of interpretations according to the principles of love of God and neighbor (Augustine) or "community, cross, and new creation" (Richard Hays)[92] is as likely to produce hermeneutical debate as hermeneutical closure. Second, any given rule of moral-theological adjudication will stand in tension with competitors. Which moral-theological norms should govern? How will they be established from scripture? The problem of identifying and applying substantive moral-theological guides for interpretation shows the limits of the rule. However, as a way of taking responsibility for our interpretations, the rule has important hermeneutical significance.

A final criticism is that the rule of moral-theological adjudication is not a rule for adjudicating after the exegetical results are in (and competing reasonable interpretations have presented themselves) but simply one more interpretive or exegetical principle among others. This is not so much a criticism of the rule as a point about how to conceive the place of the rule in the hermeneutical process. The rule can certainly be conceived as part of an integrated interpretive approach to scripture that makes no sharp distinction between exegesis and hermeneutics. But I think the rule is better taken as hermeneutically distinct from interpretive methods in two important respects: (1) it can be used with a diverse range of methods (from the allegorizing exegesis of Augustine to contemporary socio-rhetorical interpretation) and (2) it poses moral-theological questions about choice of methods.

---

91. See chapter two on the nature of informal, case-based reasoning.
92. See note 26 above.

Conclusion

This study has identified and examined five rules for the use of scripture in moral debate. The rules are my attempt to state as precisely and as defensibly as possible certain crucial hermeneutical assumptions that are generally operative in contemporary moral appeal to scripture. Others may wish to phrase the rules differently and to provide them with somewhat different rationales or criticisms. If this study evokes that response, I will be gratified, since my ultimate aim is not to recommend or reject this or that specific rule formulation but to encourage close examination of what we are actually doing, by virtue of shared assumptions, when we appeal to scripture in moral argument.

Of course, the five rules described here are not the only hermeneutical rules at work in contemporary moral appeal to scripture.[1] Nor do I claim that these rules are shared universally by Christians. In fact, each of the five rules treated here opposes one or more hermeneutical assumptions that could also be stated as a rule. For example, the rule of purpose challenges the traditional assumption that biblical moral rules carry force for the church as rules. We might formulate this as "Take biblical moral rules as rules for us." The rule of scope, as a reflex of modern scientific understanding, responds to a medieval (and ancient) hermeneutic in which empirical

---

1. In an appendix I have given some examples of other rules. These examples are also only a further sampling.

assumptions and assertions of scripture were accorded authority. We might formulate this rule as "Take the Bible as authoritative on all the subjects about which it speaks and in all the assumptions logically entailed by what it says." The rule of countercultural witness rejects the traditional view that scripture is unified in all that it assumes or endorses. We might put this as "Interpret all the moral teachings of the Bible in a harmonizing way." The rule of analogy rejects any strict historicist doctrine of incommensurability between the Bible and modern cultures. The radical historicist verdict on traditional hermeneutics is epitomized by Robin Scroggs' suggestion (rephrasing the punch line of an old joke) that when it comes to much or most New Testament teaching, "You can't get from there to here."[2] At the same time the rule of analogy rejects the allegorist's approach, which we may express as "Every likeness veils a latent inner identity and warrants an equation."[3]

The question of what traditional assumptions are displaced by the rule of moral-theological adjudication is somewhat trickier. When conceived according to a postmodern conception of language, this rule challenges an early-modern rule, namely, the Reformation principle, "Interpret obscure parts of scripture in the light of clear parts," meaning that the obscure parts are to be treated as agreeing with the clear parts. To the extent that this Reformation principle assumes a "rule of faith," the postmodern rule of moral-theological adjudication has some affinities with it. Nevertheless, the postmodern rule of adjudication reckons with a hermeneutic circle and rests on the perception that the conflict of interpretations touches scripture pervasively and cannot be resolved by exegetical method alone. The postmodern rule of adjudication dissents from the traditional idea that by means of a rule of faith one is simply distinguishing the actual intention of this or that scripture passage from its misinterpretations.

---

2. Robin Scroggs, "The New Testament and Ethics: How Do We Get from There to Here?" in *Perspectives on the New Testament: Essays in Honor of Frank Stagg,* ed. Charles H. Talbert (Macon, GA: Mercer University Press, 1985), 77-93. See also Scroggs' article, "The Bible as Foundational Document," *Interpretation* 49 (1995): 17-30.

3. Umberto Eco describes this as an aspect of what he terms "Hermetic semiosis," which involves an extremely generous view of similarity and operates by the principle that "[i]f two things are similar, the one can become the sign for the other and vice versa." See Eco, *Interpretation and Overinterpretation,* with Richard Rorty, Jonathan Culler, and Christine Brooke-Rose, ed. Stefan Collini (Cambridge: Cambridge University Press, 1992), 45-47.

Hermeneutical Rules as Rhetorical Assumptions

The five rules treated in this study express what are usually unexpressed assumptions of Christian moral appeal to the Bible. Identifying these assumptions requires mapping the logic of an argument to discover what presuppositions are necessary to make the argument persuasive. Filling in these gaps, as part of making sense of another's argument, sometimes leads us to grasp presuppositions that the speaker self-consciously affirms. At other times, identifying unexpressed assumptions is a way of confronting a speaker with his or her own unanalyzed presuppositions. Arguing is learned by imitation and sometimes we take over arguments from others without fully realizing the assumptions on which those arguments are based. The discipline of scrutinizing our assumptions (or the assumptions of the arguments we find appealing) helps us test our consistency in appealing to scripture.

Every major premise of a moral argument is a kind of rule. If I argue that 'X' is the case by developing an argument in which 'Y' is a major premise, I am invoking Y as a rule covering the case of X. For example, if I argue that the natural habitat of the manitee should be protected because the manitee is an endangered species, I am invoking as an implicit rule that "the habitats of endangered species should be protected." The five hermeneutical assumptions discussed in this book belong to a common fund of major premises in argument from scripture. As such, they are hermeneutical rules. Consider the following example, based on the discussion of lending at interest in chapter one. A speaker, whom we will call Anne, makes the following argument as part of a larger case from scripture in support of a proposal that her church should assist in establishing lending institutions in economically depressed areas to help foster cottage industries among the poor.

> The law of Moses prohibits lending at interest because the poor in ancient Israel were exploited by this practice. However, in contemporary economic society, lending at interest can be a way of assisting the poor and thus fulfilling the purpose of the law.

This argument is in what might be termed "colloquial" style, as opposed to a more formalistic style that spells out assumptions and arranges the argument in an orderly deductive pattern. We can map the implicit logic of this colloquial argument as follows, using a more formal, deductive style:

Major Premise 1: The church should follow the moral teachings of scripture, including the moral law of Moses.

Major Premise 2: In appropriating the moral voice of scripture for Christian practice, the church should give greater weight to the purpose of biblical teachings than to their express formulations as rules.

Minor Premise 1: The proscriptions of the Hebrew Bible against lending at interest are part of its moral teaching.

Conclusion 1: Therefore, these teachings about lending at interest carry force as guides for the moral practice of the church.

Minor Premise 2: The purpose of the proscriptions against lending at interest is to protect the poor from exploitation.

Conclusion 2: Therefore, in appropriating these teachings about lending at interest, the church should be guided primarily by the purpose of concern for the poor.

Notice that Major Premise 1 is the basic assumption that scripture carries authority for the church's moral life. We might call this assumption the "rule of scripture" (scripture as "canon"). Major Premise 2 expresses the hermeneutical "rule of purpose." In most appeal to scripture, the rule of scripture is assumed, not stated. In arguments that invoke the rule of purpose, this rule is typically unstated as well. Formulating these major premises draws attention to basic assumptions of the argument left unstated in its colloquial form.

Confronted with the formal mapping of her argument about lending at interest, Anne may object to Major Premise 2 and claim that she does not subscribe to the hermeneutical rule of purpose. In that case, Anne has two options. Either she can abandon her argument or she can substitute a different Major Premise 2 (although I can't think of what other Major Premise 2 might make Anne's argument work, except some other version of the rule of purpose).

The concept of hermeneutical rules, as used in this study, refers to rhetorical assumptions that make arguments persuasive or not. Hermeneutical rules are major premises that hearers impute to arguments in order to make sense of them; they are also major premises that speakers presume to share with their audience. Identifying and explicating such major premises as hermeneutical rules is a way of testing our guiding assumptions, so that we can discover how consistent we are in how we argue from scripture. Do we argue from the purpose of scripture's teaching when it comes to some topics and from the letter of scriptural teaching on other topics? Do we permit wide latitude for analogy on some issues but require close correspondence of terms and concepts on other issues? Close examination of our assumptions may lead us to reject some of them as untenable or to modify them in ways that are more defensible.

Comparing the Five Rules

The five hermeneutical rules are of different types. Two are decidedly modern: the rule of countercultural witness and the rule of nonempirical scope. These rules respond to conditions created by two great epochs in which we now live: the age of science and the age of liberation. The other three rules are contemporary recastings of ancient rules. The rule of analogy stands in the tradition of typology (and allegory). The rule of moral-theological adjudication is a modern revision of the rule of faith. The rule of purpose has an ancient pedigree in law and an analogue, if not a precedent, in the early Christian hermeneutical doctrine of the primacy of the spirit over the letter.

Nevertheless, the rules of purpose and analogy are also modern. They gain plausibility, at least in part, from the modern concepts of history and cultural relativity, which include the modern idea of a "culture" as an integrated meaning system in which the parts depend for their sense on their place and function within the whole. The concept of cultural relativity shows why we should favor, as a matter of hermeneutical method, the purpose over the letter of a biblical rule. This leads to something very different from older distinctions between the letter and the spirit. First, it elevates "purpose" in an absolute way over the letter, for which the only precedent in ancient hermeneutics is the elevation of the "Spirit" (as the revelation in Christ) over the letter of the Jewish scriptures. In that older distinction between letter and spirit, the church posited a hidden Christian purpose behind the Jewish scriptures — a purpose to be discovered through typology and allegory. As Hans Frei has astutely observed, this hermeneutic was not, strictly speaking, a rejection of letter for spirit. Rather, the church regarded the Christ story as the new and spiritual letter, which provides the clue for rereading and de-literalizing the Jewish law.[4] By contrast, the modern rule

4. Hans W. Frei, "The 'Literal Reading' of Biblical Narrative in the Christian Tradition:

of purpose makes the aim or rationale behind any law or moral teaching in the Bible, whether in the New Testament or the Old Testament, weightier than the letter.

Likewise, the rule of analogy, while having precedents in ancient typology and allegory, is a modern rule. Ancient (and medieval) herme-neutical assumptions about scripture encouraged expansive analogical in-terpretation (in the forms of typologizing and allegorizing), what Umberto Eco has called "unlimited semiosis."[5] By contrast, the modern rule of analogy is far more restrictive. It is a post-Enlightenment rule re-quiring analogical "reasoning." It reckons with the great cultural-historical gap between "then" and "now," and is not satisfied with "equations" that fail to do justice to original historical-cultural meanings.

The rule that comes closest to its ancient antecedent is the rule of moral-theological adjudication. The idea that a rule of faith ought to guide interpretation of scripture has regained currency in recent decades.[6] In some ways the rule of moral-theological adjudication stands within this reclaimed tradition of the ancient church, at least formally. However, its modern forms also include theories of language that are far removed from ancient conceptions of the speech of scripture. Contemporary theories of polyvalence and reader-construction of meaning give at least some con-ceptions of the rule of moral-theological adjudication a distinctively mod-ern (or postmodern) character.

An Example of Using the Rules in Combination

There is nothing about the five rules that makes them inherently compati-ble, but they lend themselves to use in combination. To illustrate this, I

Does It Stretch or Will It Break?" in *The Bible and the Narrative Tradition,* ed. Frank McCon-nell (New York and Oxford: Oxford University Press, 1986), 36-77.

5. Umberto Eco, *The Limits of Interpretation* (Bloomington, IN: Indiana University Press, 1990), 6, 27-43; also Eco, *Interpretation and Overinterpretation,* 45-66.

6. See, for example, Brevard S. Childs, *Biblical Theology of the Old and New Testaments: Theological Reflection on the Christian Bible* (Minneapolis: Fortress Press, 1992), 67-68; Ste-phen E. Fowl, *Engaging Scripture: A Model for Theological Interpretation* (Malden, MA and Oxford, UK: Blackwell, 1998), 7-9; Richard B. Hays, *The Moral Vision of the New Testament: Community, Cross, New Creation: A Contemporary Introduction to New Testament Ethics* (San Francisco: HarperSanFrancisco, 1996), 195.

have constructed a sample discourse on the New Testament and gender equality that illustrates implicit use of all five rules. Since the example is for purposes of illustration, I do not intend to defend all of its assertions. Moreover, interests of economy have led me to simplify certain issues of interpretation.

Sample Argument: Appealing to Scripture in Support of Gender Equality

Jesus as portrayed in the Gospels treats women in ways that go against the status quo; his practice transgresses the cultural norms and boundaries that define gender relations and women's proper roles in society. Likewise, Paul counts women as his partners, as patrons, as prophets, and apostles; and he teaches his churches that in Christ there is neither Jew nor Greek, slave nor free, male nor female.

Nevertheless, there are no direct prophetic admonitions or arguments in the Gospels or in Paul's letters calling for new social relations between men and women. Apart from Gospel stories that might be taken as exemplary for Christians (e.g., Jesus with Martha and Mary), instructions on discipleship and community life do not include calls for egalitarian gender practice. Moreover, where gender relations are directly addressed, the instructions for specific behaviors reinforce the cultural status quo (1 Tim. 2:11-15 being the most notable example). Thus, the New Testament writers, to the extent that they have a vision of gender equality in Christ, do not translate that vision into direct paraenesis, exhortation, or instruction for community formation.

How shall we interpret this state of affairs, and what implications does it have for us?

First, we should bear in mind that gender equality, as a practical social ideal, is a revolutionary notion in any patriarchal society *and* that social revolution was off almost everyone's map in the ancient world. By "revolution" I mean a fundamental restructuring of social relations. The idea that the world could be changed in its basic social patterns through organized human agency was virtually inconceivable. Many Stoics, for example, entertained radical views about how society ought to be, but even Stoics politically situated at the centers of power never sought to translate their social vision into social reality. One reason for this is surely that there existed no effective memory — no *history* in our sense of the word — of fundamental social change: no history of past revolution to make the possibility of present and future revolution conceivable. History itself — in the modern sense — is probably a prerequisite for programs of social revolution. Nevertheless, the utopian values, the vision of a world of equality as the *best* world, lie before us in earliest Christianity. The gospel includes the hope of equality. The ancient baptismal formula of Gal. 3:28 announces it: "there is . . . no longer male or female." This hope invites us, who live by different historical assumptions than the ancient Christians did, to embrace equality in the light of *our* historical situation, which includes the knowledge that the world can change in fundamental ways through organized human agency.

Second, it is remarkable, isn't it, that an egalitarian vision appears at all in the New Testament, given how deeply ingrained patriarchy was in the Greco-Roman world. The gospel, the experience of God's Spirit, somehow inspired breakthroughs, prophetic stances against the status quo, against the reigning patriarchal ideology. We see this, as I've said, to some extent in the teaching and practice of Jesus as portrayed in the Gospels. We see it at a few points in Paul. Moreover, the controversies over gender reflected in 1 Corinthians and, a generation later in the Pastoral Epistles, show that early Christian women found a basis for equality in the gospel and sought to practice it in anticipation of the new creation in Christ. Placed in their social context, these egalitarian impulses stand out as remarkable, courageous voices against what everyone else — most people within and without the church — took for granted. They represent a distinctive, countercultural voice against patriarchy. Jesus' relations with women go against the reigning gender ideology. Paul's egalitarian side also challenges this ideology, providing a prophetic critique of his patriarchal side. And the women silenced in 1 Cor. 14 and 1 Tim. 2 also "speak," witnessing to an alternative understanding of the gospel that challenges the powerful and privileged.

Third, it is important to inquire into the purpose behind New Testament instructions about gender relations. For example, Wayne Meeks has argued very plausibly that Paul's position in 1 Cor. 11 on the veiling of women has the following aim: Paul wants to promote the practical, functional equality of men and women but in such a way that the community is reminded that the new age has not fully arrived. Therefore, Paul accords full equal rights to women but requires that they wear veils as signs that the new creation has not yet fully supplanted the old. From a modern perspective — one might say from a perspective "after McLuhan" — we are far more aware than Paul was of how powerfully "form" or "medium" speaks. Paul may have thought that veiled women, if given full rights of speech, including authoritative prophetic utterance, could be equal partners of men. But symbols often speak louder than actions. To use some deconstructionist jargon, the veil is "always already" deconstructing the fragile equality Paul seeks to honor.

None of the preceding, however, should lessen our appreciation of Paul's purpose or intent. Instead, we must find our own ways of implementing that egalitarian intent in social forms, making sure that equality is inscribed in the symbol system at every point, including the "text" of the body.

Fourth, consistency requires that we treat gender in the Bible no differently than we treat slavery or relations between Jews and gentiles. In fact, Gal. 3:28 puts gender, slavery, and relations between Jews and Christians together, inviting us to interpret "no male or female" in the light of "no Jew or Greek" and "no slave or free." If we can claim the Bible against slavery, despite biblical texts that take slavery for granted, we can claim the Bible against patriarchy, despite biblical texts that take patriarchy for granted. Likewise, if Paul affirms the equality of Jew and gentile before God, we can draw out similar implications for gender relations.

Analysis of the Sample Argument

In the sample argument above, the numbering of points (first, second, etc.) marks invocations of the different rules. The only rule that is not represented by a particular number is the rule of moral-theological adjudication. That rule governs the whole in the sense that the whole argument depends on interpretive decisions aimed at making a plausible case from the New Testament for gender equality.

The first point assumes the rule of nonempirical scope. The authors of scripture operated with ancient understandings of history and the possibilities for sociocultural change through human agency. Modern historical knowledge and experience contradict these ancient assumptions. Since such knowledge is at least in large part empirical and depends on the historical sciences, it should be treated as lying outside the scope of scripture.

To the extent that New Testament quietism rests on ancient assumptions about history and social change, New Testament quietism should not be adopted by us.

The second point invokes the rule of countercultural witness. By drawing attention to and celebrating those voices in the New Testament that affirm or tend toward greater gender equality, the second point is recommending these voices. This has force as an argument from scripture only if one assumes that greater weight should be accorded to countercultural voices in scripture than to those that merely echo the dominant culture of the time.

The third point invokes the rule of purpose. Adopting Wayne Meeks' interpretation of the logic of 1 Cor. 11:2-16, it calls for applying Paul's underlying purpose to modern gender relations rather than adopting the rule Paul lays down in this passage and seeking to apply it in a contemporary setting. Moreover, it construes the argument from "headship" also in light of this reconstructed purpose and accords the purpose of this argument greater weight than the specific argument from headship itself. In these ways, the "letter" of Paul's teaching is relativized and Paul's purpose (a particular construal of that purpose at a particular level of its generality) is elevated as more universal.

The fourth point argues by analogy. It considers the social implications of the end of the Jew/gentile and slave/free distinctions. If the logic of this appeal were developed fully, that could best be done in two steps of analogical reasoning. First, one argues that the three pairs of opposites in Gal. 3:28 are similar, each involving some kind of hierarchy that comes to an end. This entails showing material correspondences between the three pairs, e.g., that gender hierarchy is like slavery and also like the relation of Jew and Gentile (from some traditional points of view within the early church). Next, one argues that the end of the hierarchy ought to be taken as including social relations, arguing for a social application to gender by analogy to the Jew/gentile case, which has manifestly social implications for Paul. Making this argument would involve explaining why Paul himself does not call for the end of the gender and slavery hierarchies as a matter of the church's social practice.

The sample argument as a whole can also be analyzed according to *interrelationship* between the rules. For example, the decision to adopt Wayne Meeks' interpretation of Paul's teaching about gender can be construed as follows. First, it is not the explicit commands Paul gives in 1 Cor.

11 regarding gender roles and relations but Paul's purpose that should govern the church's appropriation of this scripture passage (invocation of the rule of purpose). Second, that purpose can be reconstructed in more than one way, some reconstructions being more probable than others, many interpretations deserving rejection as implausible, but no one interpretation being so superior that it can be accepted as proved on historical grounds. Wayne Meeks' interpretation of Paul's purpose is as probable as its competitors. Moreover, it commends itself for moral-theological reasons growing out of modern knowledge about gender considered in the light of the Bible's portrayal of God as especially concerned to defend the oppressed (invocation of the rule of moral-theological adjudication). Further, Meeks' interpretation is also cast in modern conceptuality (using a distinction between symbols and functions), which can be justified only as an analogical contemporizing interpretation of Paul's own purpose (invocation of the rule of analogy).

To take another example, using the rule of purpose together with the rule of countercultural witness requires that the countercultural be found at the level of purpose in order to carry weight. In the sample argument above, this requirement is met, for example, in the special weight assigned to the countercultural *purpose* of Paul's instructions about gender roles and dress. By contrast, consider the claim sometimes made that the "household code" of Ephesians goes against dominant cultural norms because it calls for masters to treat slaves in a kindly fashion and for husbands to love their wives as themselves (Eph. 5:21–6:9). If one treats only the ostensible content of the household code in Ephesians, without attending to its purpose, one can spin out a set of highly countercultural teachings: treating slaves kindly must ultimately entail freeing them, and husbands loving their wives as their own bodies must ultimately require equal status in the flesh. But when one considers the purpose of the household codes by examining similar language in the writings of Greek and Latin moralists, it becomes evident that the purpose of the Ephesians code is to conform the church to a Christian way of living in the established order, not to challenge or undermine that order. If the rule of countercultural witness can gain a foothold here for an emancipatory interest, it must do so at the level of a deeper purpose of the code (that is, through appropriation at a different level of generality).

The Reasons for the Rules

In an interesting study of the purpose and force of rules, Thomas Schelling considers "rules we enforce on ourselves," as opposed to those imposed and enforced on us by others.[7] The hermeneutical rules I have described are rules that carry force, if at all, only if we enforce them on ourselves. The question is why we should devise and hold ourselves to such rules. I have in view *shared* rules. Why should we adopt and enforce shared hermeneutical rules on ourselves?

As pointed out in the introduction, one reason for shared hermeneutical rules has to do with consistency. Hermeneutical rules are one way we promote consistency and fairness in our use of scripture. If I insist that the Levitical rule against homosexual practice should be taken according to its letter but that the dominical rule of selling all and giving the proceeds to the poor should be interpreted according to its intent (and therefore with due attention to cultural differences between Jesus' time and our own), am I being consistent in my use of scripture? Can I be consistent without operating by some kind of hermeneutical rule? The answer is no. I may opt for some *other* hermeneutical rule than the rule of purpose or the rule of the letter to deal with the question of how to treat the Levitical teaching about homoerotic practice in a way that is consistent with how I appropriate Jesus' call to poverty. But, whatever my approach to consistency, it will lend itself to formulation of a hermeneutical rule of some kind or other.

The intrinsic link between consistency and rules does not mean that any hermeneutical rule I may formulate will be analyzable in a critical-rational fashion. I may declare as my hermeneutical rule that I always follow the "leading of the Spirit" in my interpretations and appropriations of scripture. If by "leading of the Spirit" I mean an event of illumination that stands outside any testing by shared norms, then my rule may be consistent but it does not count as a *shared* hermeneutical rule.

A second reason for shared hermeneutical rules has to do with their function as assumptions enabling the church to function as a responsible moral agent through community deliberation, which includes persuasion

---

7. Thomas Schelling gives many examples of the practical reasons for giving rules to ourselves. See Thomas C. Schelling, "Enforcing Rules on Oneself," *Journal of Law, Economics & Organization* 1 (1985): 357-74.

and accountability. Without shared assumptions about appropriate ways of appealing to scripture, we can't influence, much less persuade one another, by our arguments from scripture. Nor can we meaningfully challenge one another's appeals to scripture. As a result, we are not accountable to other Christians for our uses of scripture. Without shared hermeneutical rules, everyone's interpretation is equally valid for the vapid reason that no interpretation can be tested. Everyone's interpretation is equally valid and equally powerless to contribute to any progress in understanding or judgment.

Other Rules

The five rules surveyed in this study are not the only hermeneutical rules by which modern Christians interpret and appropriate scripture. They are simply prime examples of how the conditions of modernity (and postmodernity) have shaped appeals to scripture in moral argument. What follows are some brief examples of other hermeneutical rules.

Rules of Discrimination

A longstanding type of hermeneutical rule goes under the contemporary name of "canon-within-the canon." Positing an inner canon is a substantive means of differentiating between those parts of scripture that carry authority and those that do not — or for judging the *degree to which* this or that scriptural witness has a claim on the church. Luther's dictum that the highest norm in scripture is "that which promotes [*treibet*] Christ" is perhaps the most famous example. Moreover, the doctrine of justification by faith has been treated by many within and without the Lutheran tradition as a key to discern the promotion of Christ in scripture. In the last thirty years or so, various liberationist canons have also emerged as hermeneutical norms. A particularly bold example is James Cone's assertion in *The God of the Oppressed* that Christ as liberator of black people and known as such by black people in their interpretation of the Bible is a critical norm for theology today.[1] Another example is the feminist position that women's experience is a norm for discerning what in the tradition, including the Bible, is theologically valid. "Women's experience" includes women's self-knowledge of their equality and rights to equality with men. "What promotes women's liberation" in this sense becomes a basic hermeneutical norm for judging and appropriating the tradition.

I have not treated canon-within-the-canon hermeneutics in this study since they have received so much discussion by others over the years. However, the rule of moral-theological adjudication has affinities with canon-within-the-canon approaches. Nevertheless, it is important to see the difference between the postmodern rule of moral-theological adjudication and the concept of a canon-within-the-canon. The rule of moral-theological adjudication applies to competing *interpretations* of scripture, not competing *parts* of scripture. Thus, the rule of moral-theological adjudication helps one to judge between mutually exclusive but more or less equally plausible interpretations of, say, Paul's teaching about government in Romans 13, while a canon-within-the-canon may lead one to opt for the Apocalypse against Romans 13 on the question of the church's obligations to "Caesar." However, if the question is posed, "What is the witness of the Bible *as a whole* on the question of the church's relation to government?" then a canon-within-the-canon hermeneutic and the postmodern rule of adjudication may operate in very similar ways.

The Weight of Scripture as a Whole

It is common for many who acknowledge diversity in scripture to argue for a particular moral or theological position on the basis of the weight of scripture as a whole, understood as what the majority of the biblical writings teach and (or) what is most central to scripture. Thus, Richard Hays argues for Christian pacifism by observing that the New Testament, with very few exceptions (perhaps only one), stands unequivocally on the side of non-violence and that non-violence is also central to the teaching of Jesus and the New Testament ethic of discipleship in the way of the cross.[2]

---

1. James H. Cone, *The God of the Oppressed* ([no city]: Seabury Press, 1974), 16-29.
2. Richard B. Hays, *The Moral Vision of the New Testament: Community, Cross, New*

Related to these considerations is that of proportion. For example, in an article on the church and homosexuality, Luke Timothy Johnson asks "whether the church's concentration on sexual behavior corresponds proportionally to the modest emphasis placed by scripture."[3]

It may seem obvious that the weight of scripture — with its dimensions of majority voice, centrality, and proportionality — should be decisive in defining the authoritative voice of scripture on a particular topic. However, the rule of countercultural witness challenges this assumption by according special significance to peripheral, minority voices in scripture. Moroever, there are ways of defining centrality that put centrality in tension with majority. For example, Bruce Birch calls for giving precedence to the Old Testament's "broader vision" against certain "morally objectionable perspectives" in scripture, such as slavery and patriarchy.[4] According to Birch, the broader perspective of "love, justice, and wholeness" is likely to lead us to positions that "go beyond what the biblical community could have imagined."[5] This is really a rule of higher generality, which gives greater importance to those general principles that can be said to be central to scripture than to specific moral teachings that have pervasive support in scripture.

Relevance

Another hermeneutical rule is the preacher's axiom that scripture must be interpreted as far as possible in ways that make it relevant, meaningful, practical. This rule is in effect when preachers judge between competing interpretations within biblical scholarship (e.g., in the commentaries) by considering, as at least one factor, which interpretations best lend themselves to contemporary application. The cliche, "Will it preach?" expresses

---

Creation: A Contemporary Introduction to New Testament Ethics (San Francisco: HarperSanFrancisco, 1996), 317-46.

3. Luke Timothy Johnson, "Debate and Discernment, Scripture and the Spirit," in *Virtues and Practices in the Christian Tradition: Christian Ethics after MacIntyre*, ed. Nancey Murphy, Brad J. Kallenberg, and Mark Thiessen Nation (Harrisburg, PA: Trinity Press International, 1997), 218.

4. Bruce C. Birch, *Let Justice Roll Down: The Old Testament, Ethics, and Christian Life* (Louisville, KY: Westminster/John Knox, 1991), 42-43.

5. Birch, *Let Justice Roll Down*, 43.

this hermeneutical norm. Behind this question is the assumption that the Bible does preach and therefore that interpretations that radically distance the biblical text from contemporary life are suspect. Daniel Patte's criterion of "plausibility" is a rule of relevance.[6] The rule of relevance is in fact an ancient rule, as James Kugel and John Barton have recently pointed out.[7]

Rules of Canonical Interpretation

Other hermeneutical rules may be described as "canonical," because they derive either from the assumption that scripture is a kind of whole, producing "canonical effects," or from observations about the "canonical process," the way in which authoritative traditions were interpreted and used in ancient Israel and the church, including interpretive intertextuality within the Bible itself.

Rules of Canonical Structure

"Interpret scripture according to its overall shape and structure" is an axiom of newer canonical approaches with antecedents in older approaches to scripture. The traditional conception of the Christian Bible as consisting of "Old" and "New" Testaments imparts a structure to scripture that has encouraged subordinating its first "Old Testament" part to its second "New Testament" part. The structure of the Bible has also invited salvation-history interpretations in which the story of redemption moves from creation through the covenants with the patriarchs and the people of Israel to the coming of the Messiah and on to a final new creation. Salvation-history patterns are, of course, dependent on the content of scripture, but we perhaps underestimate how our sense that scripture tells a story of redemption is shaped by the placement of Genesis at the beginning of the collection, Revelation at the end, and the arrangement of the other books in something of a chronological order according to the time they purport to describe.

6. See the discussion of Patte in chapter five.
7. See below under "Historical Rules as Hermeneutical Rules."

Brevard Childs has called for a methodologically rigorous investigation of canonical structure with attention paid to the canonical shaping and arrangement of biblical books.[8] Older material is incorporated into a new framework (Judges); a closing redactional commentary provides a particular theological perspective on the whole (Ecclesiastes); separate literary units are woven into a single literary whole (Philippians).[9] Arrangement of books is another form of canonical shape. For example, according to Childs, the grouping of Matthew, Mark, Luke, and John as a fourfold witness to the person and mission of Jesus has the following canonical effect: "the unity [of these witnesses] is asserted but never established in a fixed literary form. . . . the unity must be determined from reading the four, but no one definitive entrance — neither literary, nor historical, nor theological — has been established by the shape of the canonical text."[10] At a larger and more complicated level, the creation and joining of the two Testaments puts these two bodies of writings in a mutually interpretive relation.[11]

A basic question about the rule of interpretation according to canonical shape and structure is whether this is another form of historical-intentionalist interpretation or a kind of non-intentionalist literary criticism (along the lines of New Criticism or other post-structuralist approaches). Childs speaks in ways that suggest his approach is both historical-intentionalist and literary non-intentionalist. This may not be a fatal confusion, but the credibility of canonical interpretation depends at least in part on clarification of questions about locus of meaning and the epistemological status of unintended meaning.[12]

8. See Brevard S. Childs, *Biblical Theology of the Old and New Testaments: Theological Reflection on the Christian Bible* (Minneapolis: Fortress Press, 1992), 73-77.

9. Childs, *Biblical Theology of the Old and New Testaments*, 73.

10. Brevard S. Childs, *Introduction to the New Testament as Scripture* (Philadelphia: Fortress Press, 1984), 155-56.

11. Childs, *Biblical Theology of the Old and New Testaments*, 77.

12. On this and related issues in canonical interpretation, see Mark G. Brett's excellent study, *Biblical Criticism in Crisis: The Impact of the Canonical Approach on Old Testament Studies* (Cambridge: Cambridge University Press, 1991).

Rules of Canonical Context

Scripture can also be conceived as a "context," inviting inferences about how the larger whole of scripture suggests ways to interpret a given book. According to Childs, in some cases the mere placement of a writing in the canon suggests a new way in which it is to be read (Daniel and Romans).[13] Attending to canonical context — local or general — leads to perceptions of canonical effects, intentional or not, produced by the inclusion of so many diverse pieces of literature within the same collection.

For example, the tendency for the prophetic literature to use rhetoric of absolute judgment, only to open up new hope beyond judgment, can be taken as suggesting that all judgment language in scripture is susceptible to prophetic qualification and openness. Richard Hays draws a canonical inference of this sort. Having observed that the Gospel of Matthew pronounces a final word of judgment against Israel, Hays goes on to propose that we take this word of judgment "as analogous to prophetic judgment oracles, such as those of Amos and Jeremiah, which declare God's irrevocable sentence of destruction on Israel."[14] Although these judgment verdicts are stated as irreversible and absolute, they "never mark the absolute end of the people or of God's dealing with them. Always on the horizon is the word of promise and the hope of restoration, whether later in the same book, as in the surprising ending of Amos, or elsewhere in the canon, as in Isaiah 40–66."[15] This proposal in effect formulates a synthetic hermeneutical rule of prophetic qualification and openness, applicable to all prophetic words in scripture, including apocalyptic ones.[16] In a similar vein, I have argued that all of Paul's apocalyptic pronouncements become contingent prophecy, by virtue of their relocation into the context of scripture.[17]

13. Childs, *Biblical Theology of the Old and New Testaments*, 73.

14. Hays, *The Moral Vision of the New Testament*, 433.

15. Hays, *The Moral Vision of the New Testament*, 434.

16. Hays remarks that his interpretation "does not depend on a claim about Matthew's intention; it depends instead upon locating Matthew within a wider canonical frame of reference" (*The Moral Vision of the New Testament*, 434).

17. Charles H. Cosgrove, *Elusive Israel: The Puzzle of Election in Romans* (Louisville, KY: Westminster/John Knox, 1997), 56-64.

Interpretive Modification

Historical studies of the way in which authoritative tradition was used in ancient Israel and the church (including the evidence of inner-biblical interpretation) have shown that ancient interpreters exercised considerable freedom. A canonical rule often derived from this evidence is that the canon itself warrants freedom of interpretation, sanctioning creative dissent and modification.[18]

Two related questions confronted by this rule are (1) whether it can be defended from the biblical tradition when we are probably not prepared to adopt the specific ancient hermeneutical methods by which much of the creative reinterpretation was done within that tradition and (2) whether interpretive freedom can be cast as a hermeneutical *rule*, rather than simply as hermeneutical license.

Historical Rules as Hermeneutical Rules

In his erudite apology for the historical-critical method, Edgar Krentz remarks that "[h]istorical criticism provides a way for the Scriptures to exercise their *proper critical function* for the church."[19] This statement articulates a pervasive assumption of historical criticism in biblical studies since the Enlightenment: the true meaning of scripture for the church is the meaning established solely by historical methods.

The modern historical approach to scripture challenged the traditional hermeneutics of the medieval and ancient church. For example, four common hermeneutical assumptions of ancient Jewish and Christian interpretation — assumptions that persisted up to the modern period (and beyond) — were rejected as *hermeneutically invalid* by many advocates of the historical approach. John Barton expresses these ancient assumptions about scripture as hermeneutical imperatives: (1) read scrip-

---

18. "The canon does not speak in a single voice. . . . That the biblical communities themselves can be seen judging and reinterpreting and measuring the tradition against their own experience of God can be read as a support for similar activity on our part." Bruce C. Birch and Larry L. Rasmussen, *Bible and Ethics in the Christian Life,* rev. and expanded ed. (Minneapolis: Augsburg Fortress, 1989), 174.

19. Edgar Krentz, *The Historical-Critical Method* (Philadelphia: Fortress Press, 1975), 65.

ture as profound, not trivial; (2) read scripture as universally relevant; (3) read biblical books as self-consistent; (4) read scripture as full of mystery beyond its surface, literal meaning.[20] One or more of these hermeneutical imperatives may be wrongheaded, but their legitimacy for a theological hermeneutic cannot be settled on purely historical grounds. Whether one should use a historical or an ahistorical hermeneutic (or some combination of historical and nonhistorical methods) cannot be decided on purely historical grounds because answering this question requires a judgment about the nature of the Bible *as scripture,* a judgment that cannot be made, except in a question-begging form, by *treating* the Bible exclusively as a collection of historical documents.

Hence, when one advocates the historical method as the only appropriate approach to the text's true meaning as scripture, one has, in effect, turned historical rules of interpretation into hermeneutical rules. Examples are: interpret each passage of scripture only in the light of its indigenous literary context (not in the light of other parts of scripture); accord theological validity only to what actually happened, not to what is reputed to have happened but did not in fact happen; locate the meaning of texts only in the verbal intentions of their authors. I do not claim that everyone who uses the historical method as a theological hermeneutic holds to these three principles, which are simply examples of some typical assumptions. Nor do I mean to suggest that historical methods have no place in a theological hermeneutic. On the contrary, I think they emphatically do have a place (and this study has assumed their validity). I aim only to point out that there is a difference between historical exegesis as one of the tools of historical knowledge and historical exegesis as a theological hermeneutic for interpreting the Bible as scripture.

20. John Barton, *Holy Writings, Sacred Text: The Canon in Early Christianity* (Louisville, KY: Westminster/John Knox Press, 1997), 134-45.

Works Cited

Adeney, Bernard T. *Strange Virtues: Ethics in a Multicultural World.* Downers Grove, IL: InterVarsity Press, 1995.

Aiken, Henry David. "Levels of Moral Discourse." In *Reason and Conduct: New Bearings in Moral Philosophy,* 65-87. New York: Alfred A. Knopf, 1962.

Amar, Akhil Reed, and Daniel Widawsky. "Child Abuse as Slavery: A Thirteenth Amendment Response to DeShaney." *Harvard Law Review* 105 (1992): 1359-86.

Aptheker, Herbert, ed. *A Documentary History of the Negro People in the United States.* Vol. 1, *From Colonial Times through the Civil War.* New York: Carol Publishing Group, 1990.

Augustine, *De Doctrina Christiana.* Edited and trans. by R. P. H. Green. London: Clarendon Press, 1995.

Baer, Richard A., Jr. *Philo's Use of the Categories Male and Female.* Leiden: E. J. Brill, 1970.

Balch, David L. "Concluding Observations by the Editor, Including a Comparison of Christian with Jewish Interpretation." In *Homosexuality, Science, and the "Plain Sense" of Scripture,* ed. David L. Balch. Grand Rapids: Wm. B. Eerdmans, 2000.

Barker, Stephen. *The Elements of Logic.* 2d ed. New York: McGraw-Hill, 1974.

Barr, James. *The Concept of Biblical Theology: An Old Testament Perspective.* Minneapolis: Fortress Press, 1999.

Barth, Karl. "Von der Paradoxie des 'positiven Paradoxes': Antworten und Fragen an Paul Tillich." In *Anfänge der dialektischen Theologie.* Part 1, 2d ed. Edited by Jürgen Moltmann. Munich: Chr. Kaiser Verlag, 1966.

Barthes, Roland. "Requichot et son corps." In *L'obvie et l'obtus: Essais Critiques III.* Paris: Suil, 1982.

————. *Writing Degree Zero.* Translated by Annette Lavers and Colin Smith. New York: Hill and Wang, 1968.

Barton, John. *Ethics and the Old Testament.* Harrisburg, PA: Trinity Press International, 1998.

————. *Holy Writings, Sacred Text: The Canon in Early Christianity.* Louisville, KY: Westminster/John Knox Press, 1997.

Bassler, Jouette M. *1 Timothy, 2 Timothy, Titus.* Abingdon New Testament Commentaries. Nashville: Abingdon, 1996.

Beker, J. Christiaan. *Paul the Apostle: The Triumph of God in Life and Thought.* Philadelphia: Fortress Press, 1980.

Betz, Hans Dieter. *The Sermon on the Mount: A Commentary on the Sermon on the Mount, including the Sermon on the Plain (Matthew 5:3–7:27 and Luke 6:20-49).* Edited by Adela Yarbro Collins. Hermeneia. Minneapolis: Augsburg Fortress, 1995.

Birch, Bruce C. *Let Justice Roll Down: The Old Testament, Ethics, and Christian Life.* Louisville, KY: Westminster/John Knox, 1991.

Birch, Bruce C., and Larry L. Rasmussen. *Bible and Ethics in the Christian Life.* Rev. and enl. ed. Minneapolis: Augsburg Fortress, 1989.

Blenkinsopp, Joseph. *Wisdom and Law in the Old Testament: The Ordering of Life in Israel and Early Judaism.* Oxford: Oxford University Press, 1995.

Block, Daniel I. *The Book of Ezekiel, Chapters 1–24.* The New International Commentary on the Old Testament. Grand Rapids: Wm. B. Eerdmans, 1997.

Bonhoeffer, Dietrich. *Letters and Papers from Prison.* Enl. ed. Edited by Eberhard Bethge. New York: Macmillan, 1972.

Borchert, Gerald L. "1 Corinthians 7:15 and the Church's Historic Misunderstanding of Divorce and Remarriage." *Review and Expositor* 96 (1999): 125-29.

Bornkamm, Günther. "Das Doppelgebot der Liebe." In *Neutestamentliche Studien für Rudolf Bultmann* (2nd ed.), 85-93. Berlin: Alfred Töpelmann, 1957.

Boswell, John. *Christianity, Social Tolerance, and Homosexuality: Gay People in Western Europe from the Beginning of the Christian Era to the Fourteenth Century.* Chicago and London: The University of Chicago Press, 1980.

Boyarin, Daniel. *A Radical Jew: Paul and the Politics of Identity.* Berkeley and Los Angeles: University of California Press, 1994.

Brennan, William J., Jr. "The Constitution of the United States: Contemporary Ratification." In *Interpreting the Constitution: The Debate over Original Intent,* ed. Jack N. Rakove, 23-34. Boston: Northeastern University Press, 1990.

Brett, Mark G. *Biblical Criticism in Crisis: The Impact of the Canonical Approach on Old Testament Studies.* Cambridge: Cambridge University Press, 1991.

Bright, Pamela. *The Book of Rules of Tyconius: Its Purpose and Logic.* Notre Dame, IN: University of Notre Dame Press, 1988.

Brooten, Bernadette J. *Love Between Women: Early Christian Responses to Female Homoeroticism.* Chicago: University of Chicago Press, 1996.

————. "Paul's Views on the Nature of Women and Female Eroticism." In *Immaculate Conception: The Female in Sacred Image and Social Reality,* ed. Clarissa W.

Atkinson et al., 61-87. Harvard Women's Studies in Religion. Boston: Beacon, 1985.

Brueggemann, Walter. *Theology of the Old Testament: Testimony, Dispute, Advocacy.* Minneapolis: Fortress Press, 1997.

————. "Trajectories in Old Testament Literature and the Sociology of Ancient Israel." *Journal of Biblical Literature* 98 (1979): 161-85.

Bultmann, Rudolf. "New Testament and Mythology: The Mythological Element in the Message of the New Testament and the Problem of Its Re-interpretation." In *Kerygma and Myth*, vol. 1. Edited by Hans Werner Bartsch. Translated by Reginald Fuller. New York: Harper & Row, 1961.

Calvin, John. *Ioannis Calvini opera quae supersunt omnia.* Edited by W. Baum, E. Cunitz, and E. Reuss. 59 vols. Braunschweig: C. A. Schwetschke and Son, 1863-1900.

Cardozo, Benjamin. *The Nature of the Judicial Process.* New Haven: Yale University Press, 1921.

Catechism of the Catholic Church. English translation. Washington, D.C.: United States Catholic Conference, 1994.

Childress, James F. "Scripture and Ethics: Some Reflections on the Role of Scripture in Moral Deliberation and Justification." *Interpretation* 34 (1980): 371-80.

Childs, Brevard S. *Biblical Theology in Crisis.* Philadelphia: Westminster Press, 1970.

————. *Biblical Theology of the Old and New Testaments: Theological Reflection on the Christian Bible.* Minneapolis: Fortress Press, 1992.

————. *Introduction to the New Testament as Scripture.* Philadelphia: Fortress Press, 1984.

Clarke, D. S., Jr. *Practical Inferences.* London: Routledge & Kegan Paul, 1985.

Cohen, H. H. "Usury." *Encyclopaedia Judaica*, vol. 16. New York: Macmillan, 1971.

Cole, Stephen. "Voodoo Sociology: Recent Developments in the Sociology of Science." In *The Flight from Science and Reason*, ed. Paul R. Gross, Norman Levitt, and Martin W. Lewis, 274-87. New York: The New York Academy of Sciences, 1997.

Collins, John J. "The Exodus and Biblical Theology." *Biblical Theology Bulletin* 25 (1995): 152-60.

Condit, Celeste Michel, and John Louis Lucaites. *Crafting Equality: America's Anglo-African Word.* Chicago: University of Chicago Press, 1993.

Cosgrove, Charles H. "The Declaration of Independence in Constitutional Interpretation: A Selective History and Analysis." *University of Richmond Law Review* 32 (1998): 107-64.

————. *Elusive Israel: The Puzzle of Election in Romans.* Louisville: Westminster/ John Knox Press, 1997.

————. "The Justification of the Other: An Interpretation of Rom. 1:18–4:25." In *Society of Biblical Literature 1992 Seminar Papers*, ed. Eugene H. Lovering. Atlanta: Scholars Press, 1992.

————. "Rhetorical Suspense in Romans: A Study in Polyvalence and Hermeneutical Election." *Journal of Biblical Literature* 115 (1996): 271-87.

———, ed. *The Meanings We Choose: Hermeneutical Ethics and the Conflict of Inter-pretations*. Sheffield: Sheffield Academic Press, forthcoming.

Cosgrove, Joseph K. "Technology, Philosophy, and the Mastery of Nature." Ph.D. diss., Catholic University of America, 1996.

Cox, Archibald. *The Court and the Constitution*. Boston: Houghton Mifflin, 1987.

Crapanzano, Vincent. *Serving the Word: Literalism in America from the Pulpit to the Bench*. New York: The New Press, 2000.

Crenshaw, James L. "Ecclesiastes." In *Harper's Bible Commentary*, ed. by James L. Mays. San Francisco: Harper & Row, 1988.

———. *Old Testament Wisdom: An Introduction*. Atlanta: John Knox, 1981.

———. *Prophetic Conflict: Its Effects upon Israelite Religion*. Berlin and New York: Walter de Gruyter, 1971.

———. "The Wisdom Literature." In *The Hebrew Bible and Its Modern Interpreters*, ed. Douglas A. Knight and Gene M. Tucker, 369-407. Minneapolis: Fortress Press, 1985; Atlanta: Scholars Press, 1985.

Dahl, Nils A. "Trinitarian Baptismal Creeds and New Testament Christology." In *Jesus the Christ: The Historical Origins of Christological Doctrine*, ed. Donald H. Juel. Minneapolis: Fortress Press, 1991.

Davies, W. D., and Dale C. Allison, Jr. *A Critical and Exegetical Commentary on the Gospel according to Matthew*. 3 vols. The International Critical Commentary. Edinburgh: T. & T. Clark, 1988-1997.

Donaldson, Terence L. "The Law That Hangs (Matthew 22:40): Rabbinic Formulation and Matthean Social World." *Catholic Biblical Quarterly* 57 (1995): 689-709.

Douglas, Mary. *Purity and Danger: An Analysis of Concepts of Pollution and Taboo*. London: Routledge & Kegan Paul, 1966.

Douglass, Frederick. *The Life and Writings of Frederick Douglass*. Edited by Philip S. Foner. 5 vols. New York: International Publishers, 1950-75.

Doyle, James A., and Michele A. Paludi, *Sex and Gender: The Human Experience*. 2d ed. Dubuque, IA: Wm. C. Brown Publishers, 1991.

Dworkin, Ronald. *Law's Empire*. Cambridge, MA: Harvard University Press, 1986.

———. "The Model of Rules." *The University of Chicago Law Review* 35 (1967): 14-46. Reprinted in *Taking Rights Seriously*. Cambridge, MA: Harvard University Press, 1977.

Eco, Umberto. *Interpretation and Overinterpretation*. With Richard Rorty, Jonathan Culler, and Christine Brooke-Rose. Edited by Stefan Collini. Cambridge: Cambridge University Press, 1992.

———. *The Limits of Interpretation*. Bloomington, IN: Indiana University Press, 1990.

Edel, Abraham. *Ethical Judgment: The Use of Science in Ethics*. Glencoe, IL: The Free Press, 1955.

Eichrodt, Walter. "Does Old Testament Theology Still Have Independent Significance within Old Testament Scholarship?" In *The Flowering of Old Testament*

Theology, ed. Ben C. Ollenburger, Elmer A. Martens, and Gerhard F. Hasel, 30-39. Winona Lake, IN: Eisenbrauns, 1992.

————. *Theology of the Old Testament*. Vol. 1. Translated by J. A. Baker. Philadelphia: Westminster Press, 1961; London: SCM Press, 1961.

Ernesti, Johann August. *Elementary Principles of Interpretation*. 3d ed. Translated by Moses Stuart. Andover: Gould & Newman, 1938.

Evans, Donald. "Paul Ramsey on Exceptionless Moral Rules." In *Faith, Authenticity and Morality*, 160-96. Toronto: University of Toronto Press, 1980.

Fausto-Sterling, Anne. *Myths of Gender: Biological Theories about Women and Men*. New York: Basic Books, 1985.

Fierro, Alfredo. "Exodus Event and Interpretation in Political Theologies." In *The Bible and Liberation: Political and Social Hermeneutics* (rev. ed.), ed. Norman K. Gottwald, 473-81. Maryknoll, NY: Orbis Books, 1983.

Finley, M. I. *Ancient History: Evidence and Models*. New York: Viking Penguin, 1986.

————. *Ancient Slavery and Modern Ideology*. New York: Penguin, 1980.

————. "Utopianism Ancient and Modern." In *The Use and Abuse of History*. New York: Viking Press, 1975.

Firmage. Edwin. "Zoology." *Anchor Bible Dictionary* 6: 1124-25. New York: Doubleday, 1992.

Fishbane, Michael. *Biblical Interpretation in Ancient Israel*. Paperback edition with new material. Oxford: Clarendon Press, 1988.

Fletcher, Joseph. *Situation Ethics: The New Morality*. Philadelphia: The Westminster Press, 1966.

Florovsky, Georges. "The Function of Tradition in the Ancient Church." In *Bible, Church, Tradition: An Eastern Orthodox View*. Belmont, MA: Norland Publishing Company, 1972.

Fowl, Stephen E. *Engaging Scripture: A Model for Theological Interpretation*. Malden, MA and Oxford, UK: Blackwell, 1998.

Fowl, Stephen E., and L. Gregory Jones, *Reading in Communion: Scripture and Ethics in Christian Life*. Grand Rapids: Wm. B. Eerdmans, 1991.

Frei, Hans W. "The 'Literal Reading' of Biblical Narrative in the Christian Tradition: Does It Stretch or Will It Break?" In *The Bible and the Narrative Tradition*, ed. Frank McConnell, 36-77. New York: Oxford University Press, 1986.

Furnish, Victor Paul. "The Bible and Homosexuality: Reading the Texts in Context." In *Homosexuality in the Church: Both Sides of the Debate*, ed. Jeffrey S. Siker, 18-38. Louisville, KY: Westminster/John Knox, 1994.

————. *The Moral Teaching of Paul: Selected Issues*. 2d ed. Nashville: Abingdon, 1985.

Gabler, Johann Philipp. "An Oration on the Proper Distinction between Biblical and Dogmatic Theology and the Specific Objectives of Each." Translated by John Sandys-Wunsch and Laurence Eldridge. *The Scottish Journal of Theology* 33 (1980): 133-44.

Gadamer, Hans Georg. *Truth and Method*. 2d ed. New York: Continuum, 1989.

Gager, John G. *Moses in Greco-Roman Paganism*. Nashville: Abingdon, 1972.

Gardner, Anne. "Genesis 2:4b–3: A Mythological Paradigm of Sexual Equality or of the Religious History of Pre-Exilic Israel?" *Scottish Journal of Theology* 43 (1990): 1-18.

Gaston, Lloyd. "Paul and the Torah." In *Paul and the Torah*. Vancouver: University of British Columbia Press, 1987.

Gerber, Scott. *To Secure These Rights: The Declaration of Independence and Constitutional Interpretation*. New York: New York University Press, 1995.

Gerhardsson, Birger. "The Hermeneutic Program in Matthew 22:37-40." In *Jews, Greeks, and Christians*, ed. R. Hammerton-Kelly and Robin Scroggs, 129-50. Leiden: E. J. Brill, 1976.

Gese, Hartmut. "Tradition and Biblical Theology." In *Tradition and Theology in the Old Testament*, ed. Douglas A. Knight, 301-26. Philadelphia: Fortress, 1977.

Gilkey, Langdon. *Religion and the Scientific Future: Reflections on Myth, Science, and Theology*. New York: Harper & Row, 1970.

Goetz, Ronald. "Confessions of an Academic Liberationist: Riding the Tiger of Liberation." In *Standing with the Poor: Theological Reflections on Economic Reality*, ed. Paul Plenge Parker, 60-81. Cleveland: The Pilgrim Press, 1992.

Goppelt, Leonhard. *Theology of the New Testament*. Vol. 2, *The Variety and Unity of the Apostolic Witness to Christ*. Edited by Jürgen Roloff. Translated by John E. Alsup. Grand Rapids: Wm. B. Eerdmans, 1982.

Gottwald, Norman K. *The Tribes of Yahweh: A Sociology of the Religion of Liberated Israel, 1250-1050 B.C.E.* Maryknoll, NY: Orbis Books, 1979.

Grafton, Anthony. *New Worlds, Ancient Texts: The Power of Tradition and the Shock of Discovery*. Cambridge, MA: Harvard University Press, 1992.

Gunkel, Hermann. *Schöpfung und Chaos in Urzeit und Endzeit: Eine religionsgeschichtliche Untersuchung über Gen 1 und Ap Joh 12*. Göttingen: Vandenhoeck und Ruprecht, 1895.

Gustafson, James M. "Context versus Principles: A Misplaced Debate in Christian Ethics." *Harvard Theological Review* 58 (1965): 170-202.

———. "The Place of Scripture in Christian Ethics: A Methodological Study." *Interpretation* 24 (October 1970): 430-55. Reprinted in James M. Gustafson. *Theology and Ethics*. Philadelphia: United Church Press, 1974.

Gutiérrez, Gustavo. *Teología desde el reverso de la historia*. Lima: CEP, 1977.

———. *A Theology of Liberation: History, Politics and Salvation*. Translated and edited by Sister Caridad Inda and John Eagleson. Maryknoll, NY: Orbis, 1983.

Habermas, Jürgen. *Moral Consciousness and Communicative Action*. Translated by Christian Lenhardt and Shierry Weber Nicholsen. Cambridge, MA: The MIT Press, 1996.

Hägglund, Bengt. "Die Bedeutung der 'regula fidei' als Grundlage theologischer Aussagen." *Studia Theologica* 12 (1958): 1-44.

Hanson, Paul D. *The Dawn of Apocalyptic*. Philadelphia: Fortress Press, 1975.

———. *The People Called: The Growth of Community in the Bible*. San Francisco: Harper & Row, 1986.

———. "The Theological Significance of Contradiction within the Book of the Covenant." In *Canon and Authority: Essays in Old Testament Religion and Theology*, ed. George W. Coats and Burke O. Long, 110-31. Philadelphia: Fortress Press, 1977.

Hanson, R. P. C. *Tradition in the Early Church*. Philadelphia: The Westminster Press, 1962.

Hare, R. M. *The Language of Morals*. Oxford: Clarendon Press, 1952.

Harrelson, Walter. *The Ten Commandments and Human Rights*. Philadelphia: Fortress Press, 1980.

Hartlich, Christian, and Walter Sachs. *Der Ursprung des Mythosbegriffes in der modernen Bibelwissenschaft*. Tübingen: J. C. B. Mohr (Paul Siebeck), 1952.

Hasel, Gerhard F. "The Future of Old Testament Theology: Prospects and Trends." In *The Flowering of Old Testament Theology: A Reader in Twentieth-Century Old Testament Theology, 1930-1990*, ed. Ben C. Ollenburger et al., 373-83. Winona Lake, IN: Eisenbrauns, 1992.

Hays, Richard B. *The Moral Vision of the New Testament: Community, Cross, New Creation: A Contemporary Introduction to New Testament Ethics*. San Francisco: HarperSanFrancisco, 1996.

Heisenberg, Werner. *The Physicist's Conception of Nature*. Translated by Arnold J. Pomerans. New York: Harcourt Brace, 1958.

Hennepin, Father Louis. *A New Discovery of a Vast Country in America*. Vol. 2. Chicago: A. C. McClurg, 1903; reprint of 1698 London edition.

Hirsch, E. D., Jr. "Counterfactuals in Interpretation." In *Interpreting Law and Literature: A Hermeneutic Reader*, ed. Sanford Levinson and Steven Mailloux, 55-68. Evanston, IL: Northwestern University Press, 1988.

———. "Three Dimensions of Hermeneutics." In *The Aims of Interpretation*. Chicago and London: The University of Chicago Press, 1976.

———. *Validity in Interpretation*. New Haven, CT: Yale University Press, 1967.

Holladay, William L. *Long Ago God Spoke: How Christians May Hear the Old Testament Today*. Minneapolis: Augsburg Fortress Press, 1995.

Jasanoff, Sheila, et al., eds. *Handbook of Science and Technology Studies*. Thousand Oaks, CA: Sage Publications, 1995.

Jeanrond, Werner G. *Texts and Interpretation as Categories of Theological Thinking*. Translated by Thomas J. Wilson. New York: Crossroad, 1988.

Jewett, Paul K. *Man as Male and Female: A Study in Sexual Relationships from a Theological Point of View*. Grand Rapids: Wm. B. Eerdmans, 1975.

Johnson, Luke Timothy. "Debate and Discernment, Scripture and the Spirit." *Commonweal* (January 1994): 11-13. Reprinted in *Virtues and Practices in the Christian Tradition: Christian Ethics after MacIntyre*, ed. Nancey Murphy, Brad J. Kallenberg, and Mark Thiessen Nation, 215-20. Harrisburg, PA: Trinity Press International, 1997.

———. *1 Timothy, 2 Timothy, Titus*. John Knox Preaching Guides. Atlanta: John Knox, 1987.

Jones, Scott J. *John Wesley's Conception and Use of Scripture*. Nashville, TN: Kingswood Books, 1995.

Jonsen, Albert R., and Stephen Toulmin. *The Abuse of Casuistry: A History of Moral Reasoning.* Berkeley: University of California Press, 1988.

Kaiser, Walter C., Jr. *Toward Old Testament Ethics.* Grand Rapids: Zondervan, 1983.

Käsemann, Ernst. "The Problem of the Historical Jesus." In *Essays on New Testament Themes.* Translated by W. J. Montague. Philadelphia: Fortress Press, 1982.

Kaser, Max. *Roman Private Law.* 4th ed. Translated by Rolf Dannenbring. Pretoria: University of South Africa, 1984.

Keck, Leander E. *Paul and His Letters.* Proclamation Commentaries. Philadelphia: Fortress Press, 1979.

Kelsey, David H. *The Uses of Scripture in Recent Theology.* Philadelphia: Fortress Press, 1975. Reprinted as *Proving Doctrine: The Uses of Scripture in Modern Theology.* Harrisburg, PA: Trinity Press International, 1999.

Kennington, Richard. "The 'Teaching of Nature' in Descartes' Soul Doctrine." *Review of Metaphysics* 26 (1977): 86-117.

Klatt, Werner. *Hermann Gunkel: Zu seiner Theologie der Religionsgeschichte und zur Entstehung der formgeschichtlichen Methode.* Göttingen: Vandenhoeck & Ruprecht, 1969.

Kleppner, Daniel. "Physics and Common Sense." In *The Flight from Science and Reason,* ed. Paul R. Gross, Norman Levitt, and Martin W. Lewis, 126-30. New York: The New York Academy of Sciences, 1997.

Kornfeld, Walter. "Die Unreinen Tiere im Alten Testament." In *Wissenschaft im Dienste des Glaubens: Festschrift für ABT Dr. Hermann Peichl,* ed. J. Kisser et al., 11-27. Vienna: Catholic Academy of Vienna, 1965.

Krentz, Edgar. *The Historical-Critical Method.* Philadelphia: Fortress Press, 1975.

Kugel, James L. *Traditions of the Bible: A Guide to the Bible as It Was at the Start of the Common Era.* Cambridge, MA: Harvard University Press, 1998.

Kuhn, Thomas S. *The Copernican Revolution: Planetary Astronomy in the Development of Western Thought.* Cambridge, MA: Harvard University Press, 1957.

———. *The Structure of Scientific Revolutions.* 2d ed. Chicago: University of Chicago Press, 1970.

LaFargue, Michael. "Are Texts Indeterminate? Derrida, Barth, and the Role of the Biblical Scholar." *Harvard Theological Review* 81 (1988): 341-57.

Lampe, G. W. H. *A Patristic Greek Lexicon.* Oxford: Clarendon, 1961.

Lanigan, Richard L. "From Enthymeme to Abduction: The Classical Law of Logic and Postmodern Rule of Rhetoric." In *Recovering Pragmatism's Voice: The Classical Tradition, Rorty, and the Philosophy of Communication,* ed. Lenore Langsdorf and Andrew Smith, 49-70. Albany, NY: SUNY Press, 1995.

Lanser, Susan S. "(Feminist) Criticism in the Garden: Inferring Genesis 2–3." *Semeia* 41 (1988): 67-84.

Larrain, Jorge. *The Concept of Ideology.* Athens, GA: The University of Georgia Press, 1979.

Ledewitz, Bruce. "Judicial Conscience and Natural Rights: A Reply to Professor Jaffa." In Harry V. Jaffa et al., *Original Intent and the Framers of the Constitution: A Disputed Question,* 109-113. Washington, D.C.: Regnery, 1994.

Lerner, Gerda. *The Creation of Patriarchy.* New York: Oxford University Press, 1986.

Levenson, Jon D. *The Hebrew Bible: The Old Testament and Historical Criticism.* Louisville, KY: Westminster/John Knox Press, 1994.

Levi, Edward H. *An Introduction to Legal Reasoning.* Chicago: University of Chicago Press, 1949.

Levinson, Bernard M. *Deuteronomy and the Hermeneutics of Legal Innovation.* Oxford: Oxford University Press, 1997.

Lincoln, C. Eric. *The Black Muslims in America.* 3d ed. Grand Rapids: Wm. B. Eerdmans, 1994; Trenton, N.J.: Africa World Press, 1994.

Long, Thomas G. "Living with the Bible." In *Homosexuality and Christian Community,* ed. Choon-Leong Seow, 64-73. Louisville, KY: Westminster/John Knox Press, 1996.

Maccoby, Eleanor Emmons, and Carol Nagy Jacklin. *The Psychology of Sex Differences.* Stanford, CA: Stanford University Press, 1974.

McDonald, J. I. H. *Biblical Interpretation and Christian Ethics.* Cambridge: Cambridge University Press, 1993.

MacIntyre, Alasdair. "Does Applied Ethics Rest on a Mistake?" *The Monist* 67 (1984): 498-513.

Mannheim, Karl. *Ideology and Utopia: An Introduction to the Sociology of Knowledge.* Translated by Louis Wirth and Edward Shils. New York: Routledge and Kegan Paul, 1972.

Martin, Dale B. "*Arsenokoitês* and *Malakos:* Meanings and Consequences." In *Biblical Ethics and Homosexuality: Listening to Scripture,* ed. Robert L. Brawley, 117-36. Louisville, KY: Westminster/John Knox Press, 1996.

———. "Heterosexism and the Interpretation of Romans 1:18-32." *Biblical Interpretation: A Journal of Contemporary Approaches* 3 (1995): 332-55.

Meeks, Wayne A. "The Image of the Androgyne: Some Uses of a Symbol in Earliest Christianity." *History of Religions* 13 (1974): 165-208.

———. *The Moral World of the First Christians.* Philadelphia: Westminster Press, 1991.

Merritt, H. Wayne. "Paul and the Individual: A Study in Pauline Anthropology." *Journal of the Interdenominational Theological Center* 17 (Fall 1990): 31-60.

Meyers, Carol. *Discovering Eve: Ancient Israelite Women in Context.* New York: Oxford University Press, 1988.

Middleton, J. Richard, and Brian J. Walsh. *Truth Is Stranger Than It Used to Be: Biblical Faith in a Postmodern Age.* Downers Grove, IL: InterVarsity Press, 1995.

Miller, Patrick D., Jr. "God and the Gods: History of Religion as an Approach and Context for Bible and Theology." *Affirmations* 1 (1973): 37-62.

Morgan, Edmund S. "Back to Basics." *New York Review of Books* 47 (July 20, 2000): 47-49.

Mottessi, Osvaldo Luis. "A Historically Mediated *Pastoral* of Liberation: Gustavo Gutiérrez's Pilgrimage Toward Socialism." Ph.D. diss., Emory University, 1985.

Nelson, William E. "The Impact of the Antislavery Movement on Styles of Judicial

Reasoning in Nineteenth Century America." *Harvard Law Review* 87 (1974): 513-66.

Nisbet, Robert. *History of the Idea of Progress.* New York: Basic Books, 1980.

Nussbaum, Martha C. *Love's Knowledge: Essays on Philosophy and Literature.* Oxford: Oxford University Press, 1990.

Ogletree, Thomas W. *The Use of the Bible in Christian Ethics: A Constructive Essay.* Philadelphia: Fortress Press, 1983.

Ollenburger, Ben C. "From Timeless Ideas to the Essence of Religion: Old Testament Theology before 1930." In *The Flowering of Old Testament Theology: A Reader in Twentieth-Century Old Testament Theology, 1930-1990,* ed. Ben C. Ollenburger et al., 3-19. Winona Lake, IN: Eisenbrauns, 1992.

Osborne, Grant R. "Hermeneutics and Women in the Church." *Journal of the Evangelical Theological Society* 20 (1977): 337-40.

Osiek, Carolyn. "The Feminist and the Bible: Hermeneutical Alternatives." In *Feminist Perspectives on Biblical Scholarship,* ed. Adela Yarbro Collins, 93-105. Atlanta: Scholars Press, 1985.

Patte, Daniel. *The Challenge of Discipleship: A Critical Study of the Sermon on the Mount as Scripture.* Harrisburg, PA: Trinity Press International, 1999.

———. *Discipleship according to the Sermon on the Mount: Four Legitimate Readings, Four Plausible Views of Discipleship, and Their Relative Values.* Valley Forge, PA: Trinity Press International, 1996.

———. *Ethics of Biblical Interpretation: A Reevaluation.* Louisville, KY: Westminster/ John Knox Press, 1995.

Patte, Daniel, and Cristina Grenholm, eds. *Reading Israel in Romans: Legitimacy and Plausibility of Divergent Interpretations.* Romans Through History and Cultures Series. Philadelphia: Trinity Press International, 2000.

Patterson, Orlando. *Freedom.* Vol. 1, *Freedom in the Making of Western Culture.* [No city]: HarperCollins, 1991.

———. *Slavery and Social Death: A Comparative Study.* Cambridge, MA: Harvard University Press, 1982.

Phillips, Anthony. *Ancient Israel's Criminal Law: A New Approach to the Decalogue.* Oxford: Basil Blackwell, 1970.

Polanyi, Michael. *Personal Knowledge: Towards a Post-Critical Philosophy.* Chicago: University of Chicago Press, 1958.

Posner, Richard A. *Overcoming Law.* Cambridge, MA: Harvard University Press, 1995.

———. *The Problems of Jurisprudence.* Cambridge, MA: Harvard University Press, 1990.

Post, Robert C. "Theories of Constitutional Interpretation." In *Constitutional Domains: Democracy, Community, Management.* Cambridge, MA: Harvard University Press, 1995.

"Presbyterian Understanding and Use of Scripture." Position Statement adopted by the 123rd General Assembly (1983) of the Presbyterian Church in the United States. Louisville, KY: The Office of the General Assembly, 1992.

Putnam, Hilary. *Realism with a Human Face.* Edited by James Conant. Cambridge, MA: Harvard University Press, 1990.

———. *Reason, Truth, and History.* Cambridge: Cambridge University Press, 1981.

Quintilian. *Institutio Oratoria.* Translated by H. E. Butler. Loeb Classical Library. Cambridge, MA: Harvard University Press, 1921; London: William Heinemann, 1921.

Rad, Gerhard von. *Theology of the Old Testament.* Vol. 2, *The Theology of Israel's Prophetic Traditions.* Translated by D. M. G. Stalker. New York: Harper & Row, 1965.

———. *Wisdom in Israel.* Nashville: Abingdon Press, 1972.

Ramm, Bernard. *The Christian View of Science and Scripture.* Grand Rapids: Wm. B. Eerdmans, 1954.

Rawls, John. "Two Concepts of Rules." *Philosophical Review* 64 (1955): 3-32.

Raz, Joseph. *Practical Reason and Norms.* London: Hutchinson & Sons, 1975.

Ricoeur, Paul. "Preface to Bultmann." In *The Conflict of Interpretations: Essays in Hermeneutics,* ed. Don Ihde. Evanston, IL: Northwestern University Press, 1974.

———. *The Symbolism of Evil.* Translated by Emerson Buchanan. Boston: Beacon Press, 1967.

Riggs v. Palmer, 115 N.Y. 506, 22 N.E. 188 (1889).

Ripley, C. Peter, ed. *The Black Abolitionist Papers.* 5 vols. Chapel Hill, NC: University of North Carolina Press, 1985-92.

Robbins, Vernon K. "From Enthymeme to Theology in Luke 11:1-13." In *Literary Studies in Luke-Acts: A Collection of Essays in Honor of Joseph B. Tyson,* ed. R. P. Thompson and T. E. Philips, 191-214. Macon, GA: Mercer University Press, 1998.

Romer, Leroy S., ed. *Is There a Human Nature?* Notre Dame, IN: University of Notre Dame Press, 1997.

Rose-Ackerman, Susan. "Inalienability and the Theory of Property Rights." *Columbia Law Review* 85 (1985): 931-69.

Ross, J. F. *Portraying Analogy.* Cambridge: Cambridge University Press, 1981.

Ruether, Rosemary Radford. *Disputed Questions: On Being a Christian.* Nashville: Abingdon, 1982.

———. "Feminism and Patriarchal Religion: Principles of Ideological Critique of the Bible." *Journal for the Study of the Old Testament* 22 (1982): 54-66.

———. "Goddesses and Witches: Liberation and Countercultural Feminism." *Christian Century* 97 (1980): 842-47.

———. "Religion and Society: Sacred Canopy vs. Prophetic Critique." In *The Future of Liberation Theology: Essays in Honor of Gustavo Gutiérrez,* ed. Mark H. Ellis and Otto Maduro, 172-76. Maryknoll, NY: Orbis Books, 1989.

———. "A Religion for Women: Sources and Strategies." *Christianity and Crisis* 39 (1979): 307-11.

Rutledge, David. *Reading Marginally: Feminism, Deconstruction and the Bible.* Leiden: E. J. Brill, 1996.

Sawyer, John F. A., ed. *Reading Leviticus: A Conversation with Mary Douglas.* Sheffield: Sheffield Academic Press, 1996.

Schauer, Frederick. *Playing by the Rules: A Philosophical Examination of Rule-Based Decision-Making in Law and in Life.* Oxford: Clarendon Press, 1991.

Schelling, Thomas C. "Enforcing Rules on Oneself." *Journal of Law, Economics & Organization* 1 (1985): 357-74.

Schipani, Daniel S. *Conscientization and Creativity: Paulo Freire and Christian Education.* Lanham, MD: University Press of America, 1984.

———. *Religious Education Encounters Liberation Theology.* Birmingham, AL: Religious Education Press, 1988.

Schmid, H. H. *Wesen und Geschichte der Weisheit: Eine Untersuchung zur altorientalischen Weisheitsliteratur.* Berlin: Alfred Töpelmann, 1966.

Schmithals, Walter. *An Introduction to the Theology of Rudolf Bultmann.* Translated by John Bowden. Minneapolis: Augsburg, 1968.

Scholder, Klaus. *The Birth of Modern Critical Theology: Origins and Problems of Biblical Criticism in the Seventeenth Century.* Translated by John Bowden. Philadelphia: Trinity Press International, 1990.

Scholer, David M. "The Authority of the Bible and Private Interpretation: A Dilemma of Baptist Freedom." In *Baptists in the Balance: The Tension between Freedom and Responsibility,* ed. Everett C. Goodwin, 174-93. Valley Forge, PA: Judson Press, 1997.

———. "Feminist Hermeneutics and Evangelical Biblical Interpretation." *Journal of the Evangelical Theological Society* 30 (1987): 407-20.

———. "1 Timothy 2:9-15 and the Place of Women in the Church's Ministry." In *Women, Authority, and the Bible,* ed. Alvera Mickelsen, 192-219. Downers Grove, IL: InterVarsity Press, 1986.

Schrage, Wolfgang. *The Ethics of the New Testament.* Translated by David E. Green. Philadelphia: Fortress Press, 1988.

Schüssler Fiorenza, Elisabeth. "The Ethics of Interpretation: De-Centering Biblical Scholarship." *Journal of Biblical Literature* 107 (1988): 3-17.

———. *In Memory of Her: A Feminist Theological Reconstruction of Christian Origins.* Tenth Anniversary Edition. New York: Crossroad, 1995.

Schüssler Fiorenza, Francis. "The Crisis of Scriptural Authority: Interpretation and Reception." *Interpretation* 44 (1990): 353-68.

Scroggs, Robin. "The Bible as Foundational Document." *Interpretation* 49 (1995): 17-30.

———. "The New Testament and Ethics: How Do We Get from There to Here?" In *Perspectives on the New Testament: Essays in Honor of Frank Stagg,* ed. Charles H. Talbert, 77-93. Macon, GA: Mercer University Press, 1985.

———. *The New Testament and Homosexuality.* Philadelphia: Fortress Press, 1983.

Segundo, Juan Luis. *Liberation of Theology.* Translated by John Drury. Maryknoll, NY: Orbis, 1976.

Seow, C. L. *Ecclesiastes: A New Translation with Introduction and Commentary.* Anchor Bible. New York: Doubleday, 1997.

Sheppard, Gerald T. "Between Reformation and Modern Commentary: The Perception of the Scope of Biblical Books." In William Perkins, *A Commentary on Galatians*, ed. Gerald T. Sheppard, xlviii-lxxvii. New York: The Pilgrim Press, 1989.

Siker, Jeffrey S. "Homosexual Christians, the Bible, and Gentile Inclusion." In *Homosexuality in the Church: Both Sides of the Debate*, ed. Jeffrey Siker, 178-94. Louisville, KY: Westminster/John Knox Press, 1994.

————. *Scripture and Ethics: Twentieth-Century Portraits*. Oxford: Oxford University Press, 1997.

Smith, Wilfred Cantwell. *What Is Scripture? A Comparative Approach*. Minneapolis: Fortress Press, 1993.

Snodgrass, Klyne R. "Matthew's Understanding of the Law." *Interpretation* 46 (1992): 368-78.

Spohn, William C., S.J. *What Are They Saying About Scripture and Ethics?* New York: Paulist Press, 1984.

Staerk, Willy. "Religionsgeschichte und Religionsphilosophie in ihrer Bedeutung für die biblische Theologie des Alten Testaments." *Zeitschrift für Theologie und Kirche* 31 (1923): 289-300.

Stamm, J. J., and M. E. Andrew. *The Ten Commandments in Recent Research*. London: SCM Press, 1967.

Sunstein, Cass. "On Analogical Reasoning." *Harvard Law Review* 106 (1993): 741-91.

Swartley, Willard M. *Slavery, Sabbath, War, and Women: Case Issues in Biblical Interpretation*. Scottdale, PA: Herald Press, 1983.

Sweeney, Eileen C. "Hugh of St. Victor: Augustinian Tradition of Sacred and Secular Reading Revised." In *Reading and Wisdom: The* De Doctrina Christiana *of Augustine in the Middle Ages*, ed. Edward D. English, 61-83. Notre Dame, IN: University of Notre Dame Press, 1995.

Swinburne, Richard. "Meaning in the Bible." In *Religion, Reason, and the Self: Essays in Honour of Hywel D. Lewis*, ed. Stewart R. Sutherland and T. A. Roberts, 24-25. Cardiff: University of Wales Press, 1989.

Tannehill, Robert C. "Freedom and Responsibility in Scripture Interpretation, with Application to Luke." In *Literary Studies in Luke-Acts*, ed. Richard P. Thompson and Thomas E. Philips, 265-78. Macon, GA: Mercer University Press, 1998.

Theissen, Gerd. *Biblical Faith: An Evolutionary Approach*. Translated by John Bowden. Philadelphia: Fortress Press, 1985.

Tigay, Jeffrey H. *Deuteronomy*. The JPS Torah Commentary. Philadelphia: The Jewish Publication Society, 1996.

Tillich, Paul. "The Demonic: A Contribution to the Interpretation of History." In *The Interpretation of History*. New York: Scribner, 1936.

Toulmin, Stephen Edelston. *The Uses of Argument*. Cambridge: Cambridge University Press, 1964.

Toulmin, Stephen, Richard Rieke, and Allan Janik. *An Introduction to Reasoning*. 2d ed. New York: Macmillan, 1984; London: Collier Macmillan, 1984.

Trible, Phyllis. "Eve and Miriam: From the Margins to the Center." In Phyllis Trible et al., *Feminist Approaches to the Bible: Symposium at the Smithsonian Institution, September 24, 1994*, 5-26. Washington, D.C.: Biblical Archeology Society, 1995.

———. *God and the Rhetoric of Sexuality*. Philadelphia: Fortress Press, 1978.

Troeltsch, Ernst. "The Dogmatics of the 'Religionsgeschichtliche Schule.'" *American Journal of Theology* 17 (1913): 1-21.

Tuchman, Barbara W. *The March of Folly: From Troy to Viet Nam*. New York: Alfred A. Knopf, 1984.

Turner, Mary, ed. *From Chattel Slaves to Wage Slaves: The Dynamics of Labor Bargaining in the Americas*. London: James Currey, 1995.

van Iersel, Bas, and Anton Weiler, eds. *Exodus: A Lasting Paradigm*. Concilium 189. Edinburgh: T. & T. Clark, 1987.

Vatke, Johann K. W. *Die biblische Theologie wissenschaftlich dargestellt*. Vol. 1, *Die Religion des Alten Testaments nach den kanonischen Büchern entwickelt*. Berlin: Bethge, 1835.

Verhey, Allen. *The Great Reversal: Ethics and the New Testament*. Grand Rapids: Wm. B. Eerdmans, 1984.

———. "Scripture and Ethics: Practices, Performances, and Prescriptions." In *Christian Ethics: Problems and Prospects*, ed. Lisa Sowle Cahill and James F. Childress, 18-44. Cleveland: The Pilgrim Press, 1996.

Wawrykow, Joseph. "Reflections on the Place of the *De doctrina christiana* in High Scholastic Discussions of Theology." In *Reading and Wisdom: The De Doctrina Christiana of Augustine in the Middle Ages*, ed. Edward D. English, 99-125. Notre Dame: University of Notre Dame Press, 1995.

Weber, Max. *The Methodology of the Social Sciences*. Translated and edited by Edward A. Shils and Henry A. Finch. Glencoe, IL: The Free Press, 1949.

Westermann, Claus. *Elements of Old Testament Theology*. Translated by Douglas W. Scott. Atlanta: John Knox, 1982.

———. *Genesis 1–11: A Continental Commentary*. Translated by John J. Scullion, SJ. Minneapolis: Fortress Press, 1994.

Wink, Walter. *Engaging the Powers: Discernment and Resistance in a World of Domination*. Minneapolis: Fortress, 1992.

———. *Naming the Powers: The Language of Power in the New Testament*. Philadelphia: Fortress Press, 1984.

———. *Unmasking the Powers: The Invisible Forces That Determine Human Existence*. Philadelphia: Fortress, 1986.

Wright, G. Ernest. *The God Who Acts: Biblical Theology as Recital*. London: SCM Press, 1952.

Zimmerli, Walther. *Ezekiel: A Commentary on the Book of the Prophet Ezekiel, Chapters 1–24*. Translated by Ronald Clements. Philadelphia: Fortress Press, 1979.

———. "Promise and Fulfillment." In *Essays on Old Testament Hermeneutics*, ed. Claus Westermann and trans. James Luther Mays, 89-122. Richmond, VA: John Knox Press, 1963.

Subject Index

adjudication. *See* moral-theological adjudication, rule of
adultery, 22-23
analogical reasoning (analogizing), 51-89; and the Bible, 66-72, 85-89; and the exodus, 72-75, 79-81; and liberation theology, 79-81; nature of, 53-55; ostensible and oblique analogies, 63-66; and slavery, 75-78; and Thomas Ogletree, 81-85
analogy, rule of, 3, 51-89, 182, 185-86, 190-91. *See also* analogical reasoning
anti-Jewishness, 173

Bible: authority of, 2, 9-11, 17-18, 24-25; compared to U.S. constitution, 29, 30-31; empirical assumptions, 134-48; feminist interpretation of, 99-104; moral voice as concrete and particular in, 67-68; moral significance of biblical narratives, 65n.26, 68-69; moral rules/prescriptions in, 17-18; and patriarchy, 98-104, 143-48, 165-67; progressive moral development in, 104-9; and social justice, 44-45; symbolic world of, 18; trajec-tories in, 104-9; as a whole, 49, 195-96
Biblical Theology movement, 90, 94-95, 131

canonical interpretation, 171-76, 197-200
canon-within-the-canon, 195
case-based reasoning. *See* analogical reasoning
Cathechism of the Catholic Church, 48-49
countercultural witness, rule of, 3, 43, 90-115, 182, 185, 190-91; Biblical Theology movement, 94-95; and feminist interpretation, 99-104; in Israel, 96-99; and progressive development, 104-9; warrants for, 91-93
creation and cosmology, 117
cross-cultural relevance, 117

dietary laws, 135
divorce, 63, 70-71

empirical claims in moral reasoning, 127-28

216

Author Index

Scripture Reference Index